MUD, SWEAT AND TEARS

An Irish Woman's Journey

of Self-Discovery

Moire O'Sullivan

To Paul, for encouraging me

To Andrew, for teaching me

To Pete, for loving me, and making me write it all down

MAP OF THE WICKLOW ROUND

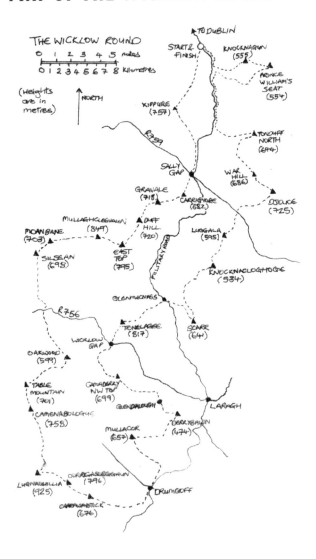

THE WICKLOW ROUND

0   1   2   3   4   5 miles
0 1 2 3 4 5 6 7 8 kilometres

(Heights are in metres)

NORTH

TO DUBLIN

START & FINISH

KNOCKNAGUN (555)

PRINCE WILLIAM'S SEAT (554)

KIPPURE (757)

R759

TONDUFF NORTH (644)

SALLY GAP

WAR HILL (686)

GRAVALE (718)

CARRIGVORE (682)

DJOUCE (725)

MULLAGHCLEEVAUN (849)

DUFF HILL (720)

LUGGALA (595)

MOANBANE (703)

SILSEAN (698)

EAST TOP (795)

MILITARY ROAD

KNOCKNACLOGHOGE (534)

GLENMACNASS

R756

TONELAGEE (817)

SCARR (641)

OAKWOOD (599)

WICKLOW GAP

TABLE MOUNTAIN (701)

CAMADERRY NW TOP (699)

GLENDALOUGH

LARAGH

CAMENABOLOGUE (758)

DERRYBAWN (474)

MULLACOR (657)

LUGNAQUILLIA (925)

CORRIGASLEGGAUN (796)

DRUMGOFF

CARRAWAYSTICK (676)

iv

Contents

1. RUNNING SCARED

I can barely walk. Blisters ooze blood between my toes. Ripped skin hangs from my feet. A web of deep scratches covers my shins. My legs ache with a pounding throb that reverberates throughout my body. My lungs are battered and bruised from too many laboured breaths. I am bent over double from the weight of the bag surgically strapped to my back. A belt of raw skin encircles my stomach, grated raw from the incessant rub of the rucksack's strap. Pain rages and runs rampant through every last muscle and every single vein. My body has reached its end.

But I will not stop. I cannot rest. I have not yet come to the end. "Run faster...try harder...move quicker," I say incessantly to myself. I know what will happen if I delay, if I'm found out here in the dark.

Less than half an hour ago, I could see Tonduff North Mountain before me clearly, its green and brown hues illuminated against the setting sun. But now, the mountain is nothing but an outline, a silhouette looming large against the nocturnal sky.

I'm scared. The mountain is slowly being engulfed before my very eyes. After all these months of hard work, of sacrifice and preparation, I'm losing it all to the night.

I can't go on. But I have no choice. I must climb to the top of the mountain. There is no other way out from this wilderness. My only escape route is from its summit.

I've run for more than twenty hours. I have climbed twenty-three mountains and covered over eighty kilometres. And with only three mountains and twenty kilometres left to go, I want to collapse and die.

I am trying to do what others have deemed impossible. I am trying to run around the whole of the Wicklow Mountains in a single, solitary day. I am trying to run over one hundred kilometres, up and down twenty-six of these mountain summits in less than twenty-four hours.

I am trying to complete the *Wicklow Round.* It's been tried, but never done before. And now I know the reason why.

But I can't let myself stop at this point. I need to snap out of this exhaustion and stay alert. There are too many dangers out here in the mountains to let myself rest yet.

It's eerily quiet out here in the Wicklow Mountains. Down below, I can see the glow of Dublin City less than thirty kilometres away whilst it busies itself with a late night of drinking and carousing. Up here in Wicklow, there's no such dancing or debauchery. There's just me and these mountains, battling it out to make the Wicklow Round a reality.

I lurch forward, onward and upward, stuttering and stammering as I go. The shin-high heather scores my legs, fresh scratches appearing on top of old scars. Eventually the bushes get the better of me. They catch my foot and I fall, hitting the ground with a thud. I lie here exhausted, my clothes and hands caked in cold brown bog. All I can see is entangled heather, lying here at ground zero.

I want to stay down here, to curl up and die.

"You've invested too much time and energy and effort already," I hear a voice imploring. "You have to continue. You have to finish. You have to get up and go on."

My body is crying surrender, my mind is pleading clemency, but somehow, somewhere an inner spirit keeps fighting and telling me to soldier on.

Slowly my eyes adjust to daylight's absence. I can still just make out Tonduff North Mountain in the distance. I have to visit its summit tonight, whether I like it or not.

Guided by my thin head torch beam, I painfully plod my way up the mountain side. As my body slows with every step, my mind begins to run riot. Thoughts of success and failure, thoughts of people and far-off places. Having already physically destroyed myself, I am now emotionally ripping myself apart.

Eventually, at the stroke of 11 pm, I reach the top. And there I stop.

There are only two more mountains to climb. I have three and a half hours left. I have in theory plenty of time.

But I don't move. I stay where I am.

My body and mind have made their decision.

I cannot go on.

And with the relief of knowing it is over, I crouch down on the mountain top. And one by one, tears of disappointment, relief, obsession and exhaustion begin to trickle slowly down my face.

2. MOUNTAIN MAYHEM

"If you ever end up in Dublin," Avril says to me, "you should call my little brother." Avril is trying to help.

I've decided to leave Kenya after seven long years of stay. Avril is helping me make the transition, but it's not an easy move to make. I look up at her through bleary eyes and agree I should track him down. Not that I'll ever live in Dublin. Not when all I can think of is Kenya and how much I will miss my African home.

Now three months on, I accidentally find myself in Ireland's capital, just as Avril prophesised. I have a brand new job and a lovely new house. But I still lack the abundant friendships that Kenya always had.

Distant memories of Avril's offer slowly come to mind.

"He's into running and biking and does lots of mad adventures," Avril had explained, as I sadly packed my bags. "Could maybe introduce you to a few people, invite you to some races."

I had always liked running. And I did need some new friends. So, with some shy reluctance, I decide to contact her brother. No harm in making new acquaintances whilst doing a bit of sport.

"You're just in time. The season is about to kick off," Paul tells me enthusiastically on the line. He turns out to be a veritable mine of information, cataloguing a long list of races around the country: everything from ten kilometres runs to marathons to ultras, right through from running to biking to kayaking.

"But then again," Paul starts to ponder, "maybe you'd be interested in real races, ones that involve running up mountains."

Running? Up mountains? Did I hear him right?

Well I love running. And I like racing. But combining these two activities in the mountains? Is that safe or even wise? How would I even run up a mountain? Would my lungs not collapse and my legs instinctively die? And what if I fall and do myself damage? What if I get totally lost and horribly die?

It all sounds so dangerous. And yet so oddly appealing.

It's been nearly three months since I left Africa. And Ireland is terribly sedate in comparison. There's no danger or disease or threats to make my daily life more exciting. Dublin has no power cuts or water shortages or food rationing. Bus drivers don't yell insults at me. Men don't leer at my white skin. There are no corrupt police officers to hassle me or civil servants to demand a blatant bribe. There are no street kids to pick-pocket me or threaten to smear me with human excrement.

Dublin is boring me to tears. I need something to recreate the flagrant danger that is intrinsic to Nairobi's daily grind. I need a challenge of some sort. And running up mountains could be the death defying activity that I'm so yearning for.

"Sure, why not? Count me in."

"Great stuff," replies Paul. "The next race is up Corrig Mountain this Wednesday. 7.30 pm start. Just a short jaunt of six kilometres. Shouldn't be a bother to a runner like yourself!"

Wednesday evening arrives and I'm feeling more than pre-race nerves. In the days since our conversation, I've begun to think that I may have bitten off far more than I can chew. True, I need a challenge, but running up mountains might be going one step too far.

I have noticed these mountains that Paul speaks of, barely visible from the Phoenix Park where I do my daily training runs. They look like a set of harmless bumps just perched beyond the city's limits. But I know deep down they are treacherous and wild, full of every danger my mind can conjure up.

I am scared of Ireland's mountains.

Sometimes the things that frighten us the most also fascinate us the most. I resolve to stick to my mountain running plan.

Paul suggests that I hitch a lift from him to the race. "Meet me just off the M50 motorway," he says. It is good of him to offer.

"How will I recognise you, Paul?" I ask.

"It'll be hard to miss me," he says. "I'll be the one driving a blue van with a big red boat on top. Not many vehicles like that around Dublin you know." He's teasing me in the way that only Irish lads know how. I've missed that sarcastic Irish sense of humour.

It's wet and windy on Wednesday night, a typical Irish summer's evening. I'm waiting by the roadside, getting more and more drenched by the non-stop dreary rain. I'm starting to feel cold and increasingly fed-up. And there's no sign of Paul or blue vans or red boats floating down the road to hoist me out of my misery.

The longer I wait, the more time I have to convince myself that this is a genuinely bad idea. The mountains are meant to be just background scenery, something I should look at from afar as I run my merry way around Dublin's flat Phoenix Park.

And anyhow, maybe I don't need to always go searching for challenges. Sometimes it's good to live a banal, stress-free life in a non-third world country. And sure, isn't even the rain trying to tell me to give up and go home. It must be a sign.

Suddenly lying horizontally on the couch in my sitting room seems far more fun than trying to run vertically up a hill.

But just as I turn towards home, there's the van and the boat and Paul himself driving the lot down the road. It's too late to retreat.

I can tell straightaway that Paul Mahon is a huge fan of the great outdoors. His van not only has a kayak on top, but it is crammed full of mountain bikes, climbing harnesses, wetsuits, running shoes, maps, survival bags, waterproof clothing and backpacks. His face too looks taut and tanned from years of exposure to the elements. And there's not an inch of fat on the guy, all burnt off from hours of mad runs around the wilderness.

Paul knows I'm out of sorts, being back in Ireland after so many years camped out in Africa. And his sister Avril has already handed him specific instructions to look out for me, to help me settle back into Irish life once more. It's with this sense of obligation that he makes polite conversation as we drive towards the race start.

There's no let up in the drizzle as we drive towards Corrig. In fact, the closer we get to the mountain, the heavier the rain seems to fall. 'Surely the race won't go ahead in this weather,' I silently think to myself, hoping and praying for a last minute cancellation. "Great mountain running weather or what?" Paul happily chirps up, secretly reading my mind. It seems that my reticence about this whole mountain running expedition is inversely proportional to Paul's excitement about the conditions. All of a sudden I feel very soft, not hard and rugged like a proper mountain person is meant to be. I thought my years in Africa would have toughened me up, but I'm abruptly finding it quite the opposite.

Paul is not alone in his enthusiasm. Cars clutter the tiny country road leading to the base of Corrig Mountain, the start of

7

tonight's mountain race. With Dublin a mere thirty minutes' drive away, runners have already arrived in their droves from their offices and homes, utterly undeterred by the prospect of running up a mountain on a cold, wet evening after work.

The race has been organised by the aptly named Irish Mountain Runners Association or IMRA, as it is known for short. The registration process is surprisingly fast and efficient despite our desolate mountain location. From the back of a car someone has conjured up tables and chairs, forms and pens, race numbers and pins, as well as a laptop and fully functioning printer. I line up, pay the race fee and membership and get myself a number. Within a few minutes I become IMRA's newest member.

With the administrative side all sorted, I now get a chance to check out the type of people who turn up to such events. Without wanting to sound too desperate, I'm silently hoping that there'll be some people here with new best friend potential. It's a real mixed bunch that I see bounding up and down the hill. There are guys and girls, both young and old, all happily chatting to each other as they stretch out their arms and legs. There are kids as young as fourteen, pensioners over seventy and every possible age in between.

I am hoping that I won't seem too out of place at the race. I am new to the mountains, but not to running. My plan is to blend in inconspicuously by wearing some appropriate athletic gear. Back home, I had hummed and hawed over what to wear. Eventually I opted for a running T-shirt, jumper, jacket on top and a pair of tights down below. It seemed a functional and comfortable composition designed to keep me warm and dry.

At the bottom of Corrig, my choice of clothing is just about holding out against the cold. However, in comparison with the others, I look positively over-dressed. The vast majority of runners are sporting shorts and singlets and seem immune to the dropping temperature. Though I am indeed desperate to blend in, I cannot forego any of my three layers of clothing. I've become too accustomed to Africa's heat to suddenly warm to Ireland's weather.

'Well at least I've got good road running shoes,' I think in consolation, looking proudly down at my clean pair of trainers. 'Hopefully they'll still think I'm some sort of athlete.' My gaze passes furtively to their footwear and my stomach begins to turn. Their shoes look different to anything I've ever seen before. On the bottom they have knots and knobbles for holding fast in mud, none of the sleek flatness that is required for running on roads.

My disguise has completely and utterly failed.

But what makes me stand out like a sore thumb is my slightly pudgy physique. The majority here are wafer thin figures, floating gracefully up and down the hill as they effortlessly warm up before the race start. All of a sudden, in addition to feeling too soft, I now feel horrendously fat. It seems that the mountains have honed these people into finely tuned athletes with perfectly toned muscles and not a gram of excess flab. They have evolved into the perfect aerodynamic shape for flying up and down mountains, whilst my more rounded shape is only fit for pushing me up to the top and rolling me back down again.

So my shoes aren't right, I have too many clothes and my body is comparatively verging on obese. The only way left to camouflage my rookie status is to mimic them and their warm-up routines. I cross the starting line and jog up the initial incline. Those around me are gliding up and down the hill still in mid-conversation. I, on the other hand, have lost the ability to speak and am stumbling more than gliding. I am so out of my depth and so out of their league. If I had my own car now, I would get into it and drive straight back home. But Paul has the keys and is nowhere in sight. There's nothing for it but to stay.

By 7.30 pm around 150 people have gathered at the starting line. I huddle somewhere in the middle of the group, a bit unsure of what happens next. All around me the friendly banter continues as athletes wait for the start. The atmosphere is surprisingly informal and friendly. And I'm beginning to feel a little optimistic. Could this be the place where I form new friendships to replace those I left back in Africa?

A registration official now stands up on a dirt mound beside the raring-to-go runners. "Alright lads, enjoy it. One, two, three, go." And with that uncomplicated countdown, the race begins.

The fastest runners at the front accelerate off at high speed. The pack follows closely behind, pursuing them up the gravel track leading up towards the mountainside. I find myself in the middle of this mêlée, struggling to match the pace. All of a sudden, I feel a looming sense of failure growling deep inside me.

'Everyone's going to pass you. You're going to be last. You're going to fail. Everyone's going to laugh.'

I have no idea from where this ominous fear has surreptitiously sprung from. But just in case it's deadly, I resolve to do everything I can to prove it wrong.

The track is already at an angle and I find myself running on my tippy toes. After a few hundred metres, I have established a rhythm and seem to be not losing any ground. 'This is okay. This could be good. I can do this,' I think to myself.

I take the opportunity to look up and see where we are headed. But instead of seeing a long line of runners straight ahead of me, the lead runners are nowhere to be found. The gravel track is empty. 'Oh jaysus, where have they all gone?'

The last thing I want is to get lost. I look behind me and spot some runners directly on my shoulder. I resolve to slow and to stick to them like glue.

The track swings left, but my group goes right, over a dirt bank and straight towards some trees. There seems to be no way through the forest in front. All I can see is a jungle of low lying branches. But one after one, my group bends down and soon they disappear beneath the foliage. There's nothing else for me to do but follow. I'm too afraid to be left behind on my own.

Beyond the branches, my fellow runners have now straightened up and are just ahead, having found a break through the forest. They are following a faint trail that goes straight up through the trees and higher up the mountainside. I follow their lead and together we run up and up and up. I find myself taking smaller and smaller steps as I try to keep my legs moving up this ever increasing incline. Whilst I'm busy adjusting my stride pattern, it becomes harder and harder to find steady footing on this new muddy path we're running on. My shoes slip on the wet needles, grass and muck which constitutes this forest trail. The evening's wet weather has mixed with the undergrowth to produce treacherous terrain. And what with 150 pairs of running shoes coursing up through this forest, the ground has been churned up so badly that it has been transformed into one big muddy slide.

And whilst the forest path disintegrates, my body soon follows suit. My maiden attempt at uphill running is swiftly taking its toll. Within seconds, my lungs catch fire. I can barely breathe. Just when I most needed a glut of oxygen, my breathing faculties have opted to initiate an emergency shutdown. And whilst my lungs are busy malfunctioning, my heart hits record speeds. I can feel it beating twice as fast as normal. Indeed a heart attack feels almost imminent.

Down below, my other body parts are also struggling. After less than a minute of intensive uphill running, my legs are ready to explode. Already I can feel the heat of detonation with every uphill stride. My thighs are ticking time bombs, straining under the load. I feel each ligament igniting and burning one by one.

I have been running up this mountain for less than five minutes and already I can't bear it any more. I have covered less than five hundred metres, but running a single step more is simply a no.

I start to walk.

WALK?!! This is pathetic. I am meant to be running, not walking. I signed up for a running race, not one to find the fastest stroller.

But the walk is at least doing me some good. I have stopped hyperventilating, my legs have stopped squealing and I am slowly but surely making upward progress. I also take solace in the fact that others around me have also adopted a walking strategy. True, the lead runners ahead of us have scooted up through the forest with a bounding running stride. But we decide to leave those guys to it, as the rest of the pack and I content ourselves with a gentrified walk through the woods.

Just as I'm starting to enjoy this, I see a light at the end of the trees. Soon enough, the path peters out, the forest falls away and we emerge onto the open mountainside. Foolishly, I had thought that the little winding path up through the forest qualified as hardcore mountain running. Never before have I been further from the truth that I'm now on the verge of discovering.

Up here, all mountain hell is breaking loose. The wind is screeching. The rain is swirling. And whilst I'm busy absorbing this Irish Hades, my fellow mountain runners are disappearing further and further into the mist. I have to stick with them if I'm not to lose them and be lost forever on this ferocious, deserted mountain.

But keeping up with them is an entirely different matter. There are no well worn tracks or paths to follow. Instead, there are furrowed breaks through a knotted mesh of heather that totally submerges Corrig Mountain. These breaks expose bare bog lurking underneath the vegetation. And thanks to another Irish summer of unending precipitation, this bog has been transformed into a slippery swamp of gooey mud on which my feet find zero traction. The more I try to run forward, the more I slide off to the side. Desperately I bog skate my way towards the summit, cursing my sleek but rubbish road running shoes.

The ground is still heading upwards, but this time I can't afford to adopt a leisurely walk. If I walk, the other runners will definitely get away. Many of them have already delved and disappeared into the mist less than fifty metres ahead. And herein lies my dilemma. If I look up to keep them in sight, I cannot also look down and check where my feet are going. A slight glance upwards and my feet end up stuttering and stammering over grass, rocks and rutted bog. And so I resign myself to looking straight ahead whilst tripping and lurching forwards, onwards and upwards in what I hope is the right direction.

By now the physical pain of uphill running has been subsumed into a greater, broader torture. The war is no longer just with my body, but with the weather, the terrain, the mountain and ultimately, my mind.

'Why are you doing this? Why don't you give up and go home?' I begin to hear my head questioning. 'Paul is going to be so embarrassed by this performance. He's going to wish he never brought you here. You're such a disappointment.' As if I don't have enough to contend with already, my mind is now harassing me.

'But if I just continue on a little longer, maybe it'll get better,' I answer, trying to convince myself. 'Just finish the race. Giving up is worse than coming last. Come on Moire, you'll be fine.'

After what seems like a never ending battle with a mind-without-mercy, towards a mountain without a top, I start to make out a stationary figure decked out in arctic gear. He is barely visible under his multitude of layers, as he tries to protect himself from the rain and wind that bounce off his waterproof pants and jacket. What anyone would be doing standing out here in these conditions is beyond comprehension.

But then I work out that he is standing to show us where the uphill finishes. He is standing on the summit.

With the last ounce of adrenaline left in my drained body, I push myself towards the marshal. I soon become the 90th person that day to conquer Corrig summit.

Now all I have to do is get back down to the bottom of the mountain. I quickly turn around at the top and search for a fellow runner to follow. But as I change direction, the wind picks up and it rams me straight off my feet. I hadn't noticed, but on the way up the wind and I had been going in the same direction, giving me the benefit of a wind-assisted ascent. But now running in the opposite direction, the gale is delivering me a full frontal body slam and is determined to push me backwards up the slope. But I don't want to go back there, to the summit or its marshal. Right now I've had enough and all I want to do is go home. This leaves me with no other option but to lean into the wind and to fight my way frantically forward.

Not content with the mere use of brutal force, the gales enlist more subtle tactics to confuse even my senses. The wind howls so loudly that I can no longer hear anything bar my deep and laboured breathing. It rams into my eyes and makes me cry, leaving me with teary blurry vision. It breaks through my clothing and extracts all warmth from within me, leaving me cold and wet and miserable and still so far from the finish.

If not the source of enough misery, the wind whips up even more mist to hide my fellow racers. I am left with the distinct illusion that I am out here all alone in my mountainous struggle. And whilst all this is happening, I am still trying to negotiate my way through the shoe-sucking marshes and booby-trapped bog underneath, trying not to break both my ankles in the negotiation process.

"Trees! I can see the trees!" I squeal over-excitedly. It's the forest I left behind oh so long ago. It is right in front of me.

A sudden sense of relief rushes through my body. I can't contain myself. I plunge my way down the last remains of bog to reach, as fast as possible, the forest edge. Right beside the trees, there's a path, a proper path! Yes, it's still got rocks and puddles and grassy mounds, but at least I can put my foot on it without fear of falling over. And the tall tree line is the perfect barrier, protecting me from the battering wind and rain. But more importantly the trees are a sign that I am closer to civilisation and to the prospect of finishing this horrendous mountain race.

My senses slowly start to thaw as I finally enter the forest. It's all downhill from here. And for the first time my legs feel the freedom of running downwards, of turning off the brakes and letting gravity bring me to speeds simply not possible on flat boring roads. I let myself fall freely down the slope, faster and faster, until I reach a speed where my legs can no longer keep up. I feel like a child again, a child without a care in the world. I plummet down the hill, filled with innocent, infantile fun, leaving behind as I go all my worries, my stress, my loneliness, my pain back up on the turbulent mountainside.

I hurtle round a corner and through the trees, the finish is in sight. One final last effort and I reach the end in a little under fifty minutes. I collapse across the line, absolutely relieved, totally traumatised, utterly exhausted and completely exhilarated.

Paul finished the race fifteen minutes ago. He has already warmed down and changed and is busy catching up with fellow runners as they come across the line. He seems a cheerful and popular character within the mountain running circle, talking to all and sundry about tonight's race and their forthcoming mountain adventures.

"So how did it go?" he asks me once he sees I've caught my breath. I'm really not too sure what to say. Do I tell him how terrified I was out on the mountain? How I'm so unfit that I could barely run half of the course? How disappointed he must be in my final time and position? How all I want to do now is curl up in the car with a sleeping bag and with the heat on full blast?

Or do I launch into an impromptu counselling session, describing how this mountain mayhem has momentarily let me forget my loneliness and fears? Or do I tell him that I'm an adrenaline junky and ask him why he thinks I need the mountains to scare me just like Africa used to do?

However, I don't want to sound like the soft, slightly fat, psychotic wimp that tonight I've discovered I am. "Hmmm, it wasn't really what I expected," is all I can muster up. I need to divert him away from the subject of my own dismal performance, my nearly coming last in the race. "So how did you get on yourself?" I enquire right back. "Ah sure, not too bad. Could have been better," is the eventual reply I get.

"Not too bad" is an understatement. Against a tough field, Paul has just finished twelfth in this race.

I am relieved to have finished my first ever mountain running race. Relief is also what I feel when Paul whisks me away to a nearby pub to join the IMRA crowd for prize giving and post race pints. It takes us less than ten minutes to drive from the desolation of Corrig Mountain to the cosiness of Scholars Pub in Firhouse, just on the outskirts of Dublin City. Compared to the blustery and damp conditions found on Corrig Mountain, Scholars is warm inside and only wet with the right kind of drink. Runners soon fill the pub with the same gusto they had when lining up on the mountain less than an hour beforehand.

The results soon roll in from the mountain and prizes are given to the night's top runners. Prizes are also given to those who had helped out with duties such as registration, course marking, first aid and results compilation. I watch to see if the poor marshal on top of Corrig summit gets something for his display of extreme valour against the foreboding Irish elements. Even if he does, I wouldn't recognise him without all those layers of clothing he has surely shed by now.

It is already 9.30 pm, over an hour since I finished, but I'm still dazed from the race's exertion. I'm also uncertain whether I enjoyed running up the mountain or if I hate the whole notion.

However, regardless of this evening's mountain race, there's another reason why I'm here. I have also come along to get to know a few people to help me settle in. Paul is busy chatting with his crowd, so I decide to talk instead to an unsuspecting mountain runner who's waiting at the bar for his pint. I've a few mountain running questions that I'd like answered, so who better to ask?

"So do those guys really run all the way up those hills?" I ask him straight out.

He looks round in my direction, surprised by the directness of my query. His skinny wind-blustered face relaxes with mild amusement as he realises that I must be a newbie.

"Well yeah, of course they do," he answers, trying hard not to sound condescending. His tone of voice is trying to tell me that that's a really obvious answer.

Figuring that I'd be satisfied with his to-the-point reply, he leans his long body back over the bar to continue with his order. But I've not finished.

"And how do they manage to run across that heather and bog?" adding, "I found it really difficult," at the end with a deferential smile.

"I suppose it's practise," he replies, shrugging his shoulders. Even though he's trying his hardest to be nice, I'm getting the impression that I'm making him feel ill at ease. His eyes have started darting around to find the barman and his pint. He's hoping to make a hasty escape. But the barman has gone looking for some peanuts for the order, so I fire another question.

"And what do you do when the path is flooded and has loads of mud on it? How do you run through that without slipping or falling over?" He turns to look down at my formerly clean road runners and silently shakes his head. "You need to get yourself some proper shoes, girl. And sure, we'll be seeing you again next week." And with that statement, his pint and peanuts arrive and raising his glass in salutation, he's off before I know it.

Next week? Hold on now, who says I going to go mountain running ever again? Certainly not after tonight's episode! There's no way I'm going back out to endure such a physical and mental massacre. Yes I love running. And yes, I like racing.

But combining these two activities together in the mountains? Now that I've tried it, I know from vast experience that it's a very bad idea.

The next morning I wake up tired and sore. Everything hurts, my legs, my lungs, my heart, my head. The mud, sweat and tears washed off in the bath last night, but my body still remembers.

It's not until that evening that the pain eventually subsides. And then my mind starts to evoke a different set of memories from the physically tortuous ones. It starts to remember the cool mountain air, the scent of the forest and the familiar smell of fresh rain. It recalls the wonder of exploring one of Ireland's mountains, albeit at far too high a speed. I reminisce about the people, those 150 runners I met last night on the hill. Never before had I seen such friendly camaraderie in the midst of serious athletic competition.

And as the physical pain finally fades away, the whole event takes on a far profounder meaning. I start to realise that last night I did something that most normal people would deem impossible.

I ran up a mountain and back down again. Most people wouldn't dare. Last night I proved to myself in a small, insignificant way, that if I put my mind to something, I can make the impossible happen.

But even if I did manage to run up a mountain last night, my 90th place in the overall race clearly testifies that I'm not very good at it at all. Maybe it is like the guy said in the pub. Maybe it will be much better if I just get some proper mountain running shoes. Maybe then I won't be afraid of falling over in all the mud and rock. With such shoes, I'll be able to run, not walk up all the mountains. If I wear such shoes, no wind will be able to blow me over. With such footwear, before I know it, I will be crowned the new Queen of the Mountains!

I go and buy some mountain running shoes. Then I turn up to my second mountain race to test out my newly spun theory.

Paul Mahon, the man who introduced me to mountain running.
Photo courtesy of 26Extreme.

3. Summer Running

Second time around, it is Howth's turn as the mid-week mountain running destination. Jutting out into the Irish Sea, Howth Head is a peninsula that's hanging on in there on the north side of Dublin Bay. And with my brand new shoes in tow and even a hill training run done that week, I know this time round everything will be good.

One of the reasons I left Ireland all those years ago was due to the country's atrocious weather. Why live in a country where it's cold, wet and windy, except for two weeks of the year and where no one knows when those two weeks of good weather will be? I soon found out there were plenty of other countries where sunshine is the year-round norm. That discovery, amongst others, made me stay away from Ireland for as long as I possibly could.

But tonight I am proven wrong. There is none of the rain, mist, wind, or mud that Ireland normally displays. Instead the weather has taken a turn for the better and Howth is displaying a picture perfect vision of a beautiful Irish summer. All I have to contend with tonight is the mountain and the run.

This evening's race is a nine kilometre circuit, with two laps of the hill to provide runners with plenty of ups and downs. And with all the same friendly informality that left such an impression on me after the Corrig Mountain race, we are soon off for our Wednesday night race at the strike of 7.30 pm.

I quickly realise my shoe philosophy is fundamentally flawed. I hit the first uphill section and my heart and lungs immediately reach their health and safety limits. My legs instantly buckle and break from my feeble attempts to gain any uphill running momentum. Even in my brand new running shoes, I'm reduced to walking my way up to the summit.

When we finally reach the top, the course brings us on a tour of the hill's flat plateau. I have discovered since Corrig that race routes are in fact marked by IMRA with little flags and tape. It means that, despite my initial conviction, it's not necessary to always have a runner in front to follow at all times. These markers I now see visibly spread along Howth's network of trails. The trails in turn transpire to be wonderfully bog-less paths made of sure footed solid stones. On either side, green gorse bushes line the path boundaries. These bushes lie close enough to define the tracks, but distant enough to avoid chance encounters with their proliferous array of thorns.

With the route well marked, the paths well delineated and the race well in hand, I take a few moments to take in Howth's stunning views. Above the summer sky is crystal blue. All around, the Irish Sea's waters are azure and clear. I smile contently inside. 'It's hard not to like mountain running when the sun is shining and the scenery is this stunning,' I think to myself between strides.

I complete the first lap and start the second, sweating now from both the heat of the race and the warm evening summer sun. Up and around the summit I go for the second time, before approaching the final downhill section that funnels straight into the finish.

The descent is a steep section on a narrow rocky path, forcing runners to go down in single file. Confident in my new mountain shoes, I throw caution to the wind and plunge my way downwards, kamikaze style. I should have read the safety instructions that came with the shoes, because before I know it, my foot clips a rock and I am sent flying forward, straight into the gorse bushes thick with their barbarous wire.

The runner behind me sees it all happening. "Are you alright?" he quickly asks. I nod in shock, surprised he hasn't used my misfortune to overtake me and gain a precious place. Without thinking he picks me out of the bushes and places me back on my two feet. I've barely time to catch my breath before he ushers me to run on. I clamber on down the hill at his behest, using my remaining reserves of adrenaline to get me to the end.

I flop over the line and immediately take a seat on the grass. It takes me a while to summon up the courage to inspect the damage from the fall. It's not as bad as I thought. Just some cuts, a bit of blood and a few hundred thorns embedded in my legs.

The guy who hauled me back to my feet comes over to check I'm still alive. "Not a bother," he courteously replies when I thank him for his help. "Those needles should pop out in the next few days. Then you'll be all fit and ready to go again next week."

I like the way he comes over to check that I'm okay. But it's not just him who's being kind. Just being with these mountain runners is helping me get back on my proverbial feet again after being away from Ireland for so long. And I am starting to get the hang of this mountain running game. I am slowly but surely getting tougher and thinner with each mountain race. So I decide to persevere. And in the end, I am right to commit.

The summer of 2006 is wonderfully warm and sunny. I turn out every Wednesday, as much for the weather as for the race. The calendar in turn never fails to produce a plethora of picturesque places and marvellous mountains to run.

The week after Howth is Paddock Lake, with its course looping up through Djouce Forest and Crone Woods via the Wicklow Way walking trail. Next is Brockagh, perched perfectly over scenic Glendalough. On to Tibradden in the

23

Dublin Mountains we go, with its unsurpassed views over Dublin City from its Fairy Castle cairn. Then it's the longest mid-week run on the calendar, Ballinastoe, a twelve kilometre loop taking in river crossings, muddy marshes and forest rides and anything else sordid that the mountain can possibly throw up. And lastly we arrive at the finale of the summer mountain running league, the Sugarloaf race and barbeque.

Sugarloaf is a lonely old hill. Huddling close to the Irish Sea, it seems cut adrift and ostracised from the nearby Wicklow Mountain range. With its distinctive steep slopes and scree-topped summit, it's the perfect place for IMRA to close its mid-week summer mountain racing season. Many come for the six kilometre circuit, with its screaming descents from its perilous peak. But many more come for the barbeque feast afterwards in the car park of the nearby Glencormac Inn.

The Sugarloaf event embodies the essence of the Irish mountain running scene. Not only do the IMRA races provide a time and place to run around Ireland's hills. They also offer a space to meet new mountain loving friends, young and old, fast and slow. At 7.30 pm, we are battling it out, adversaries on the mountain. But by 9 pm, we are in the pub together, discovering the wonderful healing powers of a proper pint.

The IMRA community is a group of people united in their love of running, of races, of mountains and of drinking. This unity they achieve regardless of their speeds, gender, ages, or abilities. And, thanks to Paul, Avril's kid brother and his companions, it is here that I am finding the new set of friends I have been longing for ever since I left the African shores.

By the end of the summer, I am addicted to the sport. But the Wednesday night races are sadly over for the year. So I search for something else that can keep me running in the mountains. I then hear about IMRA's 'Navigational Challenge

Series' and decide that this is going to be my next mountain running conquest.

Mountain running in Ireland. Photo courtesy of John Shiels, actionphotography.ie.

4. LOST

The Navigational Challenge is a set of three weekend races run across remote open mountainside. But unlike the Wednesday night season of runs, where there are a series of signposts on the mountain to show us exactly where to go, the Navigational Challenge races are completely devoid of markings. Instead, they demand 'navigational ability'. This means that I need to know how to read a map and work a compass if I want to participate.

'Sounds simple enough,' I think to myself. 'Sure didn't I use a map once to find my way around the mountains in County Donegal? Aren't the blue bits on the map water, the green bits forest and the brown bits, I think they're open land? What more would I really need to know?'

Finding out where the race actually starts is the first navigational conundrum I face. For the Wednesday set of races, clear instructions were always given on the IMRA website telling me exactly where the race would begin. They would tell me the precise roads to take, the country villages to pass through and even provide mini maps to download with exactly where to go. But for the Navigational Challenge Series, providing such information would make it far too easy. No, in fact directions to the start are purposefully omitted from the race information pack. Instead, all they give is a grid reference. Apparently the race I am attending will start at 'O 058 118'.

"Ye what?" I splutter. "Where the hell is that?" I rush to find my mountain survival books and resurrect one that explains the basics of navigation. I flick through the starting pages to figure out what the letter O and the accompanying list of six numbers means.

'The area of Ireland is divided into 25 squares, measuring 100km by 100km, each identified by a single letter. The squares are numbered A to Z, with I being omitted.'

Well that's not much help. All I want to know is where O is and then I'll be fine. And what about the 058 118 code numbers? What are these all about? And so I read on.

'A grid reference is a combination of two numbers that identify a position on a map. One number counts across from left to right (west to east) - this is the easting. The second number counts up from bottom to top (south to north) - this is the northing. The grid reference is the easting, followed by the northing.'

Already I am lost and I've not even left home. How am I meant to run this race if I can't even understand these letters and numbers, or whatever they call them, 'grid references' or something like that? How can I run if I can't even find my way to the start?

I spend the next hour pouring over my map, trying to decipher this code of 'O 058 118'. I eventually work out that the O refers to a part of the Wicklow Mountains, just south-west of Dublin. And that 058 118 is located somewhere in the middle of nowhere, a place called 'Ballydonnell'.

Through this use of secret symbols, the race organisers are sending out a clear message: If you can't understand grid coordinates and if you can't figure out where the race begins, then you don't have the elementary skills to run the race in the first place. It is blatantly obvious from this little exercise that I don't have the required skills to run. But that doesn't stop me. "Ah sure, I'll be fine," I say to myself. "Don't I understand grid references now after reading the book? It'll all be grand."

A few days later I find myself driving down a tiny country road. I'm slowly weaving my way through Grid O in the Wicklow Mountains trying to find the race start. The road is barely wide enough to take the width of my car. And with a line of Ireland's finest green grass growing right down its tarmac centre, it doesn't look like the road has seen much traffic lately, let alone this morning.

I'm beginning to wonder if I'm in the right place. Usually on Wednesdays I'd see at least a few other cars packed with thin, fit people going in my direction. But thus far this morning, I've seen absolutely no one else driving up this god forsaken road, let alone anyone who looks like they might be a mountain runner.

Thick mist is hanging menacingly low on the horizon. I look at my map and see that I should be in the Wicklow Mountains by now. Sorrell Hill and Moanbane are apparently on my left and right respectively. But looking out both my car windows, neither of them are there.

Already I'm having flashbacks of my first mountain race up Corrig. It's the same kind of mist now as I saw then, the type of mist that won't let you see further than fifty metres ahead. And it's the same type of terrain as Corrig that is now visible outside my car. To both sides, where the tarmac stops, it's all heather, bog, grass and mud stretching ad infinitum up and down the slopes.

I came very close to getting lost at Corrig. And that was fully marked with flags and tapes. 'Oh jaysus, just how lost am I about to get?' I am starting to violently fret. My stomach sinks as reality slowly settles in.

But turning back is simply not an option. 'I'm going to do this,' I tell myself, slapping my wimpy side into submission.

'Shut up and keep driving.' Like it or not, there's nothing worse in my mind than giving up before I've even tried.

I am still wondering if I have got the right grid reference when I come across a small car park hidden behind some trees. Inside it are a handful of cars, with svelte shaped people huddling behind their steering wheels. They look just like mountain runners. "This must be it!" I excitedly squeal.

I park my car and walk over to a woman hanging out by her open car boot. "Is this the start for the IMRA navigation race?" I ask. "It is indeed," she replies. I beam inside, momentarily proud that I didn't bottle out further back down the road.

I register for the race and hand over my entrance fee. She gives me in turn a plastic coated piece of paper with numbers and boxes drawn on it. "Here's your control card. You'll need it for the race." I have no idea what she's talking about. This wasn't part of the website's race briefing.

"I'm sorry," I can't help but blurt out as I take the card from her. "But what am I meant to do with this again?"

She gives me a look of mild impatience. She knows a rookie when she sees one. She's met my sort before, lads who can't use a compass, can't read a map, can't run over mountains and, hopefully, can't find their way to the start. But I've found the start. So now that I'm here, she's no option but to explain to me how this race actually works.

"There are certain places you have to visit on the course. Some of these places have marshals and they will note down that you've arrived. Other places do not have marshals. These have control flags instead." My eyes glaze over. Control flags? What are they? She can read the flagrant ignorance blazon across my entire face. She knows now that she has to start from the very, very beginning. "Control flags are orange and white cloth flags used in the sport of orienteering. They are shaped into a box and you'll see them hanging from a short bamboo stick. You'll also see hanging from the same stick a small plastic punch that resembles a mini-stapler. However, instead of staples, the punch has a unique set of pins inside. Put the control card I've just given you inside the punch, line up the control flag number with the box number on the card, press down and you'll get a unique set of pinprick holes on the card. Then when you give us back the control card at the end of the race, we'll know that you actually visited the place."

"Oh, I see," I mumble back. "Thanks for the explanation." I walk away, not having understood most of what she has just said. But I'm too embarrassed to admit my ignorance. And I desperately don't want to seem out of place. So I try to act cool like all the other competitors, by going back to my car, looking thoughtfully at my map, checking my laces, drinking some water and doing a few random stretches.

My thoughts are soon confirmed that this race at Ballydonnell is a lot less popular than the one held at Corrig. There are none of the crowds of one hundred plus runners limbering up beforehand. All that turns out to Ballydonnell on this wet and misty Sunday morning are a committed band of thirteen entrants. It could be the course length that is putting people off, Ballydonnell being over double the distance at fourteen kilometres as compared to Corrig's six. Or it could be the race's navigation element that is deterring them from running, many honestly acknowledging to themselves that they don't have the skills to run an unmarked race. Or maybe it's this morning's depressing, drizzly and misty weather that is encouraging everyone to stay in bed. But whatever the reason, the reduced number of runners means that there will be considerably less people on the course. Slowly it's starting to dawn on me that I'll probably have no one directly in front of me to follow. I may end up running much of this race on my own.

I'm starting to wonder if I made the right decision about coming to this race. 'What do all those other runners who stayed at home know that I don't know?' I begin to speculate. But then again, I kind of like the fact that there are fewer people out here this morning. I like doing things that are different, things that set me apart. I like doing things that very few other people also want to do.

I don't recognise any of the other twelve runners who are waiting at the race start. In fact, it's a completely different set of people from the usual Wednesday crowd. As I look curiously at them, I feel them staring straight back at me. "Who's she and what's she doing here?" I'm sure they are asking themselves. "Doesn't she know that this race requires navigation? Don't tell us that another mid-week runner, used to running around marked courses, thinks she can now find her way without the flags and tape? Look lads, if she gets lost, I'm not the one who's going out there to find her and bring her home again."

I have just entered the covert cell of the Irish mountain running scene. I have turned up to an event with the tough guys of mountain running. These are the mountain goats that have been to every nook and cranny of the hills and know them all like the back of their wind-weathered hands. They are the accomplished navigators and orienteers of this sport, guys who can read maps and follow compasses whilst running uphill and across bog at high speed. These are the guys who avoid the Wednesday mountain races like the plague because they find them not long enough, not steep enough and not rough enough. These are IMRA's hardcore.

And I'm starting to feel very scared.

'But it's too late,' I tell myself. 'They can't send me away now. I'm already here and I've paid my entry fee. I'm running, whether they like it or not.' Tough inner words are what I hear resounding when all I want to really do is run far, far away.

The race starts before I know it, precisely on twelve o'clock. But it's not the usual type of start where everyone lines up in a row and waits for the gun to go off. Instead, with the word 'Go', we all run straight at the race organiser who hands each of us a little piece of paper. 'Now what's this all about?' I wonder exasperatedly. 'Not more pieces of paper!' I look down at what's written on my slip.

Start O 058 118

1.   *Summit O 042 119*
2.   *River Junction O 058 084*
3.   *River Junction O 084 081*
4.   *River Junction O 066 109*

Finish O 058 118

Controls must be visited in the order given.

That's it - just a list of more secret mountain codes. These are grid references. And written beside them, to the left, a description of what I should look for when I arrive at each of these given points. But what's completely lacking is information about how I should go between these places. There's no route suggested, no designated turns given, no maps pre-drawn to show the way. Apparently, all those decisions are completely up to me.

I run as quickly as I can. Straight to my car. The plan is to lock the doors, turn on the ignition and drive the hell out of here. I am so out of my depth. Again. First it was Corrig. And now it is the turn of Ballydonnell. I'm trying to do something that I do not have the knowledge, speed, stamina, or skills for.

'Oh God, why do I do this to myself?' I moan. 'Why do I throw myself in the deep end completely convinced I can swim, even though the last time I came so close to drowning?' I did it when I swanned off to Kenya straight after university thinking I'd save all of Africa's poor. Now I'm doing it right here in the middle of Ireland's Wicklow Mountains, convinced I'll be fine despite the real possibility of getting lost out there and dying.

I don't drive off in the end, but I *do* get into my car. I need to shelter from the rain that has started pouring down just on the stroke of midday. I need to calm down and look properly at the piece of paper that I have just been given. I need to take my time, read the grid references and then find them all on my map. I also need to draw circles around them so that I can find these places later on whilst I'm in the middle of the race. If I do all this outside, the rain will turn my map into mush and will stop my pen from working. So, like everyone else in the race, I make a decisive break for shelter.

My car windows quickly steam up from the stress of trying to find the points on the map at a reasonable speed. Even though I'm trying to stay relaxed, I'm getting increasingly tense thinking about how I'm ever going to find the points out there on the real mountainside. I look up and my stress levels now increase to fever pitch. Most of the runners have already finished marking all the points on their maps. Many are already running out of the car park and up the hillside on the opposite side of the road.

'They must be heading to number 1, *Summit O 042 119,*' I guess. I jump out of my car, lock the doors and run after them with my map and compass flailing behind me. I just about manage to restrain myself from shouting after them, "Please, wait for me!"

There are no walking paths on this mountainside, only faint sheep tracks winding up through the thick heather. I take one of the sheep-formed gaps through the undergrowth and soon all lucky thirteen of us are forging our respective ways up towards the summit.

The mist is thick the whole way up. The further I go up the mountain, the more I wonder how I will ever find my way back down again. There is already no sign of the car park down below. Looking up, even the mountain's top is nowhere to be found.

I see the battered marshal before I see the summit cairn. He is decked out in waterproof mountain gear sitting on top, ready to record our arrival times. "What's your name?" he shouts, his voice straining to be heard over the by now howling wind and squalling rain. "Moire," I pant, still out of breath after the steep ascent I've just done. I see him noting my name down before sending me on my way.

I sigh with relief, happy to have found the first point. My confidence has felt a minor lift seeing that I've not got lost thus far. 'Now where's the next place I'm meant to go?' I quickly quiz myself, turning around to find the second grid reference, *River Junction O 058 084.*

From the look of my map, it lies on the far side of a forest, on the other side of the road, down at the start of a valley. What this all means is that I need to first get off this mountain and get back down to the tarmac road.

I've another reason to want to get off this mountain as soon as possible. My map is thrashing about in the gales. I need to get the hell out of here before my map gets blown or washed away. But in my haste to make a speedy descent, I forget to look at my map properly and fail to take an accurate compass bearing. Instead, I *guess* I need to head off somewhere to the left, despite 'guessing' being a complete navigational travesty. And when I see someone else going that way too, I figure that I must be right and decide to follow suit. But the runner in front is going too fast and I soon lose sight of him. Now, without a compass bearing or a fellow runner, I am lost. Totally, utterly, hopelessly, lost. All I can see are sheep, grass and heather extending in all directions. All I can do is wander aimlessly downhill, hoping that I'll sometime soon work out where I am.

Those guys were right. I am not ready for such a race. I thought I was a proper mountain running woman. But all I am is a girlie city road runner who needs the safety of sign-posted streets.

I try following some sheep out of sheer desperation. But as soon as the sheep hear me coming, they scatter in random directions. I am so off-course it's frightening. It's looking increasingly likely that the other runners will have to come out here and find me after all.

Then, much to my surprise, I run into an earth bank. And on the other side, there's the road I am looking for lying right across my path. It's a miracle! I've reached civilisation! I want to get down on all fours and kiss the tarmac in true papal style.

But, there's another problem. The road is very long. And I am not entirely sure where I am exactly on it, if I should turn left or right now so to get to the forest.

There's nothing I can do but guess again. Well I want to go *down* into the valley. And the road seems to be sloping *downhill* to the left. So, I go left. Towards the down bit. I even break into a jog, spurred on by the relief of being back on the road again. After a few minutes, I even start to make out a forest right in front. 'I must have guessed right!' I think to myself. But then I see some cars. And then I see *my* car.

"Oooh nooo," I exclaim, cursing myself for my stupidity. "I can't believe it. I've ended up right back where I started from."

I see the lady from registration wrapped up in her car, waiting for finishers to arrive. I'm totally embarrassed by the mistake I've just made. But I figure I might as well admit my error and start all over again. I run up and tap on the glass. She slowly winds her window down with a perplexed yet bored expression strung across her face.

"Hi there," I stutter. "Hmmm, I sort of got lost coming off the summit. But I'm going to go on and try and get the rest of the grid references." She looks at me, unsure of what to make of me. "Okay. Whatever you want to do," she replies in a hesitant tone. But I know what she is really thinking, "Who in their right mind would run back to the start before completing the race? Who let *this* girl enter *my* race?"

So the good news is that I know now exactly where I am. The bad news is that this is *not* where I want to be. I'm most likely in the unlucky and last thirteenth position, but I decide to make the best of a bad situation. Crouching down behind my car in its sheltered safety, I study my map once more. I find a forest track from the car park I am squatting in that will bring me within 500 metres south of the second and next grid reference, *River Junction O 058 084.*

I decide to take that route.

The forest track provides good flat running and I soon relax into my stride. All too soon however, it comes to an abrupt and decisive end. I'm forced back onto pathless open mountain right on the valley's edge. Still, I have managed to find the banks of the very river that I was desperately hunting for. All I have to do now is follow it north upstream for half a kilometre. Then I'll see the river junction and the illusive, mysterious control flag that apparently I must visit.

These 500 metres could as well be 500 *miles* as far as my legs are concerned. The river bank is a sludge-filled jungle of reeds and marsh grass that trip me up and push me over, over and over again.

'So much for mountain running,' I complain to myself, cursing the mountain, the map, the organisers and anyone else I can lay my imaginary hands on. 'I'd be better just jumping into the river and army crawling my way upstream rather than trying to fight my way through this rubbish.'

Eventually, after what seems like forever, I find the place where two streams meet. I have found the river junction. And right there on top, just as the lady had foretold, there is the orange and white control flag, the Holy Grail I have been hunting for. I can't help but let out a little scream of glee. It might be just a wretched flag, but I've worked so hard to arrive at this moment that I can't help myself and celebrate.

I take out the control card that I got at registration, the one with the boxes and the numbers. I put it between the punch and I press, the resultant pinpricks providing proof that I have indeed reached this place.

Two down. Two to go. Much to my surprise, I've made it half way round. I decide I might as well continue on and finish, seeing there's only seven kilometres left to go.

The next point on the race is another river junction, this time at grid reference *O 084 081*. The river in question is on the side of a hill, two kilometres east from where I'm standing. I look up to see the direction that I must go in and low and behold, I see someone else running across that very hill, streaking speedily into the distance. Finally, another person! It is the first time I've seen another competitor since the summit, well over an hour ago. I take off after him in hot pursuit, desperately anxious to catch him. In doing so, I forget all about looking at my own map and finding my own independent way to the river.

At this stage, I know I am probably last in the race. 'But if I only manage to pass him out,' I say, hatching my evil plot, 'then he'll be last, not me. That'll prove to the rest of them that I'm not as stupid or as slow as I may seem.'

I sprint after him across the hill. This time the route brings me right through a field of black burnt heather strewn across the hillside. This place was set ablaze during the warm summer months when the Wednesday races were on. And all the fire has left behind is the heather's hardened wooden sticks and razor-sharp stumps. Without their soft heather leaves and flowers serving as protection, a pound of flesh is soon scooped from each one of my legs.

I look down and see blood gushing from the resulting multiple scrapes and scratches. I feel squeamishly sick thinking about the bloody mess. But, in the end, I've neither the time nor the tools to stop and repair the damage right here, right now. I will have to do all that later once I get back to base.

But far worse has now happened in the interim. In the time I take to look down at my bleeding legs and back up again, my penultimate runner has disappeared into the mountain's mist.

"Damn it!" I say, cursing him for having foiled my cunning plan to bestow on him my last position. But it's too late. I've lost him. And I am right back on my own again.

I manage to find the next river and begin the trudge up its banks like before. However, it takes much longer to travel than I originally foresaw. The river goes on and on, with no apparent fork in it to be found. I start to doubt myself. Maybe I have found the wrong river. Maybe I am in the wrong valley. Am I even still in the right mountain range?

Just as I am about to turn around and head home in defeat, I spy a little tent sitting on the river side. I tentatively approach it and before I know it, a hand pops out and grabs my control card. It then hands it back to me, punched as proof of my visit.

"Well done," the hand says. "You've not far to go now. You're in fifth position. And you're the first lady to arrive."

"What? Are you serious?" I protest. "But I got lost, I mean *really* lost. So I have to be in last place."

Much as I want to stay and protest the hand's statement, the river midges are starting to bite us both. The hand makes a hasty retreat and zips up the tent, leaving me alone to accept my race status.

I can just make out the person in the distance who I now know to be in fourth place. This time I will make sure I run fast enough to keep up with him as we both go in search of the fourth and final control. I follow his trail, over the hill's crest and down to the final riverside. It is rough running all the way, with grass and heather tripping me up and mud and bog trying to slow me down. Luckily, he too is slowed down by the terrible terrain, though is still too fast for me to snare.

I eventually find the final control flag lying in wait just where the grid reference said, on the edge of a forest at the third and last river junction of the day. After one final weary punch, I battle my way back up the final hill to the car park and to the finish, after more than three hours of running.

My arrival is greeted with mellow surprise. "Isn't this the Wednesday night runner girl who we thought would get lost?" they silently murmur amongst themselves. "Maybe she *does* know how to navigate. Maybe we were wrong about her in the end."

I have fooled them all. And I have even started fooling myself. Standing at the finish, I begin to believe that I am actually a good navigator, even though the race was ample proof that I'm a total liability out on the mountains. Getting lost coming off the summit was a spectacular example of how useless my compass skills are. My thinking that I was beside the wrong river, in the wrong valley showed that maps are still a foreign language to me.

Later I find out what really happened to the other runners who finished behind me. They had, unlike me, correctly used their compasses and followed bearings off the first summit. They had also chosen much better routes between the grid references than I. However, though these routes looked great on paper, they weren't to know that one of the forests they decided to traverse was thick with closely spaced spiky Christmas trees. Many of them spent over an hour stuck underneath the foliage, army crawling their way out on their stomachs under the viciously sharp needle branches. And whilst they battled their way through the forest, idiots like me who ran all the way around the forest via the starting car park were able to slide inconspicuously up the rankings.

By pure chance, I have beaten much faster, more competent mountain runners than I could ever be. Unfortunately, I begin to believe that it is all down to my superior mountain skills and speed, even if in reality these are non-existent.

Thankfully, the second race of the Series sets my ego straight and shows me how much I still have to learn when it comes to running and navigating in the mountains. Two weeks later, I find myself in the southern part of the Wicklow Mountains, on the Military Road due south of Drumgoff.

As usual, I do a quick check of my gear before the race begins to make sure I have everything I need. I've got my map, some food and water, a waterproof jacket and my compass, everything the race rules require. I do a quick routine check of my compass before putting it into my bag, just to make sure that it is in good working order, all ready for the race.

Compasses are extremely clever gadgets. First of all, they have a needle that points due north. By knowing where north is, you can then use it together with a map to know which direction to go in. And if you want to travel between two places on a map, you can use the compass to find the bearing between these two spots. Then you plug the bearing into the compass, turn yourself around and then follow the compass's direction of travel arrow so you can reach the spot, safe and sound.

My clever compass can potentially do all these things. But today, it is not doing any of them. Instead my compass needle, which is meant to point north, is swinging wildly around and around.

'What the hell is it doing?' I wonder. 'Why is it acting up like this?' As I stare at the drunken needle, I slowly remember that I had accidentally left the compass in my bag and had gone through an airport security check earlier this week. I am now looking at its inebriated motions and wondering if the security check has de-magnetised my compass and so removed all its magical powers to navigate.

Eventually the needle manages to settle. It should show north. But instead it is pointing east. This is the wrong direction. This is a big problem. I start feeling my stomach rotating with the compass by an equal and opposite ninety degrees. I feel sick ... and stressed.

"How am I supposed to run this race if my compass doesn't even know where it is?" I scream. I want to do a hissy fit. I want my compass to behave.

"Oooh, look at that," one athlete coos as he looks right over my shoulder. He is pointing at my compass. "Wow, I've never seen a compass do *that* before!" another exclaims. "I thought they normally pointed south when they've broken down," someone else remarks, opening up the debate into a theoretical discussion that I'm not interested in hearing. Before I know it, a small crowd has gathered around me and my dysfunctional compass. But their avid curiosity is sincerely not helping matters.

"Oooh, wouldn't it be fun to try to navigate with one of those!" one chuckles.

I've had enough. 'Yeah, well if it would be so much *fun*, why don't *you* take the compass and try it yourself,' I swear inside myself, gritting my teeth, not wanting to be held responsible for my next words or actions. My stress levels are rising by the second. How am I ever going to run the navigational race if my compass doesn't even work?

Fortunately, Paul Nolan notices my panicked expression. I spoke with Paul at the end of the race at Ballydonnell where he was the overall winner. Subsequently I found out that he's one of Ireland's finest mountain runners and orienteers, speedy across all types of terrains and in all kinds of conditions. His long legs and tall thin body make him perfect material for this sport. He also seems to me a quiet, kind sort of man, who's willing to help someone out like me who wants to learn the sport. And like all good mountain runners, he has come prepared to the race and kindly lends me his spare compass.

Just in time. A few minutes later, on the stroke of noon, the race begins. Flurries of innocuous pieces of paper are flung out to all the race participants. There are more coordinates, more hills, more rivers and more valleys. There are also more runners at this race compared to Ballydonnell, nearly thirty as opposed to last time's contingent of thirteen.

I barely take the time to circle the coordinates and to double check that I've put them in the right places. Instead, I set off like a red setter along the forest track, sniffing after the first grid reference. The control flag I am looking for is planted firmly in the forest just north of Slieve Maan summit, at an intersection of fire breaks. Fire breaks are purposefully planned five to ten metre gaps running in rows through the forest designed to stop the trees from touching. In the event of a fire, such breaks would hopefully stop the flames spreading from tree to tree and from thriving indiscriminately throughout the forest.

I enter the forest through one of these breaks and soon discover that there is absolutely no fear of fires here today. The forest floor is covered in sponge-like moss and has lapped up all of the late summer's rain. We slosh our way shin deep through the water, only stopping to clamber over dead tree trunks strewn across our paths. Eventually, after fifteen minutes of wading, we intersect with another fire break. And at the centre, there's the flag and the precious punch, the purpose of our quest.

Four of us escape from the woods together, making our way to the second control on Kelly's Lough located three kilometres away. I follow in the others' footsteps, pausing for just a moment to take in the map and my surroundings. Between my looking down and back up, they disappear out of sight. But this time round I'm more relaxed about my loss as compared to that at Ballydonnell. Somehow over the fortnight since the last race I've managed to convince myself that I actually know how to navigate. 'Not a bother, I'll catch them later,' I cockily think to myself. I take another quick look at my map and set off on my own, following a track I think leads to the lake.

But before I know it, the map no longer makes any sense. The mountains are not where they are meant to be. The track I am on turns to the right when it is meant to continue on straight ahead. The rivers are in all the wrong places. Forests appear where none are planted. The map is not following my orders, just like the compass refused to obey me earlier.

I am lost. Again.

In my confusion, I run up and down the track. I run into the forest and back. I can hear myself breathing heavily, tired and traumatised from having frantically run around in all directions for over twenty minutes. Finally, after turning the map around in several 360 degree circles, I decide to run down a hill through a forest clearing. Though it eventually turns out to be another wrong route choice, it does mean I meet two fellow competitors running up the same hill, in completely the opposite direction. They too have made a navigational error. But unlike me, they have now worked out where they are and where they need to go.

"I'm lost," I mutter, hanging my head in total humiliation.

One of the runners sees my distress and comes over to help me get back in the race. "We are here," he says with magnanimous authority as he points to a precise position on my map. "And we need to be here." His finger moves and waggles over a blue watery smudge that signifies Kelly's Lough where the second control is placed.

I thank him for divulging this vital information. Taking another look on my own, it now seems simple enough on paper. The question is though, can I do it in practice?

I turn around and retrace my steps together with them, back up the hill to the forest track. From here, there are two options available to reach Kelly's Lough. The first is to run straight across Carrawaystick Mountain, a shorter distance suggested by the map. The second is to run all the way around the mountain on a firm flat gravel track. This second option is a much longer route, but one that would be easier to run on as well as one that would be much easier to navigate. The other competitors opt for the longer road around the mountain. I decide instead to take the first option and head up and over Carrawaystick Mountain.

Today I learn that going in straight lines is not always the best idea. Instead of a leisurely scenic run on a flat forest road, I end up crawling up Carrawaystick's mountainside through heaving mounds of bog and heather. My lungs crash from the uphill exertion. The terrain underfoot slows me to a walking trudge. I begin to panic. No one else is up here.

'Oh God, why didn't I follow the others and take the nice flat route around the mountain? Why do I always want to do the opposite thing from everyone when it's sometimes better to just go with the crowd?' Sometimes my incomprehensible desire to be different can really push me too far.

In the end, all three of us arrive at Kelly's Lough at the same time. However, I am significantly worse for wear than the other pair. I expended too much energy running around in circles when I got lost coming out of the forest. And now I am exhausted from having gone up and over Carrawaystick Mountain, when all I needed to do was run around it. The other two punch the control and sprint on, leaving me in last position in the race.

Thoughts of giving up slowly infiltrate my mind. 'Why don't you just drop out? Then no one will know your time and place,' My head starts listing off legitimate lies I could use to explain to others why I could not complete the race. 'Say you got injured. Or pretend you got sick. Tell them you needed to get home early. Or that you fell and lost your map,' But the more fibs I fabricate, the more guilty I feel. 'Listen,' I eventually tell myself. 'Giving up is worse than coming last. Stop being so negative and just start again. Learn from the mistakes you've already made and do things better in the second part of the race.'

So reluctantly I continue. I decide from now on that I am going to stick to tracks regardless of how long the distance is. In the end, it's the best policy. I finally emerge back on the Military Road and climb up Fananierin Ridge and Croaghanmoira Mountain where the last two controls are found.

I am so behind all the other runners that the race marshals are already coming down off the mountain, assuming that everyone has by now passed through. It's embarrassing. Without a word, I give them my control card. They punch it and give it back to me, a permanent printed reminder of my terrible performance today. But by this stage, I don't care. I just want to finish this miserable race and go home.

At Ballydonnell two weeks ago, I was so afraid of coming last. But in the end, I won the ladies' race. This time around, my deepest fears are realised. I am the last one to reach the finish line. People I would consistently beat on the Wednesday night races have finished an hour ahead of me. Even a seventy year old man has made it back before me.

I am so depressed. We head to the Drumgoff Inn for after race refreshments. But even a post-race pint cannot stem my seeping sorrows.

Mountain running was meant to get me back on my feet, meant to give me the confidence and endurance to start afresh. But coming last today makes me feel like I'm useless, that I can't even get the simplest things, like map reading, right. Being last means I inconvenience others, like the summit marshals who had to wait for me before they could pack up and go home. Being last means that I'm probably trying to do something that I can't do, making me wonder if I should even try at all.

This leaves me with two options. Either I give up now and wallow in self-pity. Or I work out what I am doing wrong and learn to get it right.

I decide to take the second option. I decide to recommit.

I begin working on my mountain navigation straight away in the pub after the race by asking my fellow runners where I went wrong. I obsessively tell them again and again how my race went, explaining every wrong turn and every useless route choice I made as I point neurotically at the poor map.

"Do you see this track? I went left instead of right. Why did I do that? How did you guys know to go right? And see here, I went all the way up and over Carrawaystick Mountain. How did you know not to go over the mountain but to go around it? And see right here, I got hopelessly lost right here. How come none of you guys got hopelessly lost out there?"

I sound utterly desperate. The well seasoned mountain runners just sit and stare. They find it hard to fathom my stupidity. And whilst I am busy throwing rapid fire questions at them, they are all the time thinking, "Did she not realise that the map showed the path was going uphill even though she was running downhill, in the wrong bloody direction?" "Did she not see the contour lines and realise that there was a feckin' big mountain right in front of her?" "Sure didn't Paul give her a compass that worked fine? And even then, could she not use it to orientate her map and figure out where she was?"

Eventually one runner finds the silence too hard to bear. He turns to me and offers the most practical advice that I can take in this afternoon. "Best to just get over it, woman," he says. "You'll feel better in the morning."

It is good advice. I am too worked up about coming last in the race to accept the reality of my multiple mistakes. And I am not yet calm enough to listen and learn from the more experienced runners who are sitting all around. For now, it is best that I calm down, go home, go to bed and get over this minor set-back.

The next morning, I am physically stiff and sore. Yesterday's three hours of mountain running has left my body wrecked. My legs are sore from the multiple scratches sustained from the mountain's gorse and trees. My mind is worn out from all the energy expended from concentrating on the map for hours. But my pride is bearing the brunt of the pain. I still can't believe the stupid navigation mistakes I made. And I still can't accept that I finished in last place.

'I'm a fast runner. This can't happen to me.'

But this isn't a bad dream that I am awakening from. The race results posted on the IMRA website are conclusive proof of my failure.

Maybe it is the subsequent physical and mental torture that drives me to this stage, but after yesterday's Carrawaystick race, I am more resolute than ever to learn how to navigate in the mountains. I simply can't give up at this point. I need to get back out there and prove that I can do this. I need to prove this to myself. And I need to prove this to the others. I want to earn their respect.

I decide to email the organisers of the Navigational Challenge Race Series and I ask them for all the grid references of all the races that have ever taken place. They send me back a long, long list of coordinates.

At home, I then take each race and plot their grid references on my map. Then, lying back in the comfort of my armchair, I study my drawing to decide the best way to go between each point. I measure the map squares to work out the distance between places. I carefully count the contour lines to work out how high up the mountain each route will climb. And when I decide the way I would run the race in theory, I drive out to the mountains over the weekend and do it for real on my own.

The first few times out, I make terrible mistakes. I run off summits in the wrong direction, heading due west instead of going east. I run straight into cliffs and boulder fields because I don't recognise their symbols on the map. I try to wade across rivers that everyone knows are too deep and wide to cross. I try to find paths marked on the map and then don't realise it when I'm standing right on top of them.

But it is okay to make such errors. Free from the pressure of racing against others, I can make as many blunders as I want in the comfort of my solo training run. And I don't have to worry about coming last, as on my training trips I am the only one out here who's running.

I wanted a challenge after my African stint. And now I have indeed found my new challenge in the form of finding my way around Ireland's wet and wild mountains.

I climb a steep learning curve with many failures along the way. However slowly but surely, my navigational skills begin to fall into place. I start finding summits and rivers and forests and paths exactly where I expect them. I learn the best way between points. I can tell what type of terrain I should find just from reading my map.

And more importantly, I start to appreciate the freedom of navigating my own way through the mountains. I can explore lakes and valleys, discover mountain tops and lap up stunning views that many cannot imagine, let alone ever see. I can run freely throughout these mountains I have just uncovered, thanks to my map and compass.

5. Mountain Marathon

I am soon itching to put my new found navigational skills to the test in another race. Eventually I find the perfect opportunity: The Mourne Mountain Marathon.

When most people think of a marathon, they think excruciating long twenty-six mile race. They see towns and streets crammed full of thousands of runners and throngs of their screaming supporters. They think elite athletes packing together at the front, vying for the title and fun runners streaming out behind them, doing it all for charity.

Mountain marathons are slightly different. First off, there's no tarmac, no roads, no signposts. Instead, the race is run over miles and miles of rough, steep, exposed and barren mountains.

And mountain marathons don't attract the thousands of competitors that regular marathons draw. Instead runners and supporters are far and few between, spread out far and wide across the mountain landscape course.

But there is one major difference I need to come to terms with. In normal marathons you compete alone. In mountain marathons, two individuals come together and compete as a team.

Mountain marathons are designed to be completed in teams of two. That's a problem for me. I'm not good in teams. I'm not a great team player. Not that I would ever admit that fact to anyone.

Team work brings out the best in most. But for some unknown reason, it can bring out my worst. I become competitive and critical. I become impatient and sharp. Its only when I totally trust my team members and I know what they expect of me, that I can slot safely into a team situation and be a help rather than a hindrance.

Learning to navigate in the Wicklow Mountains has also revealed to me how much I enjoy being alone at times. When I tell others what I'm up to, they wonder if I feel bored out there all on my own. But I tell them it's quite the opposite. That I feel at peace when I'm by myself; that I can't hurt or harm anyone around me; that others can't laugh at or criticise me.

But at the end of the day, I can't shut myself into a room and spend my days avoiding others. People I've met who've opted for such lives have appeared disconnected, disenchanted, delusional.

And I really want to do the mountain marathon. So I opt to take the team risk.

Despite my attempts at the Navigational Challenge Series and backdated races, I am still a comparative novice when it comes to map reading and compass navigation. If I want to compete in the Mourne Mountain Marathon, I need to find myself a good navigator as well as someone who's willing to team up with me.

The solution to my navigation and team dilemma materialises in the form of a young German mountain biker named Mel. I first meet Mel at an IMRA Wednesday night mountain race. She appears at first to be a prim and proper lady, with rosy cheeks, long blonde hair and a pleasant, charming smile. But beneath this delicate feminine appearance lurks a tough and determined female.

I see Mel again after the Carrawaystick Mountain Navigational race in August. She has just run the mountain race and has beaten me fair and square. I'm still sitting at the Drumgoff Inn, firing out random questions to anyone who'll listen, desperately trying to find out how to navigate.

"You need lots of practise, that's all it is," one fellow competitor advises. "Listen, why don't you do the Mourne Mountain Marathon next month up in Northern Ireland? That would be a good test of your navigation skills."

"And seeing that there'll be two of you running together in a team," someone else chips in, "you'll be able to help each other out reading and figuring out the map."

I take a few moments to consider the suggestion. "That's sounds like a good idea," I tentatively reply, whilst wondering who the hell would agree to run with me given my obviously bad navigation skills and my potentially bad team behaviour.

Mel also overhears the conversation and quickly jumps in. "I'm hoping to do the Mourne Mountain Marathon too. Would you be interested in doing it together, Moire?" she asks, brimming with enthusiasm.

Mel and I don't know each other that well. But she seems pleasant and good company. And given today's respective performances, I know she'd be well able to drag me around the Mourne Mountains. I'm scared, though, that I'll mess it up, that my Jekyll and Hyde team skills will materialise.

But I also won't know unless I try. Hopefully Mel won't hate me too much if my social flaws appear.

We eventually agree to team up and enter the mountain marathon together. Though both of us have completed many of IMRA's short mountain races, neither of us have ever done a mountain marathon before. So we decide to enter one of the middle distance classes. We are one of five all-female pairs in a total field of sixty-one teams.

It is early on a cool Saturday morning in September when we arrive at the base of the Mourne Mountains. Already hundreds of people are milling about, all ready to start their respective races.

It takes a lot longer to cover twenty-six miles in the mountains compared to the city, what with having to run up and down hills and across grassy, mucky terrain. Competitors are therefore given two days to complete the distance, with a designated overnight break in between. Mountain marathon rules therefore stipulate that you must bring everything you need to be self-sufficient in the mountains for forty-eight hours. You must bring a tent, a sleeping bag and a torch for your overnight stay. You must also bring a stove and fuel, as well as two days' worth of food. And then there are the compulsory safety requirements, a survival foil blanket, whistle, map, compass, waterproof clothing and first aid equipment. All this, you must put on your back, tighten the straps and then run with it up and over all the mountains.

By looking at everyone's bags at this morning's race start, we can tell which teams are the elite athletes vying for the title and which ones are out for a fun run.

The fun runners have enormous baggage strapped to their backs. They are bringing warm clothes, roomy tents, as well as bottles of whiskey for the evening and salted bacon for the morning. In comparison, the elite runners have what look like miniature purses. They have brought no creature comforts. They are wearing skimpy shorts to save on heavy clothing, have brought two matchsticks to light their stove instead of a 'heavy' box of matches and will squeeze themselves into a tiny one person tent even if the team is composed of two big strapping men.

Mel and I have opted for an intermediary approach. We've left the whiskey and bacon at home and have brought instead lots of dehydrated food. Already we are looking forward to tonight's sumptuous dinner of dry pasta with a powdered soup sauce, followed by a delectable dessert of powdered custard.

We've also packed tomorrow's breakfast sachets of freshly freeze dried coffee and porridge, a caffeine and carbohydrate concoction that will hopefully give us enough energy to keep us going for a second day. We have a spacious two person tent and two warm sleeping bags, but have decided to forego the sleeping mats. Instead, I'm going to spend the night on bubble wrap, a much more lightweight option than a half kilo pad. Mel has decided to go for an even more hardcore sleeping arrangement. She will lie on a thin foil blanket, with her map strategically placed underneath for extra insulation.

The two of us are feeling nervous as we start our race on the stroke of half past eight. Just as in the Navigational Challenge Series back in the Wicklow Mountains, we are handed a piece of paper with a list of grid references and descriptions. I take a quick glance. They've given us a frightening long itinerary of places to visit. Eleven controls over twenty-six kilometres with an ascent of 1500 metres. It's going to be a long, long first day on the hills.

After marking our maps with the whereabouts of the eleven controls, we jog off in search of the very first one.

Less than five minutes into the race, my back starts to complain. The burden of all the equipment is starting to weigh me down. The shoulder straps dig lines into the sides of my neck. The waist band is gradually rubbing at my stomach's skin. If this continues on, my body will have a big red welt the shape of my bag by the end of Day One.

Mel too is suffering from all this additional weight. "How exactly are we meant to run up and down mountains with this great big load hanging off our shoulders?" Mel protests.

"I know. If this was a normal marathon, there'd be none of this running-with-rucksacks rule," I whinge back in agreement.

At least our team has found some common ground to complain about early on in the race.

But we both know that this is what we've signed up to. We've just got to grin and bear it. So I tighten all the straps I can find and bolt the bag solidly to my back. With it now firmly in place, Mel and I agree on a running strategy for the day.

"Why don't we do this? We walk uphill and jog downhill. And we'll do a mixture of walking and jogging on the flat."

I nod in agreement to Mel's suggestion. Trying to run uphill with these packs will kill us within a few hours. We need to conserve our energy and use gravity when we can.

Mel's coming up with some great ideas. It's good. I'm glad. She's actually the type of person I often work well with. I need someone to take control, to tell me what they need me to do. Show uncertainty and I'll panic, I'll try to take over and then I'll create the havoc that has ruined too many relationships already.

With the first control safely found and our card punched, we take a look at the map to find the second control of the day. It's not good. The next control is a quarter of the way down the map, seven kilometres away from the start, just north-east of Chimney Rock Mountain. And right between us and the second control is Slieve Donard, Northern Ireland's highest mountain.

"I'm not climbing up and over that," protests Mel. I'm glad she says it before me. I'm already thinking the same thing. So we sit down and study the map's terrain.

There are only two realistic ways to get to Chimney Rock Mountain. We could take the long climb up the Glen Path River to The Castles, cross the Mourne Wall, then follow the Brandy Pad to the Bog of Donard before meeting the path that leads to Chimney Rock.

Or, we could run straight out of the forest and run right around the Mourne Mountains on the main A2 road from Newcastle. The road route would be much longer distance-wise, but it would totally avoid the steep mountain terrain. We could cover ground more quickly and save our legs for later mountain climbs. Already I'm having flashbacks from Carrawaystick Mountain, when running around the mountain was definitely the better option.

Mel also likes the idea of doing some tarmac road running. So off we trot, exiting the forest and turning right onto the A2. We can't help but giggle together at our unorthodox route choice. We've decided to momentarily flout the mountain part of the race and to just do the marathon bit instead. Cars slow down in sheer curiosity as they see two girls sprinting down the road with oversized rucksacks on.

"Hey Mel, why don't you let your hair down and stick out your thumb?"

"Yeah and you can flutter your blue eyes and hitch us a lift to the next mountain!"

Mel and I are having such fine ideas this morning. And it's good. I'm having fun. This team work hang-up I've been having, I was blowing it out of proportion.

Eventually we leave the A2 and follow the mountain path up along Bloody Bridge River. We are both tired already from ninety minutes of running. But we feel in good spirits as we head towards Chimney Mountain and to our second control of the day.

Up until now we have only seen two or three teams out on the course. But as the ground finally levels off and our control comes into sight, we suddenly see dozens of other teams descending like vultures into the control from an assortment of random directions. In the mêlée for the punch, I see Paul

Mahon, Avril's brother, the guy who first introduced me to mountain running back at Corrig Mountain. He's got one of those miniature rucksacks on and is sprinting towards the control. He's obviously one of the elite athletes who are out here for the win.

"How's the form, Moire?" he asks, as he punches his own card. "Mel and you going strong, I see," he says with a cheery, cheeky grin. I'm amazed that even when he's in the heat of the battle, he's still got time to put in a friendly word. And though Mel and I might be going strong according to him, he's literally flying around the course with his team-mate.

"Not too bad," we both reply, Mel flashing back one of her infamously radiant smiles. It's good to see someone out here like Paul giving us a bit of support and encouragement.

But there's no time for proper chat. We all have our races to run. "Sure we'll catch up with you at the overnight camp tonight. Have fun out there!" Paul shouts after us as he gallops on up the hill.

Mel and I continue collecting our own controls, up and over Chimney Rock Mountain, around Slieve Donard, across the Mourne Wall and down into the Annalong Buttress. We soon realise that the Mourne Mountains are much larger and more impressive than the gentle rolling hills of Wicklow. All around us are towering mountains, sheer cliffs and deep valleys, interspersed with crystal blue rivers and reservoirs. And today, blue skies light up the Mournes, making it a scenic setting for our first ever mountain marathon.

By now, we are half way around the course. But despite the beauty of the surrounding scenery, the distance, the climbs, the wet terrain and our heavy rucksacks are all taking their toll. Mel has to put up with all this and more. As our team's navigator, she is draining herself mentally as well as physically, expending energy as she continually tries to read the map and keep us on course. As she tires, she slowly starts to slip behind.

"I think I need a break, Moire," she shouts after me. "Just a short sit down."

I'm not in favour of stopping, but seeing that she's struggling, I reluctantly agree.

"Can you pass me that sugary roll?" Mel asks as she settles down on a stone.

"Sugary what?"

"Sugary roll... you know the sugar... that's in the roll." I think hard. What could she possibly mean? "Ooooh, you mean the fruit pastille sweets that you have in the back of your bag," I eventually translate. I reach into her backpack and pull them out for her. I can't help but chuckle.

"They're called sweets, Mel."

"Oh yeah," she replies with an embarrassed grin. Her Germanic command of the English language is faltering as tiredness ominously creeps in.

She swallows a few. And then gets back up on her feet. But her speed simply doesn't return.

It's not looking good as we head up Slievelamagan for our sixth control of the day. And I'm beginning to get more and more frustrated.

'She's meant to be the strong one. She's meant to lead,' I find myself ranting, terrified that her physical demise will also signal the end of our excellent team dynamics that have been so good up until now.

Memories of my last place at the Carrawaystick Navigational Race start flooding back as well.

"I don't want to be last. I want for us to do well. Come on, Mel. Speed up, will you?"

My impatience and selfishness are rapidly surfacing. I can see myself repeating the same mistakes that I have previously made. Just when I have the chance to do things differently with Mel and to redeem a piece of me.

I've no right to be annoyed at Mel. But I can't let this happen. I have to do something. But it must be constructive.

"Why don't I carry your bag for a while, Mel?" I suggest. "That will at least force me to slow down and allow you to speed up."

"Yeah, I wouldn't mind thanks," Mel replies. "I'm not feeling the best. Running without the bag will at least allow me a little rest."

So I take Mel's bag. I hook hers on my front, with my own bag still on my back. We agree that I'll keep her rucksack until she recovers.

And it seems to do the trick. She soon perks up and sets off with renewed vigour. She leads us over Ben Crom dam, up the Shannagh River to its Lough, back over the Mourne Wall and on to Butter Mountain for the last few controls of the day.

I don't let Mel know of the internal battle I'm having. As far as she's concerned, we're working as every team obviously should. Even though I'm desperately struggling to figure out the right thing to do, the right things to say to keep our team fully functioning.

It is around 6 pm when we reach Craigdoo. Just below us we can see a field covered in hundreds of brightly coloured tents planted randomly at the bottom of Butter Mountain. It's today's finish line and the overnight camping ground. Many teams have already finished their courses, have set up camp, are cooking their freeze-dried dinners and are catching up with friends.

The scene below feels like home. I can't wait to get down there to eat my dinner and fall fast asleep. All we have to do is find our final two controls and we'll be able to descend to the field of tents too.

But there is a problem. We can't find our second last control. The race description says that it is at the start of the river above Lugagour crags. But we have gone up and down the river for the last ten minutes and we cannot find the flag. Mel and I are in a state of sheer panic. The mountain marathon rules says that you have to find *all* the controls if you want to finish. If we miss one, even if we get ten out of the eleven, our race will be deemed over and we will be disqualified. As much as I want to run straight down to the finish and start setting up our tent, we have to stay up here on the mountain until we find this feckin' flag. But the more we search, the more we panic and the more tired we eventually become. We begin to wander about aimlessly up and down the river, bereft of a strategy of where to look next.

After what seems like forever, we see another team heading up high above us in the gully. We follow them and finally see the flag that we have been endlessly searching for. It is hidden behind some reeds, making it hard to see unless up close. We realise that we had been searching too far down the mountain and neither us had an altimeter to alert us to the fact that we had descended too low.

But at long last, we have found it. We can finally head towards the last control and then on to the finish!

After nine hours thirteen minutes of mountain running, Mel and I finally cross the line. Sore and hungry, yet elated that it's all over for today, we search for Paul and his friends and set up tent with them.

It's only now that I appreciate the load that we have been carrying throughout the day. Everything we need is right in our bags. Some extra clothes to keep us warm, something to eat, a place to sleep. It all seems so little, but this is all we need. It's such a liberating feeling that, for just one night, we can throw off the vestiges of urban living and live straight out of a bag. And what's even better is that there are so many like-minded people around us who are also revelling in this simplicity. With no TV, no internet, no mobiles, no distractions, everyone is hanging out and chatting, enjoying the outdoors and each other's company.

We pull out our dinner and lap up the pasta, soup powder and custard. And as everyone sits around eating and drinking, we hear the epic stories of what other teams have endured throughout today.

Out of the sixty-one teams that started our course this morning, twenty have already dropped out. For some, a team member has sprained an ankle or damaged a knee, forcing the pair to retire. For others, team members were not fit enough for the race to begin with and have become physically unwell on the course. For quite a number, navigation errors have ended their race. I hear of one team who went looking for a control on a mountain. And when they couldn't find it, they gave up, ran down to the nearest road and took the bus straight home. It looks like Mel and I have done really well just by finishing Day One.

Once we have enough energy to get back up on our feet, Mel and I wander over to the results board. Much to our surprise, out of the five all-female teams entered, only two have completed today's course. We are one of the two. We are feeling more and more proud of ourselves by the minute. Then we peer up and down the rankings and notice that the first female team came in twenty-seven minutes ahead of us. Without even saying a word to each other, we both know what the other one is scheming.

"Shouldn't we at least give those girls a run for their money tomorrow?" we simultaneously ask.

"Twenty-seven minutes? Sure that's nothing," Mel declares. "Come on. Let's go after them tomorrow." Mel is fully revived since her sugary roll incident. And she's full of fighting talk. When this girl has her sights set on something, God help whatever it is she's chasing down.

What with this being our first mountain marathon, we have absolutely no idea what we are proposing. Twenty-seven minutes, though not impossible to recover, is definitely a large lead to chase. Day Two's course is also typically shorter and therefore there is less ground to make up time. But we don't know this. At this stage, the idea of running after the other girls is like a childhood game of chase.

So, in our playful ignorance, our Day Two plot is hatched.

We hardly sleep that night. Both of us are hurting as we lie on the hard ground, every joint and muscle complaining after nine hours spent in the mountains. I also struggle to sleep without a comfy sleeping mat, not wanting to move too much lest I burst every bubble of my bubble-wrap. Mel is kept awake, jealously listening to the snores emanating from the other tents. But in the end, both of us are too excited to sleep. We can't wait to start stalking down the other girls and clawing back those precious twenty-seven minutes that separate us on the scoreboard.

We arise at dawn, stiff and sore from Day One's exertions and Night One's uncomfortable bedding. It's an 8.15 am start for everyone on the course this morning and we've just enough time to drink our coffee, take down the tent and queue for the loo before the race start.

Today is a slightly shorter course distance-wise. But what the race organisers have thrown in instead is something called a 'cluster'. A cluster is a set of controls that we can visit in *any order* of our choosing. This means that, not only can we decide how we go between points, but we can decide the actual *order* we visit these points in. Mel and I are very aware that those twenty-seven minutes we are chasing could be gained or lost just by how we make our choice.

The cluster we are given consists of five places: a river junction, a cliff, a disused sheep pen, a re-entrant (which is an indent on the hillside) and the start of a stream, all dotted randomly around the Mourne Mountains.

The stream start is where most of us choose to begin. Mel and I arrive there and punch the control. Just as we are leaving, we see the leading female team right behind us. We are only two minutes in front, but it's a good sign. We decide not to hang around and opt to visit the cliff next. We look behind but cannot see the other girls. They have chosen to go up and around Slieve Meelmore and to visit the sheep pen next instead.

Mel leads us straight to the cliff without a moment's hesitation and brings us straight up to the flag. "Good woman yourself Mel, you're really on flying form today!" I shout after her as she speeds on to find the next point.

Mel has found a new lease of life today. Since last night, I've felt guilty about having been so annoyed with her lethargic performance yesterday. I should have been more patient with her. But Mel seems completely unconcerned by my bad team behaviour. She's a woman on a mission. And I'm proud to be her teammate.

From the cliff face, the river junction is the most obvious next port of call. And somehow Mel manages to find a perfect path for us to follow to the river that is not drawn on our map. The tension and excitement is too much for me and I suddenly need to stop and pee. "Sure I can pee with you at the same time," says Mel. "That should save us some seconds." So without even stepping off the path, we look in opposite ways and momentarily relieve ourselves from all the race pressure. We are really becoming a proper team complete with excellent urinary coordination.

Onwards and upwards, we run on to the sheep pen already visited by our rivals. Then we go across to the re-entrant, before finally finishing the cluster. We are pushing ourselves and each other to the limit.

But the pace is taking its toll. Soon we start slowing down and our steps turn into a shuffle. My own legs are weak, my feet are in constant pain, my back is bent double and my balance is fast deteriorating. Mel too is suffering. But neither of us is quitting.

"Let's keep going, Moire," Mel shouts over. "Those other girls have to be as tired as we are. For all we know, they could be sick or injured. They might have even lost their map or had a big argument. We just don't know. We have to just keep going until we reach finish."

"I agree Mel," I mumble back. "We might be both feeling terrible. But the other team could be feeling even worse."

After last night's stories at the campsite, Mel and I know that anything can happen to teams on these sorts of races. We just won't know what's gone on until it's all over.

But soon things start to happen to us that neither of us expects.

Without any warning, Mel falls down a bog hole and smacks her knee sharply against a loose stone. She goes down in utter agony, screaming from the pain. From the sound of her screech, I fear that the only way she'll be getting off this mountain is on a stretcher. She lies writhing on the heather, her eyes screwed up in torture as she desperately clutches her knee. Then after a few seconds, she relaxes, sits up and rubs the wound. Mel then turns to me and says, "Okay, let's go."

"But you're hurt," I protest, wanting to get her some help. "I'll be fine," she replies. She then gets back up onto her feet and starts running off into the distance. I know Mel is a hardy mountain biker, well able to take bangs and bloody wounds. But never before have I seen someone who can endure so much pain so stoically. I feel like such a wimp in comparison as I stagger off after her.

Next it's my turn to run into trouble. We come to the final control on the mountainside before entering Tollymore Forest where today's finish lies. Between me and the flag is a large flat rock set into the ground, freshly coated in morning dew. To the right, the rock disappears over the edge to form a sheer cliff. To the left, the rock has no end. There's no room to run around it. We must run over it. Mel makes it safely across. But I am apprehensive. My shoes have already slipped several times today on wet rock. If they slip now, I'm definitely a goner.

But time is ticking and we are still trying to catch those twenty-seven precious minutes. So I jump. One foot lands on the rock and somehow stays in place. The next foot manages to land further, past the rock, on boggy ground on the other side. Mel cheers. I collapse. I hate coming this close to death.

But there's no time to hang around for theatrics. We have three final controls to get before we can cross the finish line. We punch the last one on the mountainside and then head straight towards the forest for the remaining two.

After two days in the mountains, it's great to be on relatively flat forest terrain. However, we soon get disorientated by the network of paths that run criss-cross through the trees. Our minds are so tired that we can make neither head nor tail of the tracks. What makes it worse is that we are so tantalisingly close to the finish, less than one kilometre from here. We're close to repeating yesterday's mistake, when we wandered aimlessly up and down the river looking for the missing control. So we take our time, look again at our maps and finally find the flags hidden deep in the forest and eventually the finish just beyond the trees.

We complete the day's course in five hours and forty-two minutes. The other girls' team is still behind us. But by how far, we have no idea.

Mel and I flop down on the grass beside the line, too exhausted to move. We see other teams arriving in from the mountains, but we are not interested in them. We only want to see when the other female competitors will cross the line. Our friends try to engage us in conversation, but we are too nervous to respond. Our sole focus now is on our watches and the minutes that are painfully ticking by.

We see the other female team finish, but it's too close to work out who has won. After over fifteen hours of running over forty-five kilometres and up 3,000 metres of mountains, our teams are separated by only a few minutes. We have to wait for the official results.

It is only at the prize giving that they call out the final times. Today the other team finished in six hours and twelve minutes. But when Day One and Day Two times are added together, Mel and I have not only clawed back those illusive twenty-seven minutes, but have won the female race by three minutes.

We both scream girly screams when we hear the result. We simply can't believe that we have managed to win our race category on our first attempt. The surprise and joy of it all supersedes the aches and pains of two days of mountain running.

In the end, I'm glad I raced with Mel together as a team. Thanks to her, my confidence is slowly returning. Maybe I'm not as bad a person as I sometimes come to believe. Maybe I can learn to be not a hindrance but a help, like Mel assures me this weekend I was. Though I know I'll always cherish solitude and appreciate moments away alone, maybe I can learn to also be with others and let them bring out the best in me.

The Mourne Mountain Marathon marks the official end of the mountain running season. But I've no intention of giving up at this point. I'm having too much fun to stop. So I start looking for my next big adventure that can keep me on this adrenaline rush.

Mel Spath: my formidable mountain marathon partner and kick-ass mountain biker. Photo courtesy of Alan Donnelly.

6. THE WEAKEST LINK

September arrives and the Irish mountain running season hibernates until next year. But I've a sneaking suspicion that most mountain runners aren't sitting idly at home for the winter, waiting for the race season to start again in spring. I figure they must do something with themselves during these dark and cold months to keep themselves fit and warm. I start to ask around. Because whatever it is they are up to, I want to be up to it too.

It is Avril's brother, Paul, who has again the inside line on where mountain runners go from September on. "Why don't you have a go at adventure racing? That's what most people are up to these days."

"Adventure what?"

"Adventure racing," he replies. "You've probably heard of triathlons where guys combine running, cycling and swimming in a race. Well adventure racing is a bit like doing a triathlon in the mountains, except you mountain run, mountain bike and you kayak instead of swim."

Sounds fun, except I'm still set on improving my mountain navigation skills. I don't want to drop them and forget them in the process.

"Don't worry about that. You also need navigation skills to adventure race around here. Look, the way it works is this. You're in teams of four. The race isn't marked, just like in the Navigational Series or the Mourne Mountain Marathon. So each team always needs someone to navigate for them. You'd learn loads by watching your team navigator. And if you're good enough, you might even be able to lend a hand."

Well at least I'll still be able to practise my navigation. So with that worry sorted, I bring up the only other issue that's bothering me. "Look Paul, I know how to mountain run. But I don't have the slightest idea about kayaking. And I've never mountain biked before. I'm not sure if I'd be even able to do this adventure racing thing."

"Don't worry. You'll learn. Listen, there's a three day adventure race over 250 kilometres coming up soon in the West of Ireland." He hands me a phone number. "Talk to this guy. He's looking for a fourth team member."

I'm doing it again. Throwing myself into the deep end with absolutely no idea of what I'm letting myself in for. Am I not meant to go off for a few months first and learn how to mountain bike and kayak? Should I not go away and train so that I can be fit enough for this adventure racing craziness? The Mourne Mountain Marathon was a fraction of this adventure race's distance and I could barely walk for days. How can I even contemplate being ready in a few weeks' time for this race when I haven't even tried half the sports involved?

And what's this thing about three days anyway? Triathlons take only a few hours at most. "Oh, adventure races over multiple days are totally normal," explains Paul. "At least at this one coming up the organisers let you sleep for a few hours between stages. But there are some twenty-four hour adventure races where you don't sleep at all. And then there are races over several days where you sleep for maybe an hour or two a night."

They are crazy, absolutely crazy. And I'm even crazier to agree. I pick up the phone and call the number. Ivan from Northern Ireland answers the phone. "Great stuff, Moire. Paul said you were interested alright. Good to hear you can join us.

It's hard to get a crew of four people willing to sign up for these races."

"Listen, Ivan, before you accept me on to your team, you should know that I don't know how to kayak or mountain bike. And I've never done one of these adventure races before. I'm not even sure if I'll last the three days."

"You'll be grand," Ivan assures. "Everyone has to start somewhere. Sure you'll be fine with us."

And so with these reassurances, I agree to join the Causeway Coast Adventure Racing Team for the three day Gaelforce Adventure Race in Westport, County Mayo.

The first thing I learn about adventure racing is that you need *a lot* of gear. Not a trivial two rucksacks' worth of mountain marathon kit. No, the equipment list we are given for this adventure race is pages and pages long, with each sport having a specific section with the kit that we must bring along.

Just for mountain biking I need 1) a mountain bike, 2) a helmet, 3) cycling gloves, 4) back and front lights, 5) spare light batteries, 6) bike repair kit and 7) cycling shoes. And that's just the stuff I *have* to bring as opposed to the bits and bobs that would be nice to carry along. And then there's the kit that the team must have with them at all times: food, extra clothing, first aid materials, a mobile phone, a map, a compass, group shelter, an altimeter and flares. It's like we are going on a full-on polar expedition.

I arrive in Westport on Friday afternoon, a four hour cross-country drive from Dublin. My other three team members, Ivan, Steve and Shirley are already there.

Ivan is a tall, friendly guy, fresh faced from a life in the outdoors. "How's bout ye?" he asks in his gruff Northern Irish accent that reminds me so much of home. "Grand hi," I reply, slipping back into the local lingo I remember from my childhood. "And yerself?" I ask Ivan. "Grand altogether," he says. "Glad ye could make it to the race."

He quickly makes the introductions. "That's Shirley, me sister," he says. "Pleased to meet ye," I say. "But are ye really his sister?" I can't help but ask. Never have two siblings looked so unlike. Shirley has a mohican of pink hair, electrifying when compared to Ivan's head of grey. She must have been the wild one in the family.

"And this is me mate, Steve," Ivan explains. Steve looks like Ivan's sidekick, a sturdy, short, rugby-playing kind of guy. It looks like Ivan must be the mature, responsible leader of this team, whilst Steve is the one with all the craic and the banter who's meant to keep the group's spirits high.

Though this is the first time we have properly met, we get on fine from the start. Our positive first impressions are a huge relief to us all. We're going to be spending the next seventy-two hours in very close proximity under tough race conditions, so we have to learn to get on whether we like it or not.

The race officially starts on Saturday, but we've arrived the day before for registration and outdoor skills tests. First off, we have to fill in a long medical form. I've subsequently come to learn that the medical form length is directly proportional to how dangerous the race is that you're about to attempt. And this form is pretty comprehensive. My hazard warning levels are already beginning to rise.

Next it is off to a nearby lake to test our kayaking skills. It is at this point that the penny drops with Ivan that, when I said I have *no* kayaking skills, I really meant it. I spend the next ten minutes going round and round in circles on the water, trying desperately to work out how to make the boat go forward *and* straight at the same time. The race officials verifying our skills are obviously not impressed. Fortunately, Ivan and Steve are strong paddlers and the boats we will use are for two people. We get the officials to agree that on the day, Steve and Shirley will be together and Ivan and I will pair up. At least then Ivan can do the steering and I can just paddle along.

The next test we face is our rope and abseiling skills. "You what?" I splutter. "Nobody told me anything about having to do any rock climbing. I was told it was like a mountain triathlon. You know, just biking, kayaking and running."

"Hmmm, that's sort of right," Ivan replies. "The majority of adventure races use these three disciplines. But, like in any proper real-life adventure, ye can have anything thrown at ye. In this one, there's some abseiling and a bit of climbing. But you can be asked to do all sorts of things on an adventure race like horse riding, swimming, jumaring, canyoneering, orienteering, roller-blading, heck, even mathematical puzzles."

This isn't good. Not only am I a terrible rock-climber and abseiler, but I'm also petrified of heights. "What are ye at?" Steve screams when he sees me tying myself in knots as I try to climb the ropes. "Meer till I show ye what te do," he says, taking me aside to give me a quick demo. What Steve shows me is just enough to get me through the test and for our team to just about scrape by. I'm not too sure though if I'll be able to repeat any of the moves Steve has taught me during the actual race.

By 9 pm, all the teams have registered and done their respective skills tests. However there's one last thing to do before we hit the sack. The race organisers want to give us a preview of what lies in store for us. Up on a big screen, they bring us through an animated fly-by over the whole course. Starting from Delphi mountain resort on Saturday, we are to kayak the length of Killarey Harbour, climb Mweelrea Mountain, take in a quick abseil, then arrive back at Delphi to pick up our bikes. From there, we will cycle to Croagh Patrick, go up and down that mountain and then bike back to Westport. And that's just Saturday, the end of Day One. After a few hours' sleep, it'll be an early 7 am start on Sunday morning, leaving Westport in our boats to kayak through the three hundred islands of Clew Bay all the way over to Achill Island. There we will pick up our bikes and cycle around Achill Island for the rest of the day and into the night, with some more abseiling off the coast's cliffs. Everyone has a mandatory stop for four hours to eat or sleep or rest. Then teams hike back through part of the Nephin Beg Range and finally cycle back to Westport. 250 kilometres of biking, hiking and kayaking in total. I'm tired already just thinking about it.

The six other teams look very mean and lean lining up to the race start the next day. I'm having flash-backs of the Corrig Mountain running race start when I felt so out of place. At Corrig, I felt fat in comparison to all the other competitors. Now at the start of this adventure race, I feel I'm completely the wrong shape and size. I lack the gleaming muscles and six foot heights that the other Greek gods and goddesses around me have. Adventure racing, it seems, doesn't attract too many short, squat girls like myself.

Whilst I'm still coming to terms with my dimensions, I notice that all of the other teams are composed of three guys and one girl. We are the only team here with two females and two males. One of the rules of adventure racing is that teams must be mixed or co-ed, so there are always both men and women on a team. However, it is hard to find girls to compete in the sport, so often there's a shortage of women to go round. In addition to this scarcity, there is another reason for the three to one ratio of guys to girls. Women are often regarded as the weaker sex for this kind of sport, so teams prefer to keep them to a minimum. With two women on our team, as opposed to only one, others are already dubious of our chances of even finishing.

We wait anxiously at the start, decked out in thick wetsuits ready for the initial kayak section. As the starting whistle blows, we run down the road towards Killarey Harbour, jump into our kayaks and paddle as fast as we can to the base of Mweelrea Mountain. As soon as we hit the water, my lack of experience shows. My stroke is short and powerless. I hold the paddle around the wrong way. I develop blisters on both hands. My arms are writhing in pain. Slowly our boats fall further and further behind the leaders. Ivan and Steve try hard to keep us up with them, but there is only so much the guys can do.

After ninety minutes of paddling punishment, we arrive at the mountain's base. We are in second last place. Quickly we tear off our wetsuits, put on our running clothes and begin the ascent up Mweelrea Mountain. There is not much running though to be done. We end up scrambling up the steep sides using our hands and feet. But there is nothing to hold on to except the odd tuft of grass. Foot holds are minor earth ledges or single stones. My danger warning levels are going ballistic. I try not to look down at the water below just in case my danger barometer explodes.

We can see nothing as we head further up Mweelrea and push higher and higher into the clouds. Mist is perched nonchalantly on top, oblivious to the inconvenience it is currently causing us. But Ivan is a happy navigator and has no problem finding our way through the fog. We visit the summit as required and then scramble our way back down the mountain's other side, down a treacherously slippery and stony slope. The descent is steep enough to scare me. But that's nothing compared to the abseil we are about to attempt. In reality, the abseil is down a very minor crag. But seeing that it involves heights and entrusting my life to a rope, my mind soon transforms the crag into a mammoth cliff. I am terrified. And I'm not having fun. This is going way beyond my comfort zone.

It is late by the time we get back to Delphi. We pick up our bikes for the ride back to Westport via Croagh Patrick, St. Patrick's Holy Mountain. It has been raining all afternoon and we are drenched, cold and hungry. It is in this fragile state that we get onto our bikes. Our morale and energy are quickly deteriorating and soon the idea of trekking up Croagh Patrick is too much to bear. With its sheer slopes covered in shale, we know it will be dangerous to climb it at night. And seeing that we have two more days of competition still ahead, we decide to give it a miss. We take the two hour time penalty that they'll add to our overall time instead.

By the time we arrive back in Westport, the other teams have been back for ages. Most are busy getting ready for tomorrow's race stages. Some have even finished their preparations and are sitting around relaxing and even indulging in a pint. I, on the other hand, head straight to bed and fall fast asleep.

We shake ourselves out of bed the next morning at 5.30 am to head to the shores of Clew Bay for Day Two's start. Everyone in our team is stiff and sore, but we manage to cajole each other along and keep each other going.

"Come on lads, we'll be grand," Steve tries to persuade us. Shirley and I aren't so convinced. After our dismal kayaking performance the day before, us girls are silently dreading this morning. We are to kayak from Westport to Achill Island across Clew Bay. It will take us more than five hours, more than triple the time it took to paddle the length of Killarey Harbour. And what makes it worse is that today's navigation is much more difficult than yesterday's plain sailing. Clew Bay is scattered with hundreds of tiny islands that are impossible to tell apart. We are meant to find four particular islands out of the several hundred out there.

After a couple of hours of this hide-and-seek game through Clew Bay, the weather suddenly turns foul. The wind picks up. The waves increase in size. Soon we see lifeboats coming screaming to our aid. They change our race course and divert us inland. But as we turn back towards the mainland, we meet waves pushing us onto jagged rocks. Ivan does his best to keep us away from these boulders, but the effort required is too much. As he struggles to keep us out of harm's way, severe tendonitis inflicts his left arm. He screams in pain with each paddle stroke. With one arm out of action, he tries to shout instructions to me over the deafening sound of the scowling sea. I'm scared, very scared. I'm unsure what to do and not sure if I can help. After a few narrow misses with rocky outcrops, we finally make it into calmer waters. And after six hours of paddling, we reach dry land.

There's no time for rest or reflection on what has just happened. It's out of our wetsuits and on to our bikes for a twelve hour cycle around Achill Island. My legs and backside don't know what has hit them. Never before have I been on a bike for so long, let alone straight after sitting down for six hours in a kayak. We are all physically exhausted and mentally stressed from the battering we got from the waves.

By nightfall, all of us are feeling very fragile. Steve's stomach is upset. Shirley is mentally wrecked. And I'm exhausted from not enough sleep. I don't realise how drowsy I am until I nearly fall fast asleep whilst riding my bike downhill at high speed.

Ivan sees what's happening to his team. We are all so close to breaking point. It is now the middle of the night at the end of

76

Day Two's race. We have been cycling non-stop for ten hours up and around Achill Island. Our route has now brought us to the top of a hill on Achill's coast, overlooking the whole of the Atlantic Ocean. "Let's stop here and get off our bikes," Ivan suggests to us all. I'm a bit baffled about what's going on, but I decide it best to comply. We put our bikes down, then step off the road into a field and we all lie down on the grass.

It's a beautiful, silent night. But we've been so busy huffing and puffing, racing and running, aching and moaning, that we've completely failed to look about and see the wilderness around us. It's so peaceful out here in the dead of night. I look up and see the stars. Never before have I seen constellations so clearly against such a night sky.

Ivan, Steve, Shirley and I all lie there in total silence, a silence laced with exhaustion. But it's not an uneasy silence. Rather its one completely comfortable with each others' presence. I have known these guys less than seventy-two hours and already a deep inexplicable bond has grown. We may not know each other well, but we have endured things together, have done crazy things together, have forged ourselves together into a team. That's what makes adventure racing special. Not just the sport, but the comradeship that grows when people are pushed to the limit, pushed by each other and by the great outdoors.

We lie there less than five minutes, but it is enough to revive us again. We press on, back to the race transition where we finally dump our bikes. We now have four hours to grab some sleep before going back out on the course at dawn.

We need to start the mountain hiking section at 6 am on Day Three, so we decide to wake up 5.30 am. In our utter exhaustion, everyone sets their alarms wrong. Shirley sets it for 5.30 pm in the afternoon, Ivan sets it for Wednesday instead of

Monday and I set mine for totally the wrong time. Somehow though I wake up at 5.35 am, five minutes after the supposedly alarm call and work out what has happened. 'But if I just go back to sleep,' I say to myself, 'I can pretend I didn't wake up at all. Then I can doze for a few more hours and blame the alarms for not waking us.' I am completely exhausted. Every part of my body hurts. All I want to do is sleep for several days. But I know we are so close to the finish and that we only have another six to eight hours more to go. And anyhow, the guys would never forgive me if they found out I went back to bed. My conscience gets the better of me and I shake the other three awake.

But Steve wakes up not feeling well. "You need some more food in ye," Ivan reckons. "Here, eat some of this." Ivan then proceeds to force feed Steve breakfast the only food we can find left in our gear box, a chicken masala camping meal. Needless to say it doesn't stay down too long and regurgitated chicken masala soon ends up scattered across the camping ground.

Steve braves his sickness heroically. He keeps on trekking up the first mountain, though he is noticeably quieter than before. There are no more wise cracks and chit chat coming from him. Instead, every so often, Steve stops and spews his stomach's contents onto the mountain floor. He then wipes away the debris and keeps silently hiking on. It reminds me of Mel and her knee banging incident in the Mournes. I seem to attract people who go through pain and hell right in front of me, but who just keep slogging on.

In the end, we decide to cut our trek short, to miss out some controls and take the time penalties instead. By doing this, we finish together as a team and have a final ranking. I'm secretly glad we miss out the hike. I'm so tired and sore that I can't bear the idea of going up any more mountains.

But, despite the soreness and tiredness, every trace of physical pain suddenly disappears as we cross the finish line. In an instant, the good memories of the adventure race start to filter through: the mountains and seas that we have visited, the views that we have seen, the comradeship that we have experienced are suddenly lucid in my mind. I start to feel acute euphoria, utterly proud of what we have accomplished over the last three days. We are handed a bottle of champagne to celebrate our achievement. But Steve is too sick to drink and Ivan is sensible and has to drive. So Shirley and I share it between us. The bottle is drained within seconds, us girls thirsty from dehydration and exhilaration.

The drinking continues well into the night, as the various teams descend on Westport to celebrate their race completion. It's a total cliché, but everyone is a winner tonight. Anyone who manages to get around a 250 kilometre course and doesn't lose or kill one of their team members deserves a drink or two.

When I went mountain running for the first time up Corrig, I felt terrible afterwards but loved it in the end. I'm feeling the same way now after this three day Gaelforce adventure race. My muscular pain dissipates fast. But the adrenaline and excitement of the event remains. I want more of this adventure and want to do it again.

Then once more, in typical style, I bite off more than I can chew. "Well would you like to do a seven day race in Scotland?" Paul, my mountain guru, asks. "It's 500 kilometres this time. We're looking for a few girls to fill up the spots. Let us know if you're interested." It's double the length and time of my maiden Gaelforce race. Am I totally insane? And not only that, but Scotland's wilderness is much wetter, colder and harsher than Ireland's. Will I even survive? But then again, the race that Paul is referring to is the Adventure Racing World

Championships. And it's not every day that you're invited to join an Irish national team.

I can't resist the challenge. I put my name forward and get accepted on to the squad.

Two teams are accepted from the Republic of Ireland to participate in the World Championships. The more experienced adventure racers from Ireland form the first team and I am welcomed into the second. For the next eight months, I am to train, compete and prepare with the other three members of my team: Bob, Chris and Paul McArthur.

Bob is a gentle giant of a guy, an eccentric IT consultant with a goofy head of frizzy hair and a 1970s VW Beetle van for his wheels. In terms of looks and style, Chris is quite the opposite. He's a broad stocky man and an accountant by trade. He drives a big company car and has not a single hair on his head. Despite their differences, Bob and Chris are inseparable when it comes to adventure racing. They turn out to be a great pair of lads to team up with.

Paul McArthur is the pro within our team. After years of extreme mountain climbing, he started adventure racing back in 2002. Seeing that neither Bob nor Chris nor I have done anything of this magnitude, it is Paul McArthur and the members of the first team who are to show us the adventure racing ropes.

First of all, we set out to improve our kayaking skills. So after work every Wednesday, we head down to Blessington Lake, thirty kilometres due south of Dublin. A fellow adventurer racer and outdoor instructor, Brian Keogh, has a place on the lake shore and is happy for us to train with his boats.

We tie glow sticks to the front of our kayaks to keep track of each other in the dark. And we layer up well in wetsuits, jackets and gloves to protect ourselves from the freezing temperatures. Then we do a tour of the lakes, along its banks, under the bridges and past its forest-lined edges. Sometimes we'd just float for a while, enjoying the silence and the stars. Then after an hour or two of practise, we'd head back to the boat shed to take off our wetsuits, to store our boats and to gather around a freshly blazing fire. Brian lays on mugs of tea, Kimberley Mikados biscuits, as well as ample amounts of Irish banter to warm us up before sending us on our way.

As our confidence increases on the calm Blessington Lake waters, we eventually move our practice sessions to Dublin Bay on the edge of the Irish Sea. Here we have to contend with waves and tides and proper sea conditions like we will encounter over in Scotland. We even have to keep an eye out for ferries from nearby Dublin Port and make sure we are well out of their way. Our small two person sea kayaks are no match for the bulk of an Irish Ferry ploughing its way to the UK. Most nights we kayak out from Clontarf as far as Howth Head's Martello Tower. Occasionally we are even joined by the seals from Bull Island, who swim over to join us on our Dublin Bay paddle.

Sometimes, instead of heading out to sea, we turn inland and kayak up the River Liffey that runs straight through Dublin City. It makes a nice change doing some urban kayaking instead of paddling against relentless sea waves. We kayak past the docks and ships, past the Point Depot and International Finance Centre, past the Spire and Guinness Factory. We duck under each of the River Liffey's bridges in turn: Séan O'Casey Bridge, O'Connell Bridge, Ha'Penny Bridge and Millennium Bridge, all the way up to Heuston Railway Station. As we paddle along in the river water down below, I look up at the cars up above on the Quays stuck in yet another one of Dublin's traffic jams. 'Now this is definitely the way to commute,' I think to myself. 'Forget the car or bus or bike. From now on, I'm going to work by boat!'

Though we are still busy with our kayaking, our bike skills also require some attention. Most weekends see us out on long biking spins of six hours or more across the Dublin and Wicklow Mountains. With speed and endurance already building in our legs, we spend a lot of time trying to hone our technical mountain bike skills. We start off on relatively easy mountain bike sections like the *Boneshaker* off Fairy Castle, with rocks strewn across the downhill. Soon, we increase the technical difficulty by heading to the *Ewoks* near Glendalough for steep and slippery forest descents. Finally we make it all the way to places like the *Widow Maker* and the *Rock of Death*, technical mountain biking sections if not ridden properly will see us validating these places' names.

Most of us are already mountain runners, so we are not worried about the running sections of the adventure race. But we want to get used to changing suddenly between disciplines, so at times we combine a bike ride with a run. We dump our bikes and hide our bags in the forest or heather and then go for a run up any spare mountains that we happen to find lying around.

This being a World Championship event, we know there is no way that there will just be the three disciplines of biking, running and kayaking. Just as I dreaded all along, ropes are part of the event. It's a case of facing my fear or dropping out of the team. 'I've already learnt the rubrics of mountain biking and kayaking from scratch,' I tell myself. 'Why can't I do this again with ropes?' I can't give up on the race now after already investing so much.

So I set about learning how to hang comfortably from a rope. Fortunately my teammate Chris has a rock climbing friend who brings us out to Dalkey quarry to show us the basics. He endures patiently as I cling and swing uncontrollably on the ropes, unsure of how to go up or down.

And whilst ropes are my nemesis, Chris is yet to face his. The race organisers soon reveal that there will be a swimming section during the race. Chris hates water. In fact, he can barely swim. But he too wants to race and realises that he too has to learn. So he goes for lessons and soon is happily floating around enough to be able to complete the swim section. It just goes to show if you really want to do something, it's never too late to learn.

Bob, Chris and I, being new to the sport, have so much to learn in such a short space of time. But all of us are so determined to succeed that we make the necessary sacrifices. We give up evenings and weekends, even friends and relationships, just to gain the tantalising rewards promised by this race.

Before we know it, there are less than three months to go before the World Championships at the end of May. And with less than ninety days to go, we enter the start of the Irish adventure racing season. Now we have a chance to put our training into practice and to race together for the first time as a proper team. Our winter's work pays off and we register some good results. However, I soon begin to realise that there's a lot more to racing than training.

With the extreme highs that come from adventure racing, there are also devastating lows. During long races, team members get tired, injured, sick and moody. Bikes get broken, maps get torn, shoe laces snap and survival bags get lost. It can rain relentlessly, mist can come down, winds can blow you off your feet, the cold can freeze your inner bones. Teams lose their way. They get frustrated, have fights and fall out. Someone can't keep up, someone won't slow down. Someone won't listen, someone won't shut up. And as the race goes on for longer and longer and as the teams get more and more tired, these minor inconveniences can become breaking points if not resolved in time. But just try to resolve conflict in a grown-up way when you've been racing for eight hours and you are lost in a forest and you are cold from having fallen in a river and its getting dark and your knee hurts and you can't find the energy bar you've been looking for and your teammates are shouting at each other for not having taken that other turn in the road ten kilometres back? That's why being able to work as a team in adventure racing is as important as being able to bike, kayak, or run.

Good teams are made. And we are still in the process of making ours.

But with three months to go, I'm finding it hard learning to race as a team despite my success with Mel. Firstly, I am the only girl in a group of three guys and I'm just not as fast or as strong as them. I am often under pressure to keep up and feel useless when time and again I cannot. Sure, they have ways of helping me stay with them. They put me into a two person kayak with the strongest paddler in the team. They attach an elastic cord to my waist and pull me uphill on mountain runs. They use the same cord again and attach it my bike. Then I can slipstream behind the fastest biker and be pulled along if I start to fall behind. But despite these little tricks, I'm still damning myself for not being as fit and fast as them.

At times, though, I'm not struggling to keep up. Sometimes it's the lads who are waning. There's something that happens after four to six hours where the gender divide collapses and I can become as strong as a man. They say it's to do with body fat content and endurance, but girls can start performing better as the race gets longer and longer. This too presents a dilemma. If the guy falls behind and the girl is fine, an ugly battle of egos can ensue.

And then there are the personal annoying traits that are exacerbated when in a racing scene. I know I'm impatient, I know I'm competitive, I know I push myself and others too hard. And when I'm adventure racing, these imperfections of mine are often magnified to extremes. In any other normal situation, I could walk away, rethink my actions and try again tomorrow. But when adventure racing, we have to stick together as a team at all times and keep on racing until the end. There's no time for time-out.

But there is one part of the team that is still missing and it's a part that can't be easily fixed. I soon come to realise that adventure races regularly put us in difficult and dangerous situations in the wilderness. Often we find ourselves in these situations when we are tired and not completely alert. Sure, there are safety procedures and protocols, but the great outdoors are under no one's full control. Anything can happen on mountains, rivers, or cliffs regardless of health and safety standards or briefings. So to be safe out there, you need to know what you are doing. You need to be experienced, to be able to read the signs, to know when to pull the plug. Paul McArthur has years of experience, but he is only one in the team. Bob, Chris and I are still new to the sport and very new to the extreme outdoors.

Small things happen that start to make me worried. Twice I nearly fall down steep mountain terrain and come close to breaking bones. We come close to capsizing our sea kayak, even though none of us are comfortable at rescuing ourselves at sea. During training, I fall off my mountain bike and severely damage my arm. If this had happened on an adventure race in the middle of nowhere, I would have been in real trouble. The reality is, I don't feel one hundred percent safe. And one of the reasons I don't feel safe is because I don't have the skills or the experience to ensure my wellbeing.

But I put this feeling of insecurity to the back of my mind. I am so focused on doing the World Championship adventure race that I don't want such negative thoughts to deter me.

I am so focused too that I don't even see what the training and racing is doing to me physically. I'm constantly hungry and will eat just about anything that will take the hunger pangs away. And despite all the physical activity involved, I'm putting on weight. But it's not muscle. It's fat from an improper diet, from having not enough time to cook and eat properly. My feet are a mess, layered with hardened calluses from repeated blisters on my toes, soles and heels. I notice big clumps of hair falling out when I brush the tangles out post hard races. That's in addition to feeling constantly tired. After a while though, I don't know what it's like to feel well rested any more.

But I say nothing to the others. They'd think I'm pathetic. Other adventure racers have permanent injuries and broken bones and they keep on going. My physical complaints aren't even worth mentioning in comparison to what other athletes endure.

The week of the Adventure Racing World Championships arrives and both Irish teams take the ferry across to Scotland with two vans full of gear in tow. We drive to Fort William, the site of the race headquarters, a town lying in the west of Scotland and on the shores of Loch Linnhe. I have never been to this part of Scotland before. As we drive through Glen Coe on our way to Fort William, the sheer scale and size of the

Scottish mountains suddenly hits me. They are huge in comparison to anything we'd dare to call mountains back home in Ireland. In fact, ours are mere hills when compared to these edifices. And then I see the mother of them all, Ben Nevis, Scotland's highest summit. Seeing the wilderness where we will soon be racing, I am totally terror-stricken.

And if I was intimidated by the calibre of adventure racers in Westport, I'm literally scared out of my wits by the other teams who've turned up to this race. The top teams in the world have arrived, from New Zealand, Spain, France and the States, to battle it out in the Scottish Highlands. The organisers have designed a ferocious course to test the world's best, 500 kilometres of the remotest, coldest, highest and wettest landscape that only Scotland can muster up.

It takes two days to prepare for the race. There are gear checks, skills tests, race briefings, interviews, photos and miles of maps to mark with coordinates. The organisers also provide us with GPS trackers so that they can know where we are at all times.

Finally we are taken by bus to Mallaig and ferried to the Isle of Rum where the race will begin.

The race officially starts on the Sunday morning, but we've arrived early on the island on Saturday to do a 'quick warm-up'. In adventure racing terms, that's a 500 metre open water swim and a quick half-marathon through the mountains. It's not even part of the race, but what they call 'the race prologue'.

The top teams are hungry for action. They fly through the water and bomb up the mountains and are back within a few hours. As for us, we are already suffering. Chris has an old hip wound that has started acting up and I've got blisters from my shoes. But we keep on going and finish the warm-up course together in one piece.

After a night of camping out, the race proper begins the next day. The first stage is a kayak section. We are to kayak from the Isle of Rum past the Isle of Eigg and then towards the Scottish mainland to the Morar Estuary. We are then to carry the boats to Loch Morar, kayak to Swordland, carry them again to Tarbet, then paddle across Loch Nevis to Inverie. It's a sixty kilometre kayak and we have until 2 am on Monday to complete it.

Though the sun is shining brightly on Sunday morning, the wind is whipping up impressive waves. Such waves can be disastrous for paddling, causing boats to easily capsize. It's not looking good. I'm still not the most confident kayaker and am dreading the distance that we have to cover today which will take us in excess of fifteen hours. Adding windy weather conditions into this equation will make this section extremely difficult to cover, maybe even dangerous.

Within minutes of the start, our worst fears are realised around us. Some kayaks are knocked over by the waves, tossing competitors and their gear into the water. We see other teams struggling to right themselves. We see safety boats coming to their aid. We paddle quickly past, sincerely hoping that we will not be the next to need rescuing.

But, though we stay upright, the sea is trying its damnedest to overturn both our boats. High waves hit our kayaks side-on, rolling them close to tipping point. The wind comes from behind, knocking out our steering. Even when we do reach the mainland, there is little respite there. We try to enter the channel, but the tide has turned and the wind is blowing us back out to sea. We spend the next hour paddling to stay still. I hear myself screaming above the howling wind, trying to fight against the elements whilst fighting back my own hysterical fear. Eventually the winds subside and the current dies and we round the corner into the estuary.

We reach the quiet sanctuary of the Morar Estuary and Loch Morar, but it is a sinister calm that we find. The Scottish lakes are much colder than the sea due to their superior depth and stillness. We later hear of one team who capsizes a boat within this loch. One of their team members lands in the water and quickly becomes hypothermic. Despite repeated attempts, he is unable to climb back into the boat and is lucky to be rescued alive. He can no longer go on. His team is forced to withdraw.

We just make the 2 am cut off in time. This allows us to continue on to the second section of the race, a forty-four kilometre hike with 4,400 metres of ascent across Knoydart passes and mountains to Loch Hourn.

After a full day of kayaking, I'm finding it impossible to stay awake. Bob tries to restore the team's energy by making sandwiches for us to eat. He lays down eight pieces of bread on the ground and throws ham and cheese on one side. He then folds them up and hands them out. None of us care that our sandwiches have come straight off the road and have the odd piece of grit in them. We're just glad to finally have some proper food to eat.

We start our hike in the middle of the night. I want to stop and sleep through these hours of darkness, but the rest of my team are happy to go on. We trek for four more hours before we finally find a place where we can lie down, an abandoned stone ruin without a roof. I get into my survival bag, curl up on the hard ground and pass out for two hours. It's not enough, but it will have to do. Chris, though, doesn't catch a wink of sleep. I wake to see him pacing up and down, trying desperately to keep himself warm.

We trek from 8 am on Monday until 2 am on Tuesday through steep, remote and awe inspiring mountain ranges. We have moments of utter danger and times of utter delight. But towards the end of the trek, our legs and feet are falling apart. I start to hear the guys complaining, "I hate this. Wait until I get my feckin' hands on these organisers. What sort of madness of a course is this? I've so had feckin' enough." But my exhausted brain no longer has enough wit at this stage to realise that this is just the lads' way of letting off steam. Instead, my head interprets what the guys are saying and concludes that they want to give up on the race. I start getting annoyed, then angry and after four hours of this talk, I finally explode.

"Well if you want to give up, then will you feckin' tell me?" I ominously growl at them. "I'm not going to kill myself for nothing just for you to give up half way."

"Give up?" They look at me in utter confusion. "Whatever gave you the impression we wanted to give up?"

As if men and women don't have enough problems communicating when they are in normal situations, I am now trying to understand my male teammates when we are all sore, stressed and sleep deprived. As if the physical ordeals of adventure racing weren't already enough to be dealing with.

We grab a three hour sleep before getting on our bikes early on Tuesday morning, Day Three of the race. A possible twenty-four hour cycle lies ahead. But I find it difficult to get started. My hands and feet have started to swell badly from the nonstop racing and possible dehydration. My feet can barely fit into my cycling shoes and it takes me a few minutes before I can squeeze my fingers into my biking gloves. My hands are uncomfortable and ugly to look at, but thankfully not sore.

It starts to drizzle as we set off on our cycle. And for the rest of the day, it doesn't let up. It leaves our bikes and clothes and spirits sopping wet. The sodden weight of my waterproof trousers causes them to get caught in the bike chain. The sharp chain-wheel shreds the trouser legs to bits, leaving me with rags to protect myself from the elements. Our bikes suffer repeated punctures. We stand around getting cold whilst our teammates try to quickly fix the tyres. We reach parts of the course that are too steep and rocky to ride, forcing us to physically carry the bikes up on our backs and shoulders. I get wetter and colder and more miserable. And we are still less than half way around the course.

It is 6 pm when we reach a mystery task, a minor detour devised to distract us from the day's mountain biking. It looks simple enough. There is a waterfall and a river below it. We are to jump into the river from a rock beside the waterfall. The rock is about three metres above the water. Paul does it, Bob does it, even Chris, who is so afraid of water, does it. I know I'll be able to do it too. I get to the rock edge, all ready to jump.

Then I panic. I thought I was over my fear of heights. I've just discovered I'm not. Despite getting over my rock climbing phobia, I am still petrified of falling. I try to fix my gaze straight ahead to run up and jump over the edge. But my head forces me to slow up each time, preventing my feet from leaving firm ground. "You have to feckin do this," I yell. "Feckin stupid, feckin chicken shite, bloody hell, jump will ye!" The others look on in dismay. For five full minutes I do successive false starts to the rock edge, getting angrier and more obscene.

Until I give up.

I cannot believe it. I have confronted so many of my phobias in preparation of this event. I was afraid of mountain biking and kayaking and sea swimming and climbing and I tackled all of them one by one. But what I fail to appreciate is that I overcame my fears when I was well rested and in a safe environment back home. Now, after four days of non-stop physical and mental exertion out in the middle of nowhere, I am in no fit state to face down my residual fears.

We head away from the river, back up to our mountain bikes where we left them before the water jump. "Don't worry about it, Moire," Chris says. "It's not a big deal."

"We've only received a one hour time penalty because you didn't jump," Paul McArthur explains. "Other teams decided to not jump at all and took four hours' of penalties instead."

Regardless of their attempts to console me, I am too despondent to hear. I have failed the task and am so distraught that I can barely talk as we walk. My mind starts to taunt me, 'You couldn't even make the jump. Ha! What a loser! You've just proved to all the others that you are the team's weakest link.' The stress of my failure proves too much for my system. Within a few minutes I find it difficult to breathe. Soon the lack of breath becomes a fit of hyperventilation. I begin to panic even more. "I can't breathe! I can't breathe!"

Fortunately, a nearby race official sits me down and slows my breathing back to a conventional speed. He gives me tea and talks to my teammates, reassuring them that I'll be fine. Once I'm back to a semi-normal state, we get back on the bikes and cycle off towards the final mountain section. It is getting late and dark, but my team is determined to press on. I too think I'll be fine, resolving not to slow my team up any further.

The mountain ground is rough and soaking wet, making it impossible for us to cycle. So we physically push the bikes up the mountain through the dark and rain and mist. With the darkness the demons return, determined to taunt me still. 'You couldn't even do the water jump. What sort of team member are you? You're just weak and pathetic. I can't believe the others haven't dumped you already!'

Soon I find it hard to speak. Bob asks me if I want some food. In my head I say yes, but my mouth finds it impossible to verbalise this simple word. He hears nothing from me, so rightly assumes I don't want any. My inability to talk terrifies me. How will they understand me if I don't have enough energy to communicate my thoughts?

Then as my ability to converse leaves me, I begin seeing things around me instead. Adventure racers call them 'sleepmonsters', hallucinations that stem from sleep deprivation. First I see people and houses, then people pushing wheelbarrows outside their houses. But when I turn around to look, there is nothing there. Then I see a lighthouse in the middle of the forest and start believing that boats will arrive soon. Finally I become obsessed that someone in our team is missing. Within adventure racing circles, this is called 'Fifth Beatle Syndrome' after The Beatles' fifth band member who left before their rise to fame. My head counts my team: 'One, two, three and me, that makes four. We're all here. But still someone is missing. Who is missing? I can only see three. But we are meant to be four. Where is the fourth?' My head spins around in this counting conundrum. I keep forgetting that I am the fourth team member.

The array of sleepmonsters that are now assailing me make me increasingly nervous. And whilst my brain is busy breaking down, my body is following suit. The guys see me struggling to keep up with their pace. I try to take a drink from my water bottle, but don't have enough strength to squeeze the plastic bottle's sides. They take my bike off me and tell me to walk ahead. I stagger to the left and then to the right. I need the bike to lean on. But I can no longer talk and explain to them that I need my bike back.

"She needs to sleep," Paul McArthur says. "We'll put up the group shelter at the lake just ahead." We all pile in and I fall fast asleep, rolled up in my survival bag and propped up by Chris's shoulder. We wake at dawn after a three hour rest. I'm groggy and sore but seemingly a bit better after the night of sleepmonsters.

My respite, however, is short lived. We get back on our bikes and cycle down the other side of the hill. After less than an hour, I've collapsed again on the side of the road. My team force feed me energy gels, trying to get me back on my feet. But the effects are limited.

"She needs proper food," Bob says. "There's a village just ahead on the map. Maybe we can get some there," Paul McArthur points out. For the last three days I have survived on sweets, bars, energy gels and biscuits. By now I can't stand the sight of sugar. In the absence of savoury food in my bag, I have stopped eating, just when I need food the most.

At the entrance of the village there is a tiny post office-cum-local grocery store. We go in there and proceed to clear them out of pies, to demolish their sandwiches and to consume all their coffee. I start to think it may have done the trick until we go back outside to the bikes. I pick up my bike but start to hyperventilate again, only this time I also begin to shake wildly. I can barely stand from the convulsions and I begin to sob uncontrollably. I want to go home. I don't want to be here or to race any more.

My team brings me back into the post office. The post master lies me down in a back room, my head resting on a five kilogram bag of charcoal. It's the most comfortable thing I've slept on in days and I soon begin to dose.

My team watch me and watch the clock. They are desperate to keep going. But I'm not just losing us time. I'm also threatening our race. If I drop out now, the team will be disqualified and finish unranked. A team is made up of four people. Three fails to score anything.

We have worked so hard and spent so much time, effort and money to get us to this race. How can this happen after all the high hopes that we had? But I don't want to go on. I'm too cold and miserable to get back on my bike. I can't face another 250 kilometres of this. And with my head resolutely making its own mind up, my body quickly degenerates. I develop mild hypothermia.

Eventually the race medic arrives and they bus me back to the race finish. He plonks me on the nearest couch in the race centre and I curl up in a fetal position. I sleep only a few hours, but it's sufficient to instantly regenerate me. After a quick coffee and wash, I'm feeling alive and well again.

Because of the race, I've been out of contact for the last five days, so I find a place to check my email. Suddenly, as I read through my messages, I'm hit with the full reality of what I've just done.

During the race, I always felt that we were so alone out on the course. We'd seen no other teams, no other people, not even the slightest sign of civilisation. It sometimes seemed like we were the only four people in the world on those seas and up those mountains. But I had forgotten that we were constantly carrying a GPS tracker with us. So though we were all alone, in reality people knew exactly where we were. And we were being watched. But it was not just the race officials who were keeping an eye on our journey. The GPS coordinates were also available online and friends back home could follow our progress live on maps in real-time.

And with the maps, come instant forum messages. I read the online well wishes left for us since Saturday by our friends and families. I then see our progress charted on the race website's results board. And I see the withdrawal of my team on Day Four. I then read the long list of commiserations posted today following my decision to pull out. My guilt levels grow as I read them one by one.

The website doesn't give the reason for our retirement. But I know I am the one responsible for my team's demise. I came to represent my country and I have let my country down. Back at the village's post office this morning, I didn't fathom the full repercussions of my decision and actions. But now I am the source of so much disappointment that I can barely live with myself or what I've done.

I take a notebook and start writing down every thought and feeling I have from the race. I need to get them all out of my system, to see them down on plain paper so that I can work out what really went wrong. It takes me several hours. But when I've finished writing every last drop, I read it all back to myself. Then I make a long list of resolutions to make sure that such failure will never happen to me again. I decide to make myself physically stronger and faster. I commit myself to improving my sporting skills. I decide to buy better gear. I resolve to get over my vertigo. But when I see how much I have to do, I start to question if the sport is even for me. If I have so many short-comings, am I really cut out to adventure race at all?

And even if I make all these changes and carry out these resolutions, this does not fundamentally change why I dropped out of this race. In the end, I dropped out because I was mentally not strong enough to go on. Is this a short-coming that I can even change?

Anytime I talked to friends about adventure racing, they all thought it sounded so cool. Getting to do so many adventurous sports in incredible surroundings with fun loving people is something so many people want to do. And there was definitely a part of me that did the sport because it made me sound adventurous and hip too.

But coming to this race in Scotland, I have seen a less appealing side of the sport. And it is not just the physical pains and mental breakdown that I went through that makes me think again. As I wait for my team to finish the race without me, I see other teams getting medi-vaced off the course. I see people with broken bones, cracked ribs and stress fractures from accidents whilst competing. I see people with no skin on their feet from walking too long in bad shoes. I see people covered in bacterial infections as their immune systems break down from too many days on the go. And I hear of teams pushing themselves beyond reasonable limits, people physically carrying semi-conscious team members up mountains on their backs because they can no longer walk on their own.

And when these horror stories are told, I seem to be the only one who thinks they have pushed themselves too far. Instead, everyone else seems impressed. They congratulate those that have endured longer and have pushed themselves harder, beyond their perceived physical and mental limits. I find it hard to share these same sentiments.

My team eventually come off the course twelve hours after my abandonment. When I see them, they are dirty, tired and depressed. They do not give out to me directly, but I know all of them are mad at me for quitting. According to the spirit of adventure racing, you just don't give up unless you physically can no longer go on. I am feeling much better after only a few hours. That is proof to all my teammates that I could have easily continued on. I gave up when really I should have just dug deeper.

My own team doesn't speak badly of my decision. Instead they try to understand what happened. They see my breaking point as the waterfall jump and that I rapidly deteriorated from there. To their credit, they tried as hard as they could to get me back on my feet. But for some reason, I couldn't stand up again.

I leave Scotland with a lot to think about. Up until now, I have pushed myself harder and harder and managed to muddle through. I have progressively stepped up from mountain running, to navigation races, to mountain marathons, to adventure racing in less than one year. But at this latest race in Scotland, I reached my personal perceived limits. And I'm not sure I want to go to that place again.

But more seriously, my confidence has taken a severe bashing from the event. The other Irish team end up finishing the race intact, but I forced the withdrawal of mine. I am embarrassed by my physical inabilities and mental weakness. I'm convinced that the other adventure racers are also doubtful of my competence. I am sure they all wish they had never even accepted me on to the Irish adventure racing squad.

I make up my mind. I need to prove myself to them again, to show that I am not as useless as I currently feel. And I need to get back out there and show them that I will never let down my team ever again.

7. 24 Hour Treasure Hunt

A chance for redemption soon arrives. Within days of returning to Ireland from the Adventure Racing World Championships in Scotland, I hear that the Irish twenty-four hour Rogaine Championships will take place in less than three weeks' time. I am not sure what a Rogaine is. All I know for certain is that it's a long distance race that adventure racers hold in high esteem. If I enter and finish, maybe my team will forgive me for dropping out from the Scottish adventure race. There is nothing else for it but to do the Rogaine.

I soon find out that Rogaine stands for 'Rough Outdoor Group Activity Involving Navigation and Endurance'. More simply, a Rogaine is an ultra orienteering race for teams of two people. At the start of the race, teams are given a long list of map coordinates where controls are found. These coordinates they plot on a map. They then have twenty-four hours to visit on foot as many of these coordinates as possible.

In even more basic terms, a Rogaine is like a big treasure hunt in the mountains. Whoever visits the places with the most pieces of treasure within twenty-four hours wins.

As the Rogaine acronym suggests, there are two sets of skills involved in such races. The first is endurance, the skill of being able to keep on your feet for hours on end. After my winter of adventure racing training, I know I can do this. In fact, twenty-four hours will seem like a sprint in comparison to the days we spent hiking, kayaking and biking during the Scottish adventure race.

The second skill involved is that of navigation. But the navigation required for Rogaine-ing is particularly complex.

The main skill lies in deciding the best route to take when confronted with a whole pile of points scattered across a map. The Rogaine is like an extended version of the cluster in the Mourne Mountain Marathon, whereby you can decide the order in which you visit the points. In the Mournes, we had five points to figure out the order we'd visit them in. In the Rogaine, we have to choose the order and route between thirty points or more.

But, one year on from the Navigational Challenge Series, I am still not a confident navigator. I still make obvious mistakes when out for mountain runs across new terrain. I need to find someone who is confident with a map in the mountains. I need to team up with someone who I know will not lead me astray.

Mel is the obvious answer. She was a dependable skilled navigator in the Mourne Mountain Marathon less than a year ago. And I know that she has that dogged, competitive streak that I now need more than ever in a teammate. I know I can depend on Mel to help me achieve the adventure racing redemption that I am desperately searching for.

Mel is happy with the suggestion that we team up for the Rogaine. But I am too late. She is already taken. She is racing instead with Fergal, a fellow mountain running friend.

"But have you not seen the post on the IMRA mountain running forum?" Mel asks. "There's a guy called Andrew McCarthy who is also looking for someone to team up with."

I log on that afternoon and see the post in question. I don't know Andrew that well. In fact, I've never directly spoken to him before. I have seen him at some mid-week mountain races as well as during the Navigation Challenge Series last year. I know that he's a competent navigator and quite a good runner. In fact, last year he came second in the same Rogaine. It would be good to team up with a pro like Andrew, especially when I'm entering this race for the first time.

I drop him an email in reply to his post. That week, we meet up for lunch.

Andrew is easy to recognise from afar. Just like many other mountain runners, he is tall and thin, with long legs for galloping up and down hills. If we do decide to team up, we will definitely be awarded the most lopsided team. Svelte six foot something male Andrew beside short and stocky girly me.

Despite towering above me, Andrew turns out to be exceedingly pleasant and calm. We make small talk about the Rogaine and his past two entries of the race. Despite his soft spoken demeanour, I sense a quiet determination. He understands what it takes to complete a Rogaine and to do well in the event. His calm confidence reassures me, though I barely know the man.

"My only condition for teaming up," Andrew eventually says, "is that you agree not to stop to sleep during the night. It wastes time. We'd only get stiff and cold. I want a teammate who will keep going for the whole twenty-four hours."

I'm happy enough with this rule. From my days as an adventure racer, I have learnt that staying awake and running through the night is completely normal behaviour. I agree to his condition.

By the end of lunch, we are both happy with the idea of entering the Rogaine together. We sign the entry form. We are officially a team.

There is only one Rogaine that takes place in Ireland every year. And what with this year marking the tenth anniversary, there is an impressive turnout for the event. Nearly all the adventure racers from the two Irish world championships teams have signed up. Chris and Bob have entered together. Paul

McArthur, my captain, is running with Eoin Keith from the other Irish adventure racing team. And my friend Paul Mahon has teamed up with Roisin, another adventure racer, both of whom are defending the Rogaine title that they comfortably won last year.

I am the only one from the Irish adventure racing troop who is not paired with another adventure racer. In fact, my choice of teammate looks a little strange. Adventure racers rarely break ranks to race with mere mountain runners. But I have done exactly that.

Subconsciously, though, I want time out from the adventure racing clique. Though they are all great people, amazing athletes and experienced racers, I just want to run with someone different. In order to restore my confidence, I need a change in team scenery.

Andrew and I drive down to the race start early on Saturday morning. This year, the Rogaine start is located at Aghavannagh, an hour and a half's drive from Dublin, deep in the southern part of the Wicklow Mountains.

The weather is grey and murky as we edge towards Aghavannagh. It's not unusual weather for Ireland for the month of June. But we both know it could be better. I'm well wrapped up in jumpers and jacket to protect myself from the ensuing Irish summer chill. But despite his minimal fat content, Andrew doesn't seem to mind the cold at all. He is wearing shorts and T-shirt as opposed to my full body protection. I add this fact to our obviously eschewed body dimensions to confirm just how diametrically opposed we are. I reckon that the next twenty-four hours in only each others' company could be very interesting indeed.

We arrive an hour before the midday start to register and to run through required safety checks. Andrew and I empty out our bags to prove to the officials that we have all the mandatory gear. We produce maps and compasses, extra clothes, survival bags, whistles and torches, all the items needed to survive in the mountains for twenty-four hours.

And as the contents of our rucksacks lie on the ground for the officials to scrutinize, I suddenly notice the decadent assortment of food that Andrew has brought with him for the race. For the Rogaine, we each need to carry enough food to last us twenty-four hours. Unfortunately, twenty-four hours of *nice* food weighs an awful lot. Just like in the Adventure Racing World Championships, I've opted to bring lots of sweet and sticky bars that are light and easy to carry. However, I know from experience that after only a few hours, I'll be totally sick of eating such junk food.

Instead of sugary energy bars, Andrew has a gourmet range of delectable delights all ready for a twenty-four hour's worth of feasting. He has seared beef sandwiches and roast chicken legs, almonds and bananas, dark chocolate and brownies. I am so jealous. He must notice me staring at his smorgasbord of food and the saliva dripping from my mouth because he starts to rummage around in his bag and pulls out something for me. "Here you go," he offers. "Here's a chocolate and ginger flapjack to eat on the race. I made it just yesterday." A homemade chocolate and ginger flapjack? Oh my God, I love flapjacks. And chocolate is my best friend. And putting that tangy taste of ginger into it too. I think I'm about to enter heaven.

I can't help having a nibble before the race starts. It is so deliciously chocolaty and crunchy and gingery, like nothing I've ever tasted before. I have to have another bite. And another. Soon, there is nothing left but the wrapper and a brown ring of chocolate crumbs encircling my gob.

"Oi! That was meant for the race, Moire," Andrew shouts at me when he finds out what I've done. "Couldn't you wait just half an hour until the race begins?"

"Oops, I'm sorry," I reply. I feel like a naughty schoolgirl that has been caught with my hand in the cookie jar. "But you really do make amazing flapjacks."

"Oh that's nothing. You should try the banana bread I bake. I also make these great chocolate fondants with ice cream, but that's a bit too messy to carry on a race like this."

I have just met the first mountain running culinary genius. And so begins a deep friendship based on a shared love of barren mountains and exceedingly delectable baking.

Andrew then catches sight of the sugary gunk that I have brought along. "Oh my God, you're not going to eat *that* stuff are you?"

"What? What's wrong with it?" I reply indignantly, as I stand up for my stash.

"Have you read the labels on those things? They are full of preservatives and emulsifiers and modified crap. How is your body meant to get any proper energy from stuff like that?"

I grab the bar off him and start to read in a huff. There are freeze dried fruits, defatted wheat germ, dried yoghurt powder, anti-oxidants and acidity regulators. And what the hell are humectants, I begin to wonder? I hadn't really read the label beforehand. Maybe Andrew has a point.

"We need proper normal food to get us around this course. That's what our bodies have survived on for centuries, so why change our intake now?"

And I thought I was coming here to do a long distance ultra race. It's turning out to be a nutrition lecture and that's even before the race begins! Well I'll take the berating for now. But only if he agrees to share with me later that big chocolate brownie I saw him putting back into his bag.

All this talk of food with Andrew has inadvertently served as an ideal distraction. It's already close to midday and time for the race to begin. Slowly the thirty teams gather around the race officials. And on the stroke of twelve, we grab the bits of paper on offer with the list of places to visit.

It's a long list of coordinates that they give out. It's not like the Navigation Challenge that had four or five controls to visit. This Rogaine has around thirty coordinates where control flags are hidden in the mountains for us to find. And whilst the Navigation Challenge made runners cover fourteen to twenty kilometres distance-wise, the Rogaine controls are much more spaced out. Indeed, if competitors visit them all, they will cover around one hundred kilometres.

The muggy weather breaks just as the starting gun goes. Rain begins to bucket down. Andrew and I make a break for the car. At least there we can protect our maps and lists from this sudden soggy summer downpour. Straightaway Andrew's navigational expertise comes to the fore. He finds and circles the coordinates in seconds, whilst I laboriously try to find the grid references on the map. Andrew uses my ineptitude to his advantage. Whilst I am playing hide and seek with the coordinates, he is already studying the resultant geographical paper to figure out the optimal route.

I glance over to sneak a look at where he has put his circles. But instead of happily copying his answers, I see a map that scares the living daylights out of me. There are circles all over the place, a stellar constellation of coordinates that makes no sense to me at all. There are circles on top of mountains, others in deep dark valleys. Some are hidden behind walls, others are buried in forests. The circles are all over the place. There is not a part of the map that has escaped from the rings.

The aim of the game is to work out how to visit as many of these encircled areas in the shortest and quickest way. I have not even started playing and already I want to give up. I am totally clueless as to which one to visit first, let alone the second or third. And as to the best way to get from one to another, I have absolutely no idea.

'Andrew, help!' I cry to myself. But he is in deep concentration, engrossed in reading his map. I don't want to disturb him. So I just keep on plotting the coordinates, hoping that at least some of them are in the right place.

"Finished!" I chime ten minutes later.

"Right, let's go then," he replies.

"So where are we going?" I innocently ask.

"Straight on up the track. Follow those lads in front."

I head in the direction that Andrew points. It's good to finally get going. But I'm still profoundly embarrassed by the slow pace that I plotted the map coordinates in. I have to prove that I'm still worthy to be his teammate. I mightn't be hot at navigation, but I know I'm good at running. So I start to jog after the guys ahead of us to show him that at least I'll be able to run the Rogaine.

"What are you doing?" Andrew calls after me. I stop and look round to see him slowly strolling along the track. "Don't you know this race will take twenty-four hours? You'll not last the distance if you start out that fast."

Despite the cool air, I can feel my cheeks burning with embarrassment. I go at the wrong pace, I can't read maps and I eat the wrong food. I really am a disaster of a Rogaine athlete. Maybe I need to stop doing and start listening and learning more. Andrew seems to know what he is talking about. Maybe I could learn from him.

I slow to a walk and fall into line with Andrew. Within a few minutes, I can see an orange and white cloth flag ahead with a punch inside, the first control of the day. I have our team control card, so I put it between the pins and press down. A unique set of pinprick holes are left embossed on my paper, evidence of our visit.

Whilst I am busy making pretty holes in the paper, Andrew has his head still stuck firmly in the map. He hasn't stopped walking and is still heading on down the track, saving time by not standing still to read his chart. I do a quick jog to catch back up with him.

"I think I know which way we will go," he finally proclaims. "Let's get the control at the stream on the other side of the forest and then head up Aghavannagh Mountain. What we'll try and do is climb all the high mountains today. Tomorrow we will be too tired to climb up anything too big." Sounds like a sensible plan to me.

"And I've worked out where we need to be when it's dark. It's really important that we don't find ourselves on open mountainside during the night. It is too easy to get disorientated and lost in the dark up on those non-descript heathery, boggy mountain slopes." Andrew points to the map around Glenmalure. "What we'll do is make sure we hit the tracks here around 11 pm, just when the sun sets. It is really hard to navigate at night, so it's best that we stick to obvious paths. Seeing that we won't be stopping, there seems to be enough controls around the Glenmalure area to keep us busy until dawn breaks around 3.30 am."

It all sounds very sensible. But the whole way he's planned it is totally news to me. I would never have known that I needed to work out from the beginning where to be at night.

"And do you see also these controls circled in the corners?" he continues. "These are worth more points than the controls closest to the finish. We need to make sure we visit these no matter what happens."

It's impressive listening to Andrew as he figures it all out. When I plotted my points, all I saw was a random smattering of circles across the map. Andrew has meanwhile transformed them into a child like dot-to-dot game that reveals a fabulous work of art.

The race started a little less than an hour ago. Already I'd be totally lost without him.

From the first control on the track, we head to the second one at the stream on the other side of the forest. The guys who I tried to run after at the start have already disappeared out of sight. Andrew isn't worried. He knows we've barely started the race and that there's still an awful long way to go.

Without any warning, Andrew leaves the track we are following and delves straight into the trees. I have no idea why we are leaving the track at this point. But I decide it's best not to ask. I just follow.

We arrive at the control and I take out our card to punch it. Just as I am tucking it back into my bag, the two guys who had run ahead appear from out of nowhere. They had followed the track for longer and had gone a less optimal route through the forest. Andrew, instead, had figured out exactly where to leave the track and how to arrive slap bang at the control. Just through a bit of clever navigation, Andrew and I got to the control before them, even though we were going at a slower pace.

I am overwhelmed by the sheer cleverness of it all. I want to ask Andrew how he did that, how he knew where we were and how he knew where we had to go. But there is no time. Already he has crossed over the stream and is making his way straight up Aghavannagh Mountain. I follow him in hot pursuit.

The climb up Aghavannagh is steep, up 270 metres of mountainside. He said we were going to do the big mountains today and sure enough, we are. It's impossible to run up this slope. But even whilst walking, we quickly lose our breath. All of a sudden, I start to hear a high pitched beep. It sounds just like a cardiac arrest alarm from a hospital. "Do you hear that, Andrew?" I ask in a mild panic. "Yes I do," Andrew pants back. I turn around and see him looking slightly red and puffed. "It's my heart rate monitor that's making that noise."

"A heart rate what?" I enquire.

"A heart rate monitor. It tells me how fast my heart is beating. I know that if I keep my heart beating below a certain rate, I'll burn fat as opposed to glycogen. That means I'll have more energy to last the whole course."

"So what's with the beeping? Is it going to blow up? Are *you* going to blow up?"

"Not yet," he chuckles. "I've set my monitor so that it will start beeping if my heart is beating too fast. It is hard work climbing up hills, so it is letting me know that I need to slow down a bit."

We relax our pace slightly and the beeping sound subsides. Soon we are just left with the sounds of our steps on the heather, of our lungs breathing in the mountain air and of the sweet silence that only the wilderness can provide.

We soon reach the top of Aghavannagh Mountain and register our third control of the day.

"So where are we going next?" I enthusiastically enquire. I'm already finding this expedition incredibly exciting and fun.

"We're going to follow this ridge west, then north. Then we'll drop down to the next control at the river source, just east of Slievemaan." Sounds simple enough. It looks even easy on the map, a mere two and a half kilometres' journey from where we are now. But when I look up and try and to see where we are going, all I can see is a thick wall of mist. Moreover, it's a wall of mist that Andrew is rapidly disappearing into.

I scurry after him, anxious not to get left behind. Andrew is confidently striding off into the distance, the lack of visibility not fazing him in the slightest. If I was out here alone, I'd be stopping and starting, constantly checking my map and compass, incessantly worrying that I'm going the wrong way. Andrew seems to have none of these doubts. He is the ultimate display of cool, calm and collected as he serenely turns his compass dial and faithfully follows its arrow.

"Do you have some sort of x-ray goggles on that let you see straight through the mist, Andrew?" I jokingly enquire. He turns and looks at me somewhat bemused. "No, I'm just following the compass... like you're meant to," he replies. I sound so stupid. But still, I want to know why he doesn't make all the navigational mistakes I normally make.

"Look, do you see how the land is gently falling away to our left and right. That shows that we are on the ridge," Andrew explains. "Now look at the map. See how we are crossing over contour lines. That tells us that we should be still going up. And see how the land is sloping slightly up in front of us. So that means we are going in the right direction."

"Oooh, I see," I coo back in amazement. I'd never used such subtly before whilst navigating in the mist. Normally, I would just spend ages thinking that I am lost and doomed and going to die rather than calmly looking around and using what I *can* see to find out where I am.

"So how come you know all this? Where did you learn?"

"Well I used to hill walk a lot in the west of Ireland when I was in my twenties. Over there, it's strange not to have mist when you're out and about. I spent so much time leading groups on treks on those mountains that I'm now completely comfortable navigating in low visibility conditions such as these."

Ah, so that is how he learnt. I trot alongside him, avidly watching his every move. I've never seen anything like it, his level of smoothness as he navigates seamlessly without the need to ever stop and think. I want to learn too. I want to navigate just like him.

"The control we are looking for is at that river junction over there," Andrew says, as he points to a steep section just below the mountain top. We jog towards the spot and sure enough, the control flag is right where he said it would be. With Andrew at the steering wheel, we are straight in and out in seconds.

"I think we're going to have to change our plan," Andrew soon announces. I start to worry. Has he had enough of my navigational incompetence that I've so obviously failed to hide? Is he going to drop me from our team and leave me out here, in the middle of nowhere?

But Andrew is completely oblivious to all my irrational worries. The plan he is talking about is the one we'll use to find the most controls. "Theoretically, we should try to keep up high in the mountains and get as many controls up here as possible," Andrew continues. "It's more energy efficient that way. But there are quite a number down in the valley just below us. I think we should drop down and get them and then climb back up Clohernagh Mountain."

Phew, I think. It's only a change in route as opposed to a change in team composition. But as to his proposed revision of the itinerary, I have absolutely no idea. Still, I want to at least seem like I'm contributing to team tactics.

"That's a great idea," I reply. "Was thinking just the same thing to myself," I lie.

We run down the mountainside towards the forest planted on the valley's bottom. The area is wet and boggy with awkward grassy stumps strewn right across the ground. I struggle to keep up with Andrew now, his long bare legs leaping over these obstacles with ease. I find it too tiring to lift my short stubby legs high enough to hurdle this uneven terrain. Fortunately Andrew waits for me at the forest corner and I eventually catch up with him. However I could do with a breather. Thankfully I soon find the ideal excuse to ask for a short stop.

"I'm just going to nip in here to these trees. Need to go to the toilet," I say. "That's fine," replies Andrew, even though I've probably given him too much information for his liking.

I squat down behind some pine trees. My body is relieved to be finally stationary for a few split seconds. My bladder is also glad to have a chance to empty itself. However, my bowels also want in on the relaxation act. And soon I find myself squatting for a totally different purpose.

I've forgotten to bring toilet paper. But from my days of long distance mountain hiking, I've become accustomed to cleaning up using just moss and flat stones. Fortunately in this forest there is plenty of moss growing on the ground, so I pick up a clump and swiftly wipe my behind.

Up until now, the places I have hiked in were full of deciduous soft leaved trees. The place where I am now squatting is conversely planted with coniferous pines, trees with short sharp needles that are abundantly scattered all over the ground. Unfortunately, the moss I have just used is full of these same needles. In my urge to be eco-friendly, my bum now has severe needle lacerations that I'm to suffer from for the remainder of the day.

Of course, I'm not going to admit any of this to Andrew. I pull up my pants and hobble after him, determined to grimace and bear this humiliating pain. He has run ahead and has located the next control flag on the forest edge. The excitement of yet another control so expertly found fortunately distracts me from my buttocks' pain.

We pick up another two controls in the valley. I run over to both flags and enthusiastically punch our card. Whilst I'm busy doing this, Andrew is map reading, figuring out our route and revising it as we move. We are even starting to work together as a proper team with proper allocation of tasks. My job is to run alongside and to punch the card. And Andrew's is to tell us where we're going.

We climb back up the steep sides of Clohernagh Mountain. Whilst we ascend, Andrew for the second time today, reassures his heart rate monitor that a heart attack is not impending. It seems to work. The beeping stops and we both reach the top in one piece, with the control patiently waiting for us at the summit. "Nice job, Andrew, yet another control successfully stalked down!" It's just amazing being in a team with such a competent navigator who knows exactly what he is doing.

The night before the race, I had lathered my feet in Vaseline to soften them up and to stop any blisters from forming. But despite this treatment, I am beginning to develop a small swelling on my right heel. By now, we have been on the go for over four hours, so I ask Andrew to stop for five minutes to repair the wound before it becomes a gaping sore. We sit down for the first time today and I get out my first aid kit. I then pull out a roll of industrial strength duct tape and proceed to tear off strips. "Duct tape?" Andrew questions with disgust. "Oh yes, duct tape! That's all the first aid kit I need," I reply with a wry grin. "I find it does the job just as good as plasters. Personally, I never leave home without a roll."

Despite the unorthodoxy of the method, it seems to do the trick. Soon we are scooting off the summit, down the steep drop to Art's Lough. Both of us love descending at high speed and we find ourselves squealing like little children down the perilous slope. "That was fun," Andrew exclaims when we finally reach the bottom. "Let's do that again!" I excitedly suggest. Andrew knows too well that I am joking. Neither of us wants to walk all the way back up to the top to repeat the downhill run.

We collect another few controls in Fraughan Rock Glen and around Benleagh Mountain. With seven hours of the race already gone, we find our eleventh control of the day on a river junction north of Benleagh Mountain. And sitting right beside the flag, who did we find but Mel, my mountain marathon partner and Fergal, her Rogaine teammate. They are busy having their evening sandwiches behind some river rocks, tucked safely away from the gloomy weather that now threatens to break. But there is no time to stop and talk. Andrew and I have agreed that we don't stop to eat or sleep or map read or chat. We don't want to lose time or risk getting cold from being stationary whilst sweaty and damp. As we wave to them both and walk away, Fergal holds up six of his fingers to us. "Is that the number of controls they have already visited?" Andrew and I wonder. "But we have visited eleven thus far. We must be doing okay."

It's impossible to know how other teams are doing out on this course. Mel and Fergal are the first team we've met since the start at midday. All Andrew and I can do at this point is keep going, keep collecting controls and keep hoping for the best until we reach the finish at midday tomorrow.

Once again we head through the mist across open mountain bog to get to the next control. This time round I feel completely at ease. I know that Andrew will get us across this misty mountain without the slightest stress. What with both of us feeling relaxed at how things are going, our minds begin to wander from the race and we start to engage in more diverse and interesting banter. And slowly but surely, our conversation erupts into a highly entertaining stream of latest news and gossip. I am soon in stitches with laughter as Andrew tells stories of people we both know. Time starts to race by, our amusing chat only being interrupted as we near the next control.

By 9 pm, we arrive in the valley of Glendalough right at the top edge of our maps. Glendalough is one of the most popular attractions within the Wicklow Mountains. It has two beautiful lakes, accessible walks, stunning views, ancient monastic ruins, as well as plenty of fine pubs and hotels. Normally this place is hopping with tourists visiting its many sites. But what with it being so late in the day, everyone has either gone home or retreated for a pint. We have the whole place to ourselves. "Ah, isn't it so quiet here?" Andrew peacefully contemplates. I completely agree. It's not often that I'd see Glendalough so tranquilly empty, especially during the summer months.

"I do have a confession to make though. I specifically planned our route today so that we'd have a nice stroll through Glendalough Valley this evening," Andrew admits.

"But aren't you meant to plan the route so that we get the most controls in the shortest time and distance?" I reply.

"Well yes, that's true. But we had to go through Glendalough anyhow. I just worked it out so that we'd arrive when the place had quietened down for the night." Now that's truly ingenious planning.

We break out our sandwiches in celebration and munch on them whilst strolling alongside the valley's lakeside. The trees beside us are peacefully swaying in the evening breeze and the waters are tickled by the wind. Soon the valley's silence starts me thinking. I pause for a moment between mouthfuls of my sandwich. "So, thus far we've got twelve controls, isn't it? And we did it in nine hours. Doesn't that mean that if we keep going at this rate, we should be able to get all of the race controls?"

Andrew does the mental calculation. "Well yes, I suppose you're right. Yeah, imagine if we did that. That would be absolutely brilliant!" His enthusiasm swiftly mounts as the prospect of getting all the controls becomes a distinct reality. He is encouraged, too, by my enthusiasm to keep going and to sweep up all the points on offer. But I know we can do it. We have already done so well thus far.

From Glendalough, we climb up Derrybawn on the hunt for more controls. As we near the top, we meet another team huddled away behind a bush also shovelling down their sandwiches. It is nearly 10 pm, but they look a little worse for wear. They appear cold and tired and from the way they are eating, extremely ravenous. In comparison, we realise how fresh we still are, like we've barely begun our race.

We reach the control at the forest south of Mullacor just over an hour later. It is 11 pm, exactly eleven hours into the race. Night is fast approaching. But we have reached the control bang on time. We manage to cross the last section of open mountain and we reach the forest edge just as daylight fades.

For only the second time since the race began, we stop and sit down. Last time it was to fix our feet. This time it is to put on extra clothes to guard against the impending night chill. We save time by dressing simultaneously. And within five minutes we both have extra tops and bottoms on and two torches on our heads. We are now ready to take on the next five hours of darkness.

We make our way into the forest. But the loss of light quickly affects our brains. We tire and lose our concentration. We end up lost in the entangled myriad of dark forest trails, unable to tell which trail goes where.

We eventually escape from the trees and reach the main road that runs along the base of Glenmalure valley. Our next task is to get across the Avonbeg River, to the other side of the valley, to find the next control. But try as we might, we cannot find the bridge that fords the river. We go forwards and backwards along the road, trying to find the bridge's access track. But after half an hour of searching in the dark, we give up and deem it irretrievable. We then start considering wading straight across the river. But the current is too strong and the waters too deep for me to make it across safely.

"Looks like we'll have to go all the way round and go via Drumgoff Bridge instead," Andrew resigns himself. "It will add about three kilometres to our route, but there's nothing else we can do." I agree. We just have to find an alternate route.

But the night time problems refuse to stop there. We head off to the next control. Our maps say that it is at the bottom of a cliff, up a small hillside close to Drumgoff which is two kilometres away. But when we try to head up the hill, we are met with a fortification of ferns. They have sprouted up quickly in the summer months and now, having gorged themselves on ample summer rain, the ferns stand at over six foot tall. Andrew goes ahead and tries to use his height advantage to batter down this jungle of killer weeds. I follow behind, trying to mimic Andrew's steps whilst forging my own way through the dense foliage. We cannot see if or where the wall of ferns will ever stop. All we can see in the dark is yet more ferns ahead.

Andrew stops and turns around. "I can't do this," he says, his head hanging low. "Neither can I," I reply. We give up on the control. And with that, we abandon our hopes of getting maximum points. We've struggled and failed for over an hour.

It's just past 1 am as we head back down the hill towards the road leading towards Drumgoff. Saturday social drinkers are spilling out from the Drumgoff Inn as we pass, all happy and warm from their drunken night out. In sheer contrast, Andrew and I are tired and miserable from our own night out in the cold. "Should we go in for a pint?" Andrew asks, motioning towards the inn. "Don't tempt me," I growl. I know at this stage if we go in to the pub, I'll certainly not be coming out again.

We put our heads down and keep walking. "Let's get that control we missed on the other side of the river," Andrew suggests, trying to reignite our momentum. By now we have crossed Drumgoff Bridge and there is a track beside us leading straight through the forest directly to the control we tried to get two hours ago. "I agree. Let's keep going. We'll soon get back into our rhythm."

We soon find out that the forest is a popular spot for other teams seeking out night time refuge. We find two body bags lying at the forest entrance, a team trying desperately to get a few hours kip wrapped up in their survival bags. Further on down the track, we come across a full camping cookery set pristinely laid out for the morning. This time however the team is nowhere to be seen. They have buried themselves deep in the forest to keep themselves snug and warm. In anticipation of waking up early, they have already laid out their kettle and cups in the middle of the forest track all ready for a morning brew. We tip-toe past both these teams, trying not to disturb them. We find the control, punch our card and get out of this sleepy forest as fast as we can.

It is good to get the control in the forest after the unbridgeable river and ferocious fern incidents. We emerge from the trees back on to the road with a new focus and with spirits lifted.

It is still dark by the time we get to the top of Fananierin Mountain. From here, Andrew decides that we should drop off the summit and head straight up Ballinacor Mountain. But just as we begin this proposed ascent of Ballinacor, I start to find myself staggering. We've been on the go for nearly fifteen hours and the time spent on my feet is starting to show. No matter how hard I try, I can no longer keep up with Andrew. His long legs are carrying him up the mountain with ease whilst I find myself crawling my way up its side. Despite Andrew slowing his own pace, I cannot bridge the distance between us. All I can do is look up and follow and make sure I don't lose sight of where he's headed.

Dawn breaks as we reach the control south of Ballinacor. With renewed daylight, we stop for a moment to take off our night-time wear. But I am starting to become delirious. I find it hard to work out how to undo the zips. I end up sprawled on the ground, trying to wriggle my way out from my over trousers. The more I squirm on the floor, the more my raw bottom squeals out as I rub against the needle incisions made during yesterday's forest toilet stop.

The other problem I have is with my hands. I can't get them to unbutton my jacket. Just like they did during the adventure race in Scotland, my hands have swollen up like big balloons. I can no longer see the wrinkles on my fingers, so taut the skin is from the fluid. They are disgusting to look at, like big Mickey Mouse hands swinging uselessly from my arms.

As the morning progresses, I get more and more tired and increasingly confused. Andrew too is suffering. He is desperately trying to stay awake and is finding it hard to keep concentrating on the map. His aches and pains are mounting. His morale is breaking down.

It all comes to a head when, around 6 am, we can't find a control that we are looking for in another forest. We amble around, up and down the forest track, unable to make neither head nor tail of the map or our surroundings. I eventually reach the stage where I'm too tired to look any more and just stand still miserably on the road. Andrew keeps on pacing up and down desperately looking for the flag.

"Have you eaten at all, Moire?" he asks me as he passes me for the third time. It's a question asked out of part frustration, part concern. I start to think back. The last time I ate was... I think maybe... nope, I've no idea. My brain's cogs slowly slot into place. 'I think Andrew's trying to suggest I eat something,' it concludes. 'Oh dear,' I begin to realise. 'It looks like I'm making the same mistake as I did in Scotland. I must eat or risk being medi-vaced again.' I open a pocket in my bag using my swollen stubby fingers and pull out the nearest thing I can find. It's a green apple gel, laced with caffeine. 'That should do the trick,' I think to myself. I suck it down and all of a sudden, ping! I'm totally and utterly awake.

We eventually find the control that we've been looking for, hidden away in a gully. And what with caffeine power now running through my veins, I'm fired up to find all the rest. For the next four hours, I run up and down hills, through forests and along roads, like a sniffer dog looking for control flags.

Andrew on the other hand is starting to flail. Being an avid advocate of *proper* food, he refuses to try one of my illicit energy gels. Eventually, though, he caves in and agrees to take one of my sweets instead. It is stacked with sugar and preservatives and lots of other nasty processed foods that he fervently despises. But he is feeling so poorly at this stage that he'll try just about anything... well anything apart from the gels.

It's no wonder that he is feeling tired. Not only has Andrew been on his feet for nearly twenty-four hours, he's also been concentrating on the map all this time. This mental exertion, coupled with the physical endeavour, has made his batteries run down much quicker than mine.

There is less than two hours to go before we must get back to the finish. If a team is late by even one minute, then strict time penalties are applied that quickly whittle away their score. And what with the finish time fast approaching, many teams are around the finish area picking up the last of their controls. Everyone looks tired and beaten up from the night out in the mountains. But how everyone else has done, we have still no way of knowing.

Eventually Andrew and I call it a day and head to the finish line. We have visited all of the Rogaine's controls except two of them. Sore but proud of how we have done, we painfully jog over the line together. We hand in our control cards to be verified and for our final score to be totted up. In the meantime, Andrew and I head to the finish tent, where at 10.45 am on a mid-summer's Sunday morning, I slump down and devour a burger, four sausages, a cup of tea and two bottles of cold beer. A well deserved meal after a job well done.

The other adventure racers soon arrive back at the finish. Paul and Roisin have done well, but had a rough time after an old leg injury of Roisin's sprang up. Bob and Chris, my adventure racing teammates, abandoned the race mid-way, again a result of injury. Paul McArthur, my adventure racing team captain and his partner Eoin arrive home with a few minutes to spare. They have run a good race, but are also looking a bit worse for wear.

In the end, we all have to wait for the scores to be tallied up. And to everyone's, including to our own surprise, Andrew and I have won the race outright. We are the Irish Rogaine Champions for 2007. We were definite rank outsiders. But we have beaten four former champions.

I can barely keep my eyes open as we go up to collect our prize. But I still have enough energy to smile exuberantly from ear to ear. I'm so happy that we've won. I'm so happy that I've finally redeemed myself. And I'm so happy that I've met and raced with Andrew, a real mountain wizard and a really quality guy.

Dave Weston from Setanta Orienteers (middle) presenting the Rogaine trophy and title to myself (L) and Andrew McCarthy (R). Photo courtesy of Andrew Johnstone.

8. PIONEERS

After our Rogaine success, Andrew and I keep in touch. We enter other mountain running races together. We meet to do training runs once in a while.

Often on our training runs we chat about the mountain running scene, we swap stories and scandal, we talk about this and that. One day, our discussion turns to mountain runs and races that we've always wanted to do. We talk of the Mourne Seven Sevens, runs around the Twelve Bens in Connemara and the Rab Mountain Marathon in the UK.

"But do you know what I'd really love to have a go at?" Andrew asks me. "I'd love to try the Wicklow Round."

I had heard of the Wicklow Round. Back in 2006, a group of Irish mountain runners, led by mountain veterans Joe Lalor and Brian Bell, set out to design a long distance mountain running challenge around Ireland's Wicklow Mountains. They selected twenty-six of the highest summits in the Wicklow range. They then threw down the gauntlet to athletes far and wide to visit the peaks of all these mountains within twenty-four hours. Few could even contemplate the Round. With the challenge covering over one hundred kilometres and climbing over 6,000 metres, three quarters the height of Mount Everest, it is certainly beyond the reach of most regular mountain runners.

The Wicklow Round itself is modelled on the UK's Bob Graham Round. Bob Graham was born around 1890 and ran a guest house in Keswick in the Lake District. He was a formidable hill walker and knew the local mountains well. In 1932, Bob Graham set out to visit as many summits as possible in the Lake District within twenty-four hours. In the end, he bagged forty-two peaks, one for each year of his life. In the process, he climbed over 8,200 metres and covered over one hundred kilometres. He did his Round wearing tennis shoes, long shorts and a pyjama jacket. He ate bread and butter, a lightly boiled egg, fruit and sweets to keep him going.

The feat was not to be repeated again until 1960. Gradually the Bob Graham Round, as it came to be known, has become a key milestone in the British fell running scene, being considered one of the most demanding tests of endurance for an amateur athlete or mountaineer. By the end of 2008, over 1,450 mountain runners had followed in Bob Graham's steps and scaled these same distances and height over those same forty-two peaks.

Not to be outdone by the Brits, the Irish had finally come up with their own mountain running challenge. But unlike the Bob Graham Round that was first completed by the man himself, no one had yet finished the Wicklow Round.

"Yes, I was thinking about the Wicklow Round too," I reply. "I'd love to have a go. The problem is that it would demand an enormous commitment in terms of time. I'd not only have to train properly to make sure I was fit, but there's also a huge amount of ground work to be done to figure out the route."

Given that no one has yet completed the Wicklow Round, no one actually knows the best and quickest route between the twenty-six peaks. All the rules say is that you must visit all the summits in the order in which they are stated. What they don't say is how you are actually meant to go between each one of them.

Some of the routes are obvious, with trails linking one summit to the next. However, these are the exception rather than the rule. In most places in the Wicklow Mountains, there are no paths leading directly from peak to peak. This is unlike the Lake District, where the Bob Graham Round takes place, where there are numerous walking paths all over the place. Many of the mountains selected for the Wicklow Round are in fact too remote to appeal to the majority of hill walkers. And without hill walkers, no proper paths are formed. That means you have to go out and spend time hunting for sheep and deer tracks instead that might lead between the summits.

There are also places where the route between two mountains is far from obvious. Some of the mountains selected as separated by steep valleys, thick forests, deep rivers and impassable cliffs. Travelling in a straight line between two mountains is totally impractical, if not completely impossible. The only way to find out the quickest way between two summits separated by such natural obstacles is to physically go out and run every conceivable, feasible route.

With the Bob Graham Round being in place for more than sixty years, the optimum route has already been honed. Bob Graham Round experts know unmarked secret ways that can save precious seconds and that can make all the difference between completing the Round in less or more than one day. Sixty years of work has already been invested in the Bob Graham Round. In comparison the Wicklow Round is starting from scratch.

Admittedly, I had already been out on some Wicklow Round scouting trips with other mountain runners. I joined Joe Lalor, one of the Wicklow Round's original architects, on one such run as he tried to figure out the optimal route between the mountains that he himself set. One fine Sunday morning, a group of us ran up Scarr, one of the twenty-six mountains on the Round. Once we reached the summit, we all split up and scattered in different directions. We wanted to see who would be first to reach Knocknacloghoge, the next mountain on the

Round. Some went north towards Kanturk and tried to find routes through the forest. Joe and I contoured north to Brown Mountain and tried to reach Knocknacloghoge via the mouth of Lough Dan. In the end it took us the whole morning just to figure out the route between two of the twenty-six peaks.

"Yes, you're right. It'll be a lot of work trying to figure the route out," Andrew replies. "But sure there's the whole of the winter and spring to scout it out. And then, if you want to try the Wicklow Round together as a team, you and I could do it sometime next year, probably in May."

It sounds like a very tempting offer. By now it is October. The summer and along with it this year's mountain running season are officially over. I need something to occupy my weekends and Wicklow Round preparations could potentially fill that gap.

Furthermore, since June and the Adventure Racing World Championships, I've spent a lot of time reflecting on both my aptitude and ardour for adventure racing. I've thought about everything, from my ability to compete in each discipline, to the financial cost of the sport and its physical toll on my body. I've considered team dynamics and time commitments. And I've come to the conclusion that, despite it being a tremendously cool and trendy athletic endeavour, it simply isn't the sport for me.

So, if I'm not adventure racing any more, I need to find something else to occupy my time.

"Look, if you like I could develop a training timetable for you, based on using a heart rate monitor," Andrew says. "Over the weekdays, you can do short endurance runs. And then on the weekends we can go out and run longer sections of the Round. But I'm sure we'll be both well able physically to do the

Wicklow Round. We covered the same kind of distance in a similar sort of time during the Irish Rogaine."

I welcome the offer on a number of levels. Firstly it would be interesting to do proper scientific training using heart rate data and see if it really makes any difference to my endurance and my running speed. Scouting the Wicklow Round will also mean that I'll get to know the Wicklow Mountains much better and even visit some peaks that I've never been to before.

Andrew's suggestion also gives me a chance to get back out practising my mountain navigation skills that I've severely neglected over the last year. And in particular, it'll be a golden opportunity to learn from Andrew by watching and discovering how he navigates with ease, whatever the wilderness or weather, just like he did during the Rogaine.

And after all last year's efforts spent learning how to mountain bike, kayak and climb so that I could adventure race, this plan means that I'll go back full time to the sport that I really love. For the whole of next year, I'll just be mountain running.

"Alright, let's do it," I say. It's a done deal. Andrew and I will attempt the Wicklow Round together next year, in May 2008.

In reality, I know there's absolutely no way I could attempt to do the Wicklow Round without Andrew. I simply don't have the navigational experience or prowess to envisage ever attempting such a thing. I have no idea how to decide which routes are the best through the mountains. And ultimately I'd be simply too scared to even attempt something as big as the Wicklow Round on my own.

Now if this was the Bob Graham Round in the UK, theoretically I could do it alone. In the Bob Graham Round, supporters and navigators are allowed. This means officially I could do a solo attempt but still have someone run alongside carrying my bag, food and supplies. At the same time, I wouldn't necessarily have to know any of the routes. I could go with a navigator who already has the sixty years of local knowledge who could shepherd me all the way round. So in theory, I could attempt the Bob Graham Round "on my own" but still have one or two people there with me constantly.

In fact, according to the Bob Graham rules you *have* to have someone with you at all times to prove that you have visited all the peaks. But the Wicklow Round doesn't demand such proof. Instead an honour system is in place, meaning that they trust that you visit all the mountain tops, whilst still reserving the right to put marshals on summits if they see fit.

According to the English, the sheer distance to be covered and the staggering heights to be climbed in the Bob Graham Round are sufficient tests of a mountain runner's ability and zeal. Navigational or bag carrying abilities are not tested. However, wanting as ever to get one up on our neighbours, the Irish have raised the stakes in this mountainous merry-go-round. On this side of the water, the Wicklow Round has indeed mimicked the Bob Graham Round's one hundred kilometre length and several thousand metre climb. However, the Wicklow Round rules go on to state that "competitors may run solo or in groups, on the strict understanding that all members carry their own gear and that the navigation must be done by a member doing the attempt in total... It is against the spirit of the event to have a pacing runner or navigational support". What this means is that I either learn to navigate properly and do it solo, or I tag along in a group that has a competent navigator in it. And given the fact that after more than a year I've still not mastered the basics of map reading, I think it's wise for me at this stage to do the Wicklow Round as part of a team.

128

And anyhow, regardless of all these rules, it'll be good fun running the Wicklow Round with Andrew. His company helps makes long hours and miles in the mountains disappear. He always has good stories, some gossip, or some random piece of information that distracts me completely from the hard work of mountain running. If he's not talking about heart rate training or his Pilates exercise regime, he's informing me about cookery and fashionable restaurants, or about the music scene and the latest hottest bands.

And in a way, I think I'm good for him too. Though he knows far more than me in terms of how to train, he's not always the most motivated to actually go out and do his required hours of runs. That's not to say that Andrew doesn't love the mountains or mountain running just as much as I. It is just a question of 'memory focus'. Before getting out on the mountains, Andrew can only remember the breathlessness and pain that it's definitely going to entail. Of course, mountain running is not easy. It's tiring and sore. It can be frightening and cold. And these are the realities that Andrew's mind primarily evokes before he steps out his front door.

I too know the tortures that mountain running inflict. But for some reason, my brain primarily recalls the freedom and fitness, the discovery and elation that are gained when participating in such a sport. My brain remembers the fun. Andrew's remembers the pain. My selective memory helps balance out Andrew's negative reality. My enthusiasm helps coax Andrew into coming out to play in the mountains.

We start our long Wicklow Round training runs in mid-November. First we decide to tackle those sticky summits where the routes between them remain a mystery.

We unorthodoxly start at the end, trying to work out the fastest way to run from the last summit, Knocknagun, to the finish at the start of the track up Kippure. We first try the most direct route. We soon enough realise that this is not a good idea. We end up in mucky wet marshes that try to pull our shoes straight off our feet. It being the start of winter as well, the marshes are full of cold wet water that threaten to freeze off our extremities.

Once we manage to extract ourselves from these swamps, we end up running into expansive bog cutting areas. Back in the day, my ancestors saw fit to dig up and burn the plentiful Irish bog that generously covers this land. In doing so, they rendered useful this muddy mess by using it to keep their houses warm. But in digging up the turf in rectangular shaped fields, they left behind intermittent trenches and fences of waist high bog. These we now have no choice but to clamber up and over. And once over one boundary, we fall into ditches of unevenly cut ground right on the other side. I feel like a World War I veteran in the trenches, army crawling my way through, trying to avoid the booby trapped holes, worried that I'll never make it out alive.

We hop and stagger over the rutted terrain underfoot, our ankles bending this way and that as our feet land on ground sloping at every possible angle. With the tradition of bog cutting now obsolete, the turf has now been reclaimed by thick heather and long grass that we slog and struggle through. Eventually, we escape from this quagmire and reach the finish line. It has taken us over forty minutes to cover around four kilometres. And we are both totally shattered from the effort required to traverse this terrible terrain.

"I don't think that's the way to go," I conclude as I state the bleedin' obvious.

"I agree. If that's what I had to go through at the very end of a one hundred kilometre run, I could easily do all the summits and then just give up on the whole thing whilst heading towards the finish line."

It takes us a whole morning to work out that the direct route is not the best one to take. It eventually takes us two more tries before we come up with a better option. Three attempts in total to find a four kilometre route! The whole route is over one hundred kilometres. How many attempts will we need to figure out the rest? It starts to dawn on us that trying to figure out the Wicklow Round route is going to take us an awful lot of time.

In the end, we opt to drop down to Oldboley's from Knocknagun's summit and to run back to the finish via the tarmac Military Road. It looks longer on paper but it ends up being much faster in terms of time.

Once we work out how to find our way to the finish, Andrew and I try to find the best route off Tonduff North, the third last mountain on the route. Rumour has it that there is a faint path in the high heather that comes off the summit and runs downhill left of a gully. This path then peters out after one kilometre as the hill starts to flatten out. Then another path starts some fifty metres away off to the right. This we must take so that we can descend safely through the steep and treacherous cliff lined Raven's Glen. Hopefully we'll then arrive in one piece at the forest's edge close to Ballyreagh Bridge.

Of course, none of this is marked on our maps. So we have to go out there and find it for ourselves.

We just about find the path that leaves the Tonduff North summit, a narrow affair that gets repeatedly lost and found through the thick Wicklow heather. But once this path fades on the plateau, we fail to find the next. We weave this way and that across the landscape, trying to find some footprints that might lead us to the trail. Instead we pick up sheep tracks that lead us absolutely nowhere. We find ditches that stop dead. And as we keep looking, we descend further and further into the glen. We spread out to cover more ground and to maximise our chances of finding the path. I lose sight of Andrew as he checks out a route he thinks he sees scurrying through some ferns.

After twenty minutes of clambering down through heather bushes and over steep rocky mounds, I eventually hit the forest edge. But Andrew is nowhere to be found. Normally he is quicker than me at descending through such mountainous scrub. I figure that he must have gone on ahead and is probably waiting for me at Ballyreagh Bridge. But when I get to the bridge, he isn't there either. I call his mobile. There's no answer. I start to panic. I have no idea what has happened to him.

After about ten minutes, he comes staggering along the forest boundary. He looks a little worse for wear. "What happened you? Where did you go?" I ask, looking him over for signs of broken bones. "Well, you know those rocks and boulders that are up in Raven's Glen that we have to clamber over to come down as far as here," he says, with a noticeable quiver in his voice. "Well I tried to step down one rock that the heather was hiding. I kept lowering myself down, but my feet weren't hitting any ground below." Alarm bells are ringing in my head. Andrew is over six foot tall. If I had been caught on one of those, I'd be surely dead. "Basically I was lowering myself down a cliff without even knowing it," Andrew continues with his story. "Fortunately I was able to just about climb back up again. That's what took me so long."

"This route is treacherous," I quickly conclude. "It seems like if we don't find the path, then the route is far too dangerous to follow." Eventually, after many games of hide and seek in the heather, we find the path we had been told about. And after a few practise runs, we feel comfortable that we can re-find it if we take our time and be careful. This is the route that we decide to take on the Wicklow Round.

Andrew and I next try to figure out how to get between the two mountains of Luggala and Djouce, the twenty-first and twenty-second mountains on the Round. If you want to take the most direct route, you have to jump off a cliff, either trespass through the Guinness family estate or swim across Lough Tay, climb back up through steep gorse bushes to the road, army crawl through a thick pine plantation and then eventually walk up through open mountain until you hit Djouce's cairn. Needless to say, there has to be a better way around.

Quite a number of mountain runners have already made the Luggala to Djouce route one of their favourite topics to discuss whilst drinking pints in the pub.

"Well it's obvious of course," the debate would always go. "You are meant to head south from Luggala to Pier Gates and then follow the Wicklow Way all the way to the top of Djouce."

"That's a ridiculous idea. If you do that, you have to run downhill and lose nearly three hundred of metres of height. And then you have to climb all the way back up again to Djouce. That would be far too tiring. No, what you have to do is head north, not south, towards Sheepbanks Bridge. Then head straight up from there across open mountain all the way to the top of Djouce."

"That's ridiculous. Don't you know what the terrain is like over there? South of the bridge, the ground is covered in knee high heather. And then from the bridge to Djouce, you have to trudge through thick marsh grass and rutted bog. But now if you go south via Pier's Gates, then you get a smooth grass run off Luggala, a tarmac road up to Ballinastoe and the firm Wicklow Way wooden boardwalk practically all the way to the summit."

And so the debacle would go on. What none of the bar stool debaters can be bothered to do is actually go out and run the two routes. That would be obviously far too tiring and would ultimately put an untimely end to their favourite discussion. Such people are otherwise known in this sport as 'armchair orienteers'. They make a hobby of sitting in the comfort of their own armchairs, perusing their maps and then deciding and telling everyone with an authoritative tone the best ways to go.

Unfortunately, the Wicklow Round doesn't work like that. The available maps don't give enough information to make proper route decisions whilst sitting in front of cosy, warm fires. No, Andrew and I have to get out there and find out for ourselves where the paths go and the ones that are the quickest to run.

But sometimes, even with all our weekend scouting trips, we don't find the paths that we need. Eventually, we have to turn to the experienced, older mountain runners who sit quietly at the back of the pub and silently listen to such debates without saying a word. We need to go and ask them if they know of any clandestine paths. Many of these veterans compete in the IMRA Navigation Challenge Series at the end of the summer. These are the mountain runners who have been over and back every last part of the Wicklow Mountains. They know where the paths start, where they stop and where they go. Andrew and I have to search them out, explain what we are doing and beg for their advice.

"There's a small path that leads from the river to the summit," he says while pointing to a blank part on the map. There is no dotted line there signifying a trail, but Paul Nolan knows very well that it's there. "You'll find the start by going just to the right of an earth bank that begins close to this flat piece of land right here. Remember, if you don't find this path, you're done for. Everything else is a steep exhausting climb through long heather, boulders and ferns." I trust Paul's advice. Paul is a famously fast Irish mountain runner and orienteer, speedy across all types of terrains. Not only has he represented his country at the sport, he has also run up and over every single mountain found on the whole of Ireland's isle. So if he's says that there's a path, I have no doubt there's one. He's also a kind sort, once lending me his spare compass when mine was going round in circles nearly two years ago. Now he's lending me his Wicklow Round route ideas.

We go out and find the path, just as Paul had described. The next time we see him, we ply him for more valuable information, for directions that we are currently stumped with. "What are you heading north east across that marsh land for?" Paul asks with horror as I describe one route we are proposing to take. "Why don't you just head east along the forest edge instead? There's a wide path cut along the fence that is much easier to run on." Again Paul is right. By going along the forest's side, we shave four minutes off our previous split. And yet again, there was no way of knowing about that route. The map divulges nothing except blank white open land.

But there is one question about the Wicklow Round that no one really knows the answer to, neither Paul nor Andrew nor I. It is assumed that the Wicklow Round will take someone just under the twenty-four hours to complete. And if this is the case, they will have to spend a night out in the mountains. The question is where on the route to spend those inevitable hours of darkness.

It is easy to get lost in the mountains in the dark, especially if you are travelling over barren trackless mountain. The wisest thing to do therefore is to stick to obvious walking paths, just like Andrew and I did on the Rogaine. But obvious paths are far and few between out in the Wicklow Mountains. It is not like the Mournes or the Lake District, where wide gravel paths vividly stand out from their borders of grass and green. Instead the Wicklow Mountain paths can be best described as wider patches of exposed brown bog in a sea of heather and grassy terrain. At night, these brown paths are very easy to wander off and exceedingly easy to lose. We find out that the mountains with the most obvious bog paths that we'd be least likely to stray from are from Drumgoff onwards.

Andrew and I calculate that at the end of May, there would be around six hours of darkness. If we arrive at Drumgoff at dusk, in six hours we would reach Glenmacnass via the mountains of Mullacor, Derrybawn, Camaderry and Tonelagee. We need to go out and practise these mountain sections in the middle of the night to make sure we can navigate them in the dark.

I'm amazed how little we can see in the dark tonight without the benefit of moonlight. I can only make out what my head torch beam lights up, which turns out to be masses of bog and heather all encamped around. We have to be more careful than ever. Tonight we are trying to navigate up and down Tonelagee. It's not going to be easy. Even during the day, this mountain's paths are notoriously difficult to find.

"It is really important that we use our maps and compasses precisely," Andrew reminds me. "Don't go on a path if it's leading you the wrong way." I hear what he says. But fail to follow his advice. I'm so used to following small tracks and kidding myself that they are going in the right direction. But if I do that now in the dark, we could end up totally and utterly lost.

I keep following random exposed sheep trails that are cut through the bog. But Andrew pulls me back each time and points fervently at his compass. "Don't you see that you're going the wrong way? You'll be in the valley and forests around Mall Hill before you know it."

But by now, I've become so accustomed to following Andrew that I still don't know how to navigate without him. He does such a good job of always leading us in the right direction that, though I've learnt so much from him about navigation, I still can't manage on my own. After my failed attempts tonight, I again leave the navigation to Andrew and he excels as ever in difficult, dark conditions.

I let him take the lead. From south of Lough Ouler, he takes a bearing of sixty-nine degrees from the saddle. Then, around the 550 metre contour line and after about a kilometre of running, he switches to a seventy-six degree bearing. After five hundred metres, we come across the walking path. We check its bearing, find it corresponds with the map and then we follow it all the way back to the road.

I would never have known to navigate like that. If I was alone, I would be totally lost up there. But I'm not worried. As long as Andrew is out there with me in the mountains, I know I'm totally safe.

Andrew and I continue to scout the mountains, tackling longer and longer sections each time. We find more paths. We discover better routes. We keep a record of how long it takes us to travel from each summit to the next and start to build up an idea of how long the whole Round will take us. We stick to our training plan and cover twenty, thirty, forty kilometres each time. With a bit of luck, in a few months time, we'll be attempting the Wicklow Round.

But whilst all is well in the mountains, all is even better back down in Dublin. I start to date a guy called Pete. He's a solid, dependable lad, well respected by everyone, just the kind of man I need to counterbalance my own wild streak for mad adventures.

We meet through a mutual colleague who found out about my ultra mad running exploits. Though Pete is an ex-rugby player, he has just successfully completed the Dublin marathon. He figures that, after tarmac running exploits, mountain running can't be all that hard. He asks me if we can go for a run together so that he can try out this new sport.

I end up bringing him on a four hour mountain tour of Mullacor, Derrybawn, Glendalough, the Spink, around to Prezen Rock and then back to Drumgoff via the Wicklow Way, a leisurely jaunt of around twenty kilometres. I figure that if he's done a marathon, he'd be well able for this route. Also since he is proving to be slightly cocky, I'm hoping to put him in his place.

In the end, it works. Pete collapses from exhaustion just south of Mullacor. He has brought the wrong shoes, the wrong food, the wrong drink and the wrong clothes. He's incapable of running uphill, running downhill, or running on any sort of uneven surface. I tried to tell him, but he didn't listen. Now he's paying the price for thinking that doing a marathon is some sort of licence to say you can mountain run.

"You should become either a motivational speaker or an army drill sergeant," he mumbles, as he writhes in pain on the grassy ground. I laugh and pull him back on to his feet and make him run the last four kilometres. I take pity on him in the end though and buy him a pot of tea at Drumgoff Inn. I even share my sandwich with him.

Pete and I start to go out together when I am in the middle of my Wicklow Round training. And though he has had a four hour taster of mountain running, he doesn't fully grasp what I am trying to do.

138

"Wicklow what?"

"Wicklow Round. It's a challenge to run around twenty-six peaks in the Wicklow Mountains in under twenty-four hours."

"And why would you want to do something like that?" Pete asks, trying to understand.

"Because it's there... Because I want to see if I can do it... Because I love running in the mountains and this lets me do it all the time."

The reasons seem feeble to Pete. But he's willing to accept them for now.

"And who's this guy that you are doing it with?"

"Oh, that's Andrew. He's the guy I did the Rogaine with last year."

"Should I not be weird-ed out that you are running every weekend around the mountains with another lad?"

I laugh at such a seemingly strange suggestion. "Not at all. Andrew's a friend and a running buddy. You've really nothing to worry about."

But despite the questions and answers, I can't explain and Pete can't work out, why I'm so fanatical about the whole Wicklow Round thing. It all comes to a head when he suggests we go away for the weekend to spend some time together.

"But no, I can't go away!" I immediately protest. "I've got a five hour training run to do with Andrew on Saturday and then Sunday I've got to go orienteering." Pete is surprised by my reluctance but grudgingly accepts my excuse. But when he asks me when I'll be free for another weekend trip, the answer I give is "Never".

"Are you serious?" he replies. "Yes," I answer without much thought or hesitation. "You see Andrew and I need to scout the Wicklow Round and we have these long runs that we have to do. And then, towards April the racing season starts and then this year I want to concentrate on weekend races rather than the Wednesday ones."

Pete doesn't know what to say. Does this girl not hear herself? Does she not realise that that's not how relationships work? But he keeps diplomatically quiet. He needs time to digest what just happened.

Eventually I manage to find a free weekend when we can go away. There's a mountain race down in Kerry on Carrauntoohil Mountain that I want to go to and I ask Pete if he wants to come along.

"Is she not interested in anything apart from mountain running?" Pete starts to ask himself. "This woman is totally obsessed." But at the same time, my doggedness and commitment are strangely appealing to him, so he decides to stick with me for the ride.

This behaviour of mine continues for months. Pete tries to accommodate my neurotic training schedules, whilst I try to rearrange them slightly to find time for Pete. I enjoy Pete's company immensely. We share a love for travel and for books. We enjoy good food and pints, though he can never fathom how I can eat and drink so much and still remain so petite. And Pete is good for me. He brings me back down to earth. He broadens my horizons and listens to my thoughts. He reminds me that I'm a girl and not a tomboy. He tells me that it's good sometimes to wear a dress and not to be permanently caked in mountain mud.

But despite all these positives in the relationship, I continue to unwittingly sour it with my fanaticism. That is until one day I pick up a book called, 'The Lore of Running'. This thousand page almanac contains a wealth of running wisdom, everything from the physiology and biochemistry of running to a general guide to injuries and the basics of running health.

I am interested in finding out more about how training affects the body in order to understand the training plan that Andrew has just given me. So I start to read The Lore of Running to find out more.

So there I am, flicking through this phenomenal encyclopaedia, going through the steps involved to develop a solid training foundation. I am busy thinking of mileages and times, training and racing goals, when before I know it I come across the final step, Step Number 14. I begin to read it figuring that, like most of the preceding steps, it will be completely new to me, something I have never heard of before. But much to my surprise, this Step 14 sounds all too familiar. Indeed, it is something I have successfully practised and perfected.

Step 14 is 'Selfish Runner's Syndrome'. It reads as follows, "Running can indeed become an extremely selfish activity... To put racing as the sole reason for living is inappropriate and ultimately detrimental to family life."

Alarm bells start ringing. Flashbacks are flashing. I start to remember all the arguments Pete and I have had. I think of how I spoilt nights out because I had training the next day or because I had run a tiring session already that morning. I recall refusing weekends away because there was a race I wanted to attend. I think of the weekend breaks we did take together, when I would disappear in the middle for a solitary training run.

Just like in an apparition, I see and understand in an instance how my running has taken precedence over everything, including my own relationship. The prognosis is clear: I am riddled with Selfish Runner's Syndrome. I am truly and utterly ashamed. I call Pete to tell him of my new discovery. He is not surprised. "I tried to tell you," is all he can say, tinged with a touch of sympathy.

I continue to struggle against Selfish Runner's Syndrome whilst training for the Wicklow Round. Sometimes I conquer it. Sometimes I fail. But I am fortunate to have found that single page within the one thousand that explained this common, yet poorly diagnosed, illness. Recognising this syndrome allows me in turn to forego race or runs for the occasional night out and opens up a whole new world of activities beyond my running fixation. I am fortunate too that Pete still lets me run and still loves me for the mucky, dogged, obsessive tomboy that I am.

My final good fortune is that, though there is no known cure, I find some ways to lessen the effects of Selfish Runner's Syndrome. As the Irish double Olympian, Noel Carroll once explained, "Never complain of being tired; don't always want to go home early on evenings out; don't talk running all the time (have other topics of conversation); and always play down the importance of running in your life." Now these are definitely things I need to incorporate in any new Wicklow Round training plan.

Joe Lalor (L) and Brian Bell (R), founders of the Wicklow Round. Photos courtesy of John Shiels, actionphotography.ie

9. WARM WINTER WEATHER

Andrew and I have opted to scout the Wicklow Round during the winter season. But this year Ireland's winter weather is refusing to comply. Every weekend we are hit by cold, wet and windy conditions that are utterly miserable to be out in. We are hit by freezing fog as we try to find our way off Camaderry. We are battered by sidewise sleet as we run up Scarr. I put on two jumpers and a jacket, running tights and waterproof trousers, a warm hat, a scarf and gloves for all my training runs. But despite all these multiple layers, I still end up arriving back to my car frozen to the bone. My fingers can't even untie my laces, so I resort to physically pulling my shoes straight off my feet. I have to sit in the car for twenty minutes with the heater on full blast before I can even contemplate changing the rest of me.

Every fortnight during the winter and spring, Andrew and I go out for twenty to forty kilometre runs across parts of the Wicklow Round. But straight afterwards, Andrew often catches a cold that takes him several days to recover from. Being forced to rest means that Andrew is unable to do the intervening endurance and speed work that we both need to do to survive these long distance mountain runs.

Andrew is barely better in time for the next planned long mountain run. He then comes straight out with me on another mountain reconnaissance trip. But his system is not ready for the physical strain of a mountain run combined with the harsh wintery weather conditions. Andrew falls sick again and again. But yet he perseveres, still ardently wanting to train for the Wicklow Round.

I hate the cold. And I hate this crappy weather. But I at least have a refuge from the cold winter that is battering both Andrew and I to bits.

I now work for an international aid charity that works in some of the poorest countries in the world. And though I am based in their Dublin headquarters, I regularly visit their field offices abroad. My job typically involves spending one or two weeks at a time helping the charity's field staff find local partner organisations that can do our work on a long-term, more sustainable basis.

Fortunately, the poor countries where I end up working are in Africa and Asia, places that are typically sunny and warm. And it is to developing countries like these that I flee to take a reprieve from Ireland's sodden shitty weather.

Thankfully, after a woefully bitter November and December in Ireland, I am sent on assignment to Haiti in the New Year. Haiti, along with the Dominican Republic, occupies the island of Hispaniola in the Caribbean. As the first Latin American state to achieve independence in 1804, Haiti is the only nation whose independence was gained as part of a successful slave rebellion. But decades of violence, dictatorship, environmental degradation, unemployment, inequality, sanctions and tropical storms have reduced the Haitian side of the island to one of the poorest nations in the world. There have been several coups, rebellions, US invasions and UN missions throughout the 1990s and 2000s, but the one constant throughout has been the abject poverty of local Haitians. But despite the poverty and violence, Haiti still remains vibrant with its voodoo history and culture providing a constant background of dance, music and drums. It is almost surreal that this party atmosphere can turn into violent rioting and gun battles within seconds.

For me, Haiti's bright sun and blue skies are like manna after the winter desert I have been traversing. I feel fantastically awake and refreshed to be in such a warm and tropical climate. And yet, though it is wonderful to have a two week retreat away from Ireland's dismally dark and cold conditions, there is no break from the training regime. I have to stick to doing my normal endurance and speed work if I want to be able to do the Wicklow Round route finding expeditions when I return.

My problem in Haiti is finding a place to run. The streets in the capital, Port-au-Prince, are dusty and noisy from permanent traffic gridlock. The roads themselves are broken and pot-holed, with very few pavements to run on. And despite a United Nations peace keeping mission in place since 2004, the area I am based in is notorious for car-jacking and kidnappings, with foreigners particularly targeted. To reduce any risk of kidnapping, a driver collects me from the hotel each morning and drives me directly to the office in a secure vehicle. So, if they won't even let me walk to work, there's absolutely no question of running outside. There is nothing else for it but to stick to training indoors whilst I'm based in the Haitian capital.

But I hate gyms. And I despise treadmills with a passion. I'm a mountain runner. I'm meant to run freely wherever and whenever I want to. But despite my protestations, there really is no choice. If I want to keep my fitness levels rising, I have to run indoors.

There's a gym in the hotel basement, so I'm up at 4.30 am every morning to do my cooped up seventy minute run. I have to get up this early so that I'm showered, fed and all ready to go for my secure vehicle pickup at 7 am.

It's still dark outside when I rise, but it is already warm. I switch on the lights and the air-con. Then I turn on the treadmill machine. And I run. Normally at home I can run for hours on end and barely notice the time pass. But on the treadmill I count every minute passing slowly, painfully. There is nothing to look at except my bored reflection in the gym's window pane. When the sun comes up, my reflection fades, leaving only the changing shadow of the razor wire fence to watch, as it lethally encircles the hotel edge. Even the fit US marine who comes in at 5.30 am every morning isn't enough to make the gym appeal. He turns on basketball highlights on the gym's TV and blasts it out. How I miss the silence and solitude of the mountains.

Fortunately, I get to leave Port-au-Prince and that dungeon gym after a few days and am sent to La Gonâve, a small island situated off the Haitian mainland. I go there by speedboat taxi, twenty of us packed in a boat meant for six. The captain keeps filling his vessel at the harbour, oblivious to the fact that the boat's rear end is skimming the water's surface. As a safety measure, my colleague hands me a limp, lifeless life jacket that is falling to bits at the seams. I doubt that this will save me, though by the looks of this unseaworthy vessel, it may be useful to keep.

None of the carjackers or kidnappers from Port-au-Prince have made it this far outside the capital. La Gonâve is a peaceful hilly oasis full of fishermen and farmers. However, life is hard in this apparent paradise. Rainfall is a permanent problem on this island, with drought, overgrazing and poor water utilisation forcing the 100,000 island dwellers to eke out an existence from this barren and dry reef-fringed land. We are here to visit wells that our charity is helping build and to see some schools where water pumps and toilets are being installed.

On this island, there is one road to speak of that runs the sixty kilometre length of the island. But it's not really a road, more of a dusty track hacked out of the thorny bush landscape. I decide to get up early in the morning, just as dawn breaks, to run up and down this sandy trail. I've got meetings from 8 am until 6 pm, so if I want to run my only chance is to start at 6 am.

It's blaringly hot even at this time in the morning, but I'm happy in the heat. It makes such a pleasant change from the fading memory of Ireland's wintry weather. And it's such a relief too to be able to slip on some shorts and a T-shirt and to run bare armed and legged. Back home I have to spend ten minutes covering every last part of my body to make sure the cold doesn't catch me.

The first challenge of the day is remembering how to get out of the Haitian village where we are staying. The village is infiltrated with narrow streets generating a multitude of random twists and turns before hitting the one and only main road that I am heading for. If I get lost coming or going, there's no way I'll be able to describe to the locals where I want to go. There are no signposts or street names and my command of the local language Creole after a mere four days in the country isn't good enough to communicate where I am staying.

Once I'm out of the village, I'm happy to run away from it for thirty-five minutes before turning around and heading home again. I meet a few local travellers on the road who nod their heads and greet me.

One man is stopped on the track side beside his cart full of a thousand rocks, sweat tumbling down his brown skin. I don't know where he's going with all that rubble, but it looks too heavy a load to be pulling. What people have to do for a living around here, I can only begin to wonder. And the fact that he has to pull it himself and not use a lorry just shows the level of progress on this island.

I run past him going out the road and then pass him again twenty minutes later on my way back. He and his cart are in the same position. He hasn't moved an inch. He seems more interested in my running form than in his cart of stones. "Where is that white woman running to?" he seems to ponder. "And why is she turning around and coming straight back again?"

People in rural areas of poorer countries like Haiti often don't know what to make of people who are recreational runners. "Why is she running around like that for in all this dust and heat?" they wonder. "Who is she running away from? Is she in trouble?" "Who is she running after? What have they done to her?" To these islanders, running seems like such an unnecessary, even luxurious expenditure of energy, especially as they trudge toward yet another long hard day of labour in the fields and sweltering heat.

Two weeks of Caribbean sun do me good and I return to Ireland tanned and revived. But it's not long before I'm heading to another assignment, this time to Africa and the Democratic Republic of Congo, commonly known as DRC.

DRC lies in the heart of Africa, a huge country that straddles the equator. DRC is effectively the size of Western Europe, with its landmass greater than the areas of Spain, France, Germany, Sweden and Norway combined. Its population of sixty-six million ranks it as the fourth most populous country in Africa and the continent's third largest country. DRC is richly endowed with vast reserves of natural minerals and metals. And in addition to these natural resources, its expansive rainforests contain great biodiversity, including many rare and exotic animals.

But DRC is less known for its size and diversity and more for its violent, corrupt and bloody history. The most recent war which began back in 1998 has brought the country to its knees. This war, which has involved seven different foreign armies on its territory, is the world's deadliest conflict since World War II.

It has killed 5.4 million people directly in the fighting and indirectly from disease and malnutrition. And although peace accords were signed in 2003, fighting continues in the country's east.

Despite DRC's hostile reputation as a country permanently at war, it actually ends up being a far easier country than Haiti to find a place to run. The capital Kinshasa has what's known as the Golden Mile, two parallel streets along the Congo River that flows along the city's northern boundary. The roads enclose the residences of foreign ambassadors and Congolese dignitaries, encircling the backs and fronts of their houses. Every one hundred or so metres, heavily armed army troops stand guard, protecting these wealthy people and their properties. These troops are also stationed here to keep a close eye on neighbouring Brazzaville, the city and country sited just on the other side of the river barely two hundred metres away. This is the only place in the world where two national capital cities are on opposite banks of a river, in guarded sight of each other.

The Golden Mile run is short but beautifully set. Palm trees line the smooth tarmac road. The grass on the verge is perfectly manicured and green. Beautiful French villas hide behind adorned gates. Noisy cars are banned. And as the sun sets over the Congo River, it shines brilliantly red on the waters, making a picture perfect vision of an idyllic African scene.

It makes such a change from the rest of Kinshasa, where the roads are broken, the grass is dead, the traffic is chaotic and crime is rife. Kinshasa is a crazy city full of sharp contrasts. Here affluent suburbs coexist with sprawling slums and abandoned urban areas that are worn down from years of civil war. But the rich always know how to carve out a place for themselves where peace and serenity reigns.

I've never felt so safe in all my life, running loops around Kinshasa's ambassadorial circuit. Even though I know the troops are checking out every white woman on the block, particularly those who are wearing scantily clad athletic gear, I take great comfort in their presence. I'm not worried by their stares. I'm just glad that I can keep to my training plan, whilst also taking an hour's break from the chaos that is Kinshasa.

Just like my Haiti trip, I get to escape to the countryside for a week's worth of work. I am sent to Kasongo in eastern DRC. Kasongo is on the opposite side of the country from Kinshasa. It takes a three hour plane ride across the whole country to reach the city of Goma on the Rwandese border. And from there, it's a stopover and a night's wait for another plane ride the next morning. It takes two hours to travel south to Kasongo in a small wobbly aircraft, an aircraft whose departure is totally dependent on the country's unpredictable tropical weather.

We arrive at Goma's airport, unsure if our flight will even go. Weather has been erratic in the area all month and we are still waiting on radio reports to tell us whether the rains have abated over Kasongo. If it is raining, the aircraft can't land on the grassy runway and we will just have to wait until tomorrow for another potential try.

The airfield is littered with UN cargo planes, old Russian Antonovs and army helicopters as well as missionary and aid agency run planes. There are even a few aircraft that are lying just off the runway encased in black molten lava. They have lain there un-extracted for the past six years, ever since the nearby volcanic Mount Nyiragongo erupted and covered them back in 2002. The airport terminal itself is run down, with peeling paint, grubby officials, leaking toilets and broken chairs. It is an indicative scene of a developing country where resources are tied up in fighting a never-ending civil war.

Even though we get the all clear weather-wise, I nearly don't make it onto the plane. I fail to see two army officers solemnly hoisting the DRC flag whilst I'm busy rifling for something in my travel bag. My companion for the journey quickly grabs my arm to sternly stop my search and makes me stand silently to attention. I've not the slightest idea what is going on. Once the flag is securely raised, she explains to me that traffic and pedestrians must stop everything they are doing for the raising of the national flag at 6 am and 6 pm every day. Police and military personnel have been known to detain people who neglect to show the event due respect.

We eventually make it to the plane and soon get the all clear to take off. Our plane rises and circles over Lake Kivu, then glides over small hamlets tucked away on the hills. The craft then starts to take us over hundreds of miles of green unbroken jungle. I look down and really feel like I'm travelling into deepest, darkest Africa.

Kasongo, where we are headed, is a small town of 63,000 people that lies to the east of the sprawling Lualaba River, close to Lake Tanganyika and to the west of Tanzania. Back in 1875, Kasongo was once a vibrant Afro-Arab trading post. And between 1879 and 1884, Kasongo was visited by HM Stanley on his third expedition, Stanley being the orator of the infamous quote "Dr. Livingstone I presume?" But since those epic moments back in the nineteenth century, Kasongo has been in steep decline. The area has been severely affected by the ongoing civil war. And though the hostilities have abated, hence allowing my visit, the effects of the conflict are still evident in the people and their surroundings.

Despite the work that I must do here, the Wicklow Round training must go on. I break through the mosquito net at 5.30 am the next morning. It is still dark outside. Oblivious to the time, the neighbour's cockerel has already been crowing for the last hour. I grope for my Petzl light and hit the switch. The generator is only used at night, so I have to get ready under the cover of my head-torch. I have fifteen minutes before dawn to find the bathroom, splash some water on my face from a bucket, string up my hair and tie on my shoes.

By 5.44 am, the dark is struggling to keep hold. A few stretches later and with my watch showing a quarter to, it is light enough to start the day and my run. Saluting the guard, I amble out the wooden gate. He is still fast asleep after his night-long shift. He is meant to be wide awake and standing guard, warding off potential thieves.

I know exactly which way to go. After landing in our twelve seater plane yesterday, we drove from the airfield straight into Kasongo town. It was a dirt road that linked the town and the airfield, a fifteen kilometre track wide enough for one car that I can now use to jog along.

The road is red and fresh from the morning mist. But before I know it, it quickly narrows as I leave the town, thick jungle greenery crowding in from either side. I half expect a lion or an elephant to come charging out at any second from the tangle of trees that surrounds me. But all these animals have already been eaten by the warring factions, so I am safe from such wildlife attacks.

But just as I think the foliage will engulf me and the road, I come upon large hundred metre chunks carved out of the thicket, wherein lie homes and farms and families. Some farmers are up already and busy with their daily chores. Most of the early revellers just stand and stare at me as I jog my merry way past. Others though greet me just like any other local who would be passing by at this time. "Hujambo," they shout as I run past their doors. 'Ah, so it is Swahili they speak in these parts of the woods,' I work out. I wave and I shout "Sijambo," shouting hello straight back, remembering my African words from my now fading memories spent in Kenya.

I travel out for half my run time before finally turning to run straight back. By now it is 6.30 am. In these parts of the jungle, school starts at a bright and early 7 am. As I begin my pitter-patter home, I start to come up behind groups of kids dressed all alike in green and white uniforms. They are heading the same way as me along the same road, I back to town and the office and they on to class at the local missionary run school.

As I pass a group of schoolboys, they think it fun to keep pace with me. With books tucked under arms and flip-flops flip-flopping far too fast, we jog through the jungle, the white girl and her band of merry adolescent boys. This Rocky movie recreation in Congolese style would have certainly made even Sylvester Stallone proud. I am somewhat distressed however when I look down and see some seven year old kids keeping up with me no problem, whilst I am busy sweating from the run's strain. They must be fit from long walks to school and equally long days working in the fields.

One young Congolese school boy takes the opportunity to introduce himself and to ask for my particulars. "Jina lako ni nani?" he asks, wanting to know my name. "Mo-Ra," I reply in my Africanised accent, bastardising my name so that he can understand. But when he requests my phone number and address, I strategically sprint far away. Such behaviour from a boy half my age I can hardly condone.

My sudden turn in speed drops the students, but leaves me tired as I trundle towards the forest's edge and town boundary. My amble is sufficient enough for a barefoot farmer to take up where the students have left off. He jogs happily beside me without saying a word. And then, after ten or so minutes of his

153

silent company, he turns to me and says "Asante sana!" as if this was the most normal thing in the world. And with that, he thanks me very much for the exercise and my company before returning home again.

I finally reach the town's perimeter and leave the thick jungle behind. I know I am close to base. I turn the final corner only to now run full flight into a road bursting with kids heading straight to school. There are thousands of them, a sea of brown children decked out in every shade of green, kids big and small and every size in between. Although the road is wide enough for us all, I am travelling against the flow. I am forced into the gutter with the chickens and other animals who are also trying to escape from this adolescent stampede. The children keep walking on regardless, clearly with more scholarly thoughts on their minds.

Eventually I arrive back to the house where I am staying, unscathed, sweaty and bemused. After such a running adventure in the jungle, the bucket shower is totally refreshing and the breakfast papaya tastes much sweeter than before.

But the adventures don't stop there. I'm back in Ireland from DRC for less than a month before heading off again. This time I head east, to the Lao People's Democratic Republic, or Laos for short, a landlocked country found in South East Asia.

Laos is a holiday resort in comparison to Haiti and DRC. It has none of the wars or violence characterised by my two previous field trips. Yet, it still is relatively poor with a third of the population falling below the national poverty line. After years of isolation, Laos is now opening its doors to foreigners, displaying to them its stunning mountains and historic cities imbued with the calmness and gentleness of the Laotian people.

Vientiane, Laos' capital, is a surprisingly sleepy small town on the banks of the Mekong River. Its capital is filled with silk shops and French bakeries, wide boulevards and steaming noodle-stalls, bringing alive its latent yet remnant Indochinese history.

There's no need for treadmills or Golden Mile boulevards in Vientiane. And I don't even need to wait for dawn before starting my run. The whole of Vientiane is wonderfully safe and easy to get around. My preferred route is out the hotel door and straight down towards the Mekong River. From there, I follow the roads and paths that skirt along the river's water. I pass the ornate Buddhist temples just as the orange shrouded monks leave their gates in search of their morning alms. I pass the French mansions with their impressive facades that need a lick of paint. I pass the fishing boats and crab cages, all ready to net their river fare. And I pass the homes that house ferocious, rabid dogs that love to chase white naked legs.

The dogs are the only form of life in Laos that has forgotten to be sleepy and calm. Instead, they are vicious and wild animals that are only subservient to their masters. I'm not normally scared of dogs. I'm the sort of person who stands my ground and usually chases them away. But if dogs don't listen to my shoos, then I'm at a loss at what to do.

Two Laotian dogs in particular have it in for me. Every morning they lie in wait until I run past their gate. Then they spring out of nowhere, unleashing their wildest barks and bites. Their farmer owners first seemed shocked and then amused. But by my third morning of running past their house, the farmers take absolutely no interest at all. They are too busy with the chickens, pigs and numerous children to be bothered about their dogs attacking a silly morning jogger. I eventually learn to break into a walk twenty metres before and for twenty metres after this particular gate. When I walk, the dogs don't seem interested in the slightest. I am obviously not a fast enough target to chase.

For some reason, these ferocious dogs are not unique to Laos. In fact, when I run in most developing countries, I have unfortunate encounters with canines. Dogs are often kept for security purposes rather than as docile pets. So when they see me running away from them at speed, they immediately assume I'm a thief and take off after me in hot pursuit.

However, there is one place in particular where I never have to worry about dogs. During the lead-up to the Wicklow Round, I also spend two weeks in Rwanda, working in its capital Kigali. Rwanda's name will be forever linked with the 1994 genocide. Back then, over the course of one hundred days, approximately one million Tutsis and Hutus were killed, eliminating close to twenty percent of the country's population.

One day I remark to a co-worker that I have never seen any dogs on my early morning run. She explains to me in turn that, during the genocide, packs of dogs would maraud around, feasting on the dead corpses that littered the streets. Since that time, Rwandans have had an aversion to keeping dogs in their homes.

When I am staying in Kigali, I take the same running route each time. But even with it being more than a decade after the genocide, I cannot escape the past. After less than five minutes, my route takes me past the infamous Hotel des Mille Collines, the hotel immortalised forever in the movie "Hotel Rwanda". It was there that the hotel's manager, Paul Rusesabagina, housed over a thousand Tutsi refugees during the genocide. Over the weekend I eat lunch at the hotel. It is impossible to imagine what had happened in that dining room, beside that swimming pool, at those hotel gates.

Yet despite the terrible history that Rwanda still lives with, there is considerable progress in the country. Roads are good, amenities work, investment is happening. It is still one of the world's poorest countries, but things are looking up for Rwanda. Even running is helping Rwanda heal itself. The annual Kigali marathon, I discover, is devoted towards achieving continued peace and reconciliation.

I fly back to Ireland. I've been out of the country for six of the last fourteen weeks and have been running mainly on flat tracks and roads. Because of my unexpected work travels I have not spent as much time running up and down mountains as I had originally planned. I need to get back out into the hills. I need to get my legs used to the climbs and the long distances. And Andrew and I need to finish scouting the Wicklow Round.

I am out in the Wicklow Mountains less than forty-eight hours after arriving home. I've no time for jet lag. Andrew and I have two months before our proposed attempt. I can't let another second's worth of preparation time in Wicklow go to waste.

10. ALONE

"You've done what?" I scream. "I've torn my cruciate ligament." Andrew repeats it once more for my benefit.

"But what's that? How did you do that? What does this mean?"

I'm nervous. We can't afford to have any injuries now. It is the beginning of April and there are less than eight weeks before our intended Wicklow Round attempt.

I can guess how it happened. Both us are competing today at the Leinster Orienteering Championship, which is taking place on Fair Mountain. We have both completed our courses. Only that Andrew has come back from his run parading a painful limp.

Orienteering is a sport where athletes use a map and compass to navigate between points in unfamiliar terrain. Compared to the Navigational Challenge series, the points are more numerous. Orienteering controls are also separated by much shorter distances and the sport uses maps with greater detail that require technical map reading techniques.

The orienteering course set today on Fair Mountain is in difficult and deadly terrain. We have to run around sharp cliffs, wade our way through deep marshes, climb up steep grassy slopes, traipse our way through soggy bogs and battle our way through overgrown prickly pine forests. And not only do we have to negotiate this minefield of natural obstacles, we have to also find controls that are purposefully hidden out of sight. We have to find tiny rocks embedded below hundreds of cliffs. We have to find small holes in the bog within a vast peat landscape. We have to find little ditches in the ground somewhere in the deep dark forest. And not only do we have to find these miniature features in this convoluted setting, but today at the start of April, the weather has decided to up the ante. The summer months are fast approaching. And it is officially snowing.

The sleet and the snow slam into us as we stand around the finish. Andrew and I watch runners collapse across the line from total exhaustion after their course has led them up, down, over, around and under Fair Mountain. We also see others walking dejectedly back to the start. These competitors have lost a control, got hypothermic on the course and have given up from fear of catching frost bite. Nobody has had a fun day out on this race.

"So what happened to you?" I ask Andrew, pointing at his knee.

"You know that area around the base of Fair Mountain? Well I was running along and went to put my foot on what I thought was a piece of moss. However, it turns out that the moss was hiding a rock underneath. When my foot hit it, my foot slipped straight from under me. I ended up falling and twisting my knee."

"Does it hurt?" I enquire, hoping that it's just a minor sprain that will be alright in the morning. But Andrew knows enough about training injuries to be pretty sure of his torn ligament prognosis. He heads home to rest it and to try to stop the swelling. A few hours later he sends me a text. "Knee the size of football. All I can do is RICE". He has to Rest, Ice, Compress and Elevate. Damn it. This is serious.

A few days later, we meet for lunch. He's definitely walking straighter than he did after Sunday's race. But still Andrew enters the cafe with a pronounced hobble. It's hard to make small talk when there's such an obvious question looming. How does this accident affect our attempt on the Wicklow Round?

"It shouldn't be too bad," Andrew begins. "I think I managed to reduce the swelling in time. It should be back to normal within the next six weeks."

Six weeks! That means mid-May, two weeks before we attempt. How is he ever going to be fit in time?

But the problem really isn't the knee. That can be fixed. The problem is something more serious.

"I've been thinking about all the colds I've been having over the winter and all the training sessions I've missed," Andrew explains. "This ligament issue is just another set-back to add to the long list of things that haven't gone to plan. I suppose I've just got to admit to myself what's happening. I'm just not going to be fit enough to do the Wicklow Round."

My stomach hits the floor. I lose my power of speech. I can't believe he's just said that. Does this mean that we are not going to do the Wicklow Round after all? After all the weekends we spent in Wicklow running around those mountains in freezing, shite weather. After all the mornings I got up at 5 am in Haiti, Congo and Laos to do long hot training runs when I could have been basking in bed. After all the hard work we have done, all the scouting, all the training. I can't believe it has all come to nothing because of one too many colds and one torn asunder knee.

"Well, you could try to do it on your own," Andrew quietly says under his breath. What an absurd suggestion! What a moronic proposition! Does he even realise how ridiculous this idea is?

There's no way I can do this on my own. I need him to navigate. I need him to tell me how fast or slow to go. I need him to distract me with his banter when the Round starts to get physically tough. I need him to feed me with his chocolate brownies and homemade banana bread. I've become totally and utterly dependent on him to lead me safely around the mountains. There's absolutely no way.

Secretly though, I don't think he wants me to go it alone. He has invested too much time, energy and effort in this himself to see me run off with the spoils. But Andrew has still thrown out the idea as a lifeline to me. He has given me an option. The question is whether I want to take it.

Do the Wicklow Round on my own. It's hard to even contemplate the idea. But the thought of all my hard earned winter training going to waste depresses me even more.

For the next few days I feel fed-up and let down. I know that none of this is Andrew's fault. In fact, this is the norm when it comes to doing things in teams. People get injured, they get sick, they get busy, they drop out.

I eventually berate myself into action. 'Pull yourself together, Moire. It's not the end of the world. And anyhow, how can you possibly make a decision about going solo if you don't even know what it involves? You need to go out there and try to do sections of the Round on your own. Then you can work out if it's even feasible or just a crazy idea.'

It's a valid point. So I decide to go out and do parts of the Wicklow Round alone and see how far I get.

I first try to find a route off Carrawaystick Mountain that will get me quickly to the forest road that leads all the way to Drumgoff. There are no paths off the summit marked on any of my maps. So I decide to make up my own route.

I run due east away from the peak, down a steep heathery slope with the idea of following a river source through a newly planted forest until I reach the road. The good news is that I navigate this properly and find the slope, river and forest with

161

ease. The bad news is that I've made a terrible route choice. The descent is perilous and I come close to tripping and falling down the slope several times in humpty-dumpty style. And what's more, I'm out here on my own, with no horses or king's men to pick me up and put my pieces back together again.

The route along the river turns out to be a reed infested jungle that I have to bash my way through with a pretend machete like some Amazon jungle explorer. But even famous explorers are wise enough to never go it alone. They always have their back-up crew and local native guides to make sure they survive the wilderness that they are travelling through.

Eventually I find the forest road. And though I felt hopelessly forlorn whilst I fought through the forest, now that I know exactly where I am, I feel an overwhelming sense of pride. I found the road on my own. I came off the summit safely without anyone else's help. It's this strong sense of achievement that spurs me on to go out and test my ability to do it all over again.

Next time, I try a more formidable route. I set out to scale Lugnaquillia, Wicklow's highest mountain standing at 925 metres above sea level. It's the twelfth mountain on the Round. The mountain itself is flanked north and south by impressive cliff faces, whilst flat football-like grounds lie expansively on top. This makes it a dangerous mountain. Mist can often come down quickly and what with the featureless flat top combined with sharp dramatic cliffs on either side, it is a place that you can quickly get disorientated, lost and even die. I've been warned that mountain rescue call outs are numerous for this mountain. I need to be extra careful here.

Everything looks fine as I start to run up Lugnaquillia from its northern end. It's a cold and cloudy day, but nothing beyond the norm. I can see the summit far off in the distance and know that I'm headed the right way. But the further I go up the mountain side, the harder it is to see the peak. Soon I notice the grass is getting more and more caked with frost. And with every step I take up the mountain, freezing fog closes further in. Soon I can barely see twenty metres in front of me. All I can see is flat grassy land all around. I'm also avidly aware of the cliffs that are lurking ominously to my left and right.

I panic. But the more I panic, the more I realise that losing my nerve would be a fatal mistake. I am the only one out here who can help me. If I lose the plot, there's no one else here who can save me. Normally Andrew would be here to guide us both quickly off the mountain in a calm and collected manner. Now I've got to do what Andrew does and use what I know to get me off this mountain in the most fast and efficient way.

I'm too proud to call out mountain rescue. If I call for help, I'll be the laughing stock of the mountain running community and will never be able to show my face at a race again. If I call for help, it will just verify what everyone else is surely thinking, that a girl shouldn't be mountain running on her own and pretending that she can navigate. And anyhow, by the time mountain rescue arrives, I'll be frozen stiff and most likely dead. My hat and gloves are already icing up from the freezing fog. I've no choice but to keep moving. I've just got to make sure that I am moving in the right direction.

I try to remember what Andrew has shown me. With my map and compass, I take a bearing to the highest point right in front of me. I measure the distance and height change. It's 800 metres to the point I'm aiming for, up seventy-five metres of climb. At the rate I'm going, it should take me around ten minutes to get there. I check my watch for the exact time. And I then take a look at my altimeter to verify the height. Then with all these random figures floating around in my head, I line up my compass and start to follow it, praying with each footstep that I've made all the right calculations.

I'm scared. So scared. The mist is thick. The grass is frozen stiff. The Arctic wind is blowing straight across me, eerily chilling me inside. But there's no time to be scared. I have to be rational. I have to take control. If I want to do the Wicklow Round, I have to learn to be cool, calm, collected and capable whilst in the mountains, just like Andrew was when I first saw him navigate in the Rogaine.

Ten minutes pass and the ground starts to level off. I check my altimeter. The altitude reading is right. I must be where I want to be. I must have found my way! But I've no time for proper celebrations. I'm still too far from safety. I have to repeat these calculations two more times before I find Corrigasleggaun, a smaller mountain near Lugnaquillia and from where I know my way home.

As I run downhill closer and closer to Corrigasleggaun, the mist begins to fade. The grass has thawed out at this lower altitude. And soon my gloves begin to melt. I start to see Kelly's Lough down below me, the one I visited on that second fateful Navigational Challenge race. I look back up to where Lugnaquillia should be. But as I turn around, I see no mountain, just a cloudy haze. That's the fog that I was submerged in for the last twenty minutes. That's the fog from which I have just masterminded my escape.

I severely chastise myself once I'm back on warmer, lower ground. 'That was such a stupid and dangerous thing to do. Going up Lugnaquillia in such cold, threatening weather? What was I even thinking?' But I can't help a wry smile from slowing growing across my face. 'But I did it.' I say with a victorious grin. 'I navigated off the mountain on my own. I found my way through the fog. I did it!' My heart is now beating faster than

I've ever felt it before, fast from the exertion of mountain running, fast from the exhilaration of my solo mountain rescue.

It's this adrenaline that keeps me going out for more and more solo action. I start to go out for longer and longer mountain runs over parts of the Wicklow Round. But I still know that running in the mountains can be a dangerous sport. So on each outing I bring an extensive safety kit. And I let Andrew and Pete know the route I will travel and the time they should expect me back.

Once, they don't hear from me. I've informed them that I'm going for a forty kilometre training run over nine mountains. I intend to park my car at Wicklow Gap, run down the road to Ballinagee Bridge and then do the Wicklow Round route from Oakwood as far as Camaderry. I guess it will take me eight hours.

But I don't foresee what will happen to me during the training run. First I get caught on some barbed wire whilst trying to climb over a forest fence. I end up swinging on top of it for ten minutes, with a leg straddled on either side. I'm unable to climb over. I'm too stuck to climb back. The sharp barbed wire bits lurk menacingly between my legs. I fear that I'll become another victim of female genital mutilation. If six foot something Andrew had been here, he would have easily stepped over the whole thing. I would then have lent on his shoulder and hoisted myself over too. But as a petite five foot four damsel in distress, I'm left dangling on the wire hoping that someone will hear my shrill shouts for help.

Eventually I manage to lose my balance and fall flat on my face. Fortunately I've landed on the right side of the fence. And even better, I've not received any puncture marks in the process. But I've wasted precious minutes.

This delay however isn't as bad as the next one I encounter.

For eight hours of running, I need to drink three to four litres of water. But I end up misjudging the number of rivers that I will cross on today's run. My water bottle reserves soon run dry, but I can't find any clean streams to refill them. I've also forgotten to bring iodine tablets that could clean the dirty water that I'm finding. I continue to run on regardless, but the signs of dehydration soon begin to show. I become more and more delirious and my pace begins to slow.

I had planned to arrive at the car at Wicklow Gap by 8 pm and to notify the guys that I was safe. As I reach Camaderry's summit it is already 8.30 pm and the sun is starting to set. I've forgotten to bring a head torch with me. I assumed I'd be back at the car by now. But the incidents with the fence and my dehydration have caused a huge delay. If I get caught out here in the dark without any light, it definitely will be a mountain rescue call-out.

I hear a text coming through on my mobile phone. It's Andrew. "Looking dark out there. Are you off the mountain yet?" I just about manage to text back. "No. Soon. " My brain is too tired to multi-task, to both navigate and use my phone at the same time. And anyhow, there's no time to compose elaborate text messages. I've got to get off the mountain before the sunlight completely goes.

Fortunately I can see the main road down below and the car headlights passing by. I find the tarmaced way that leads to the road and Wicklow Gap and I reach my car just in time for sundown.

In my efforts to go solo, I am making many mistakes. But I am not only committing navigation errors as I had initially feared. I am also messing up in terms of basic mountain safety by not preparing myself properly for each trip. Up Lugnaquillia, I went out in bad weather. Up Camaderry, I didn't drink enough water. At other times I go out wearing the wrong clothing, I bring the wrong food, I forget to tell someone where I'm going, or I keep running when I'm obviously unfit to continue.

Fortunately, I always manage to escape from my mistakes largely unscathed. And I soon become acutely aware that I indeed *have* to make these errors if I want to learn. When things go well in the mountains, I learn very little. And if I'm following someone around like Andrew, I'm not making the mistakes myself. But when I'm out on my own and make multiple errors in the mountains, then I know exactly what I shouldn't do and I vow never *ever* to do it again.

I conclude in due course that I need to get some proper training if I'm not to make a fatal mistake that I'm no longer alive to learn from. So I sign up for a weekend's navigation course in the UK's Lake District, two days dedicated to navigation for mountain marathons and adventure racing.

Having already filled in a form admitting how haphazard I can be at mountain navigation, it is straight down to business first thing on Saturday morning. We are divided into groups of twos and threes and are sent straight out into the mountains to learn from an experienced instructor. I am put into a group with John Allen, an experienced adventure racer and part of a team that finished nineteenth in the World Championships Adventure Race in Scotland, the race that I fatefully withdrew from.

The first thing John teaches us about is map symbols and scales. After this quick refresher, we then head further into the mountains to learn how to read our maps and to relate them to the ground around us. We practise finding river junctions, crags, ponds and spurs. John points to minute details on the map and tells us to lead the way.

And then John explains something that has always been a mystery to me. He tells us about contours, the connected lines and circles on the map that join land of equal height.

"It's like the mountain has been cut horizontally into big portions of cake of equal height and the resultant cake slices have been drawn around," John explains. Now if the explanation involves cake, or any type of confectionery for that matter, then I am bound to understand. He then tells us that, though rivers may divert and paths may fade away, these cake slice contours will never ever change. "Contours are therefore what you fundamentally navigate off, because these are never wrong."

Just to prove how crucial these contours are, he brings us into featureless terrain. This is the type of terrain that you'd find in deepest darkest Wicklow, parts of Wicklow that I typically stay well clear of. But for the Wicklow Round, I have no choice. I have to journey through such barren dull mountains. Now is my chance to learn how to safely navigate around areas such as these.

John brings us to a place where there are no paths or cliffs or rivers or forests that can help us find our way. Instead there are only rolling hills of endless grass, with every minor change on the ground carefully carved into our maps. We spend the afternoon journeying from re-entrants to ridges, from spurs to saddles using our maps. And by the end of the day, I can finally fully understand my mountain map and I feel much more confident about my navigation.

Sunday is our chance to show our instructors and ourselves what we learnt the day before. A small orienteering event is held where we have four hours to find twelve controls in whichever order we want.

This time, I find it much easier to make decisions about which route I should take. I am able to line up my map correctly with my surroundings and always know where I am on the mountain. I find the tiny spur east of Low Kop by reading the fine contour lines. And when the mist comes down over Loadpot Hill, I comfortably follow my compass and trust that I'm headed the right way. In the end, I find all the controls with forty-five minutes to spare.

"That was quick," John remarks as I sprint back to base. "And you're the first person back." I'm genuinely surprised.

"I thought you said that you didn't know how to navigate?" he asks in a baffled tone.

"Well normally I make terrible mistakes. But for some reason today, everything just made sense."

Something clicked when we were out on the hills yesterday and today. The part that was missing that slotted into place was that I needed to have some confidence in myself. I hadn't realised it, but I had already learnt a lot from watching Andrew, as well as from my own individual epic mountain runs. What I needed to learn from this course was to trust my instincts, to consistently apply what I know and most of all, to enjoy navigating in the mountains without this irrational fear of being lost or wrong.

Self-confidence was what I needed to learn. If I believe I can't, then I don't. If I say I can't, then I won't. I have to believe that I can run up the mountain. I have to believe that I won't fall coming down. And I have to believe that I can find my way by applying simple mountain rules.

Now that I feel better about my navigation skills, I decide to put them to the definitive test. I sign up for the Great Lakeland Three Day Ultra Mountain Trail, a three day navigational event in the UK's Lake District taking place at the start of May. This year's event covers over 160 kilometres of distance and 10,000 metres in climb. My rationale goes that if I can find my way over these one hundred miles of mountains, then surely I am capable of doing the Wicklow Round alone.

The event is small by UK standards, with less than fifty competitors. The organisers purposefully keep the numbers down to make the event small and friendly as a counterbalance to the tough long days on the hills. The event is organised by the same guys who arranged the navigational course, so I am happy to see familiar faces in addition to the small contingent of fellow runners.

For the next three days I will do 1.3 marathons every day up 3,000 metres, a third of the height of Mount Everest. Already I feel slightly nervous about Day One's run. Everyone else is from the UK and knows the Lake District exceedingly well. I know only the small section we explored during our navigation course and that is nothing in comparison to the areas that we are about to cover on this event.

Needless to say, within less than an hour on Day One, I'm lost. I'm looking for Kidsty Pike but I get confused around Low Raise and start looking for the Pike a kilometre too early. Fortunately I see the other runners jogging into the distance and I find the control as they leave it.

'Damn, damn, damn. When am I ever going to stop making such stupid mistakes?' one part of my brain starts berating me. But there's another part that telling me, 'Don't worry. You'll be fine. It's just taking you a while to understand the map scale. This map is 1:40000 whilst the maps at home are 1:25000. That means on this Lake District map it takes you longer to travel through the map than you'd think.'

I leave the two sides of my mind to continue fighting it out. I've got better things to do with my time, like find the next control.

Unfortunately I make another small mistake as I come up to the control on Angletarn Pikes. I head for the wrong cliff. I eventually find the control placed beside a totally different cliff when someone else points it out.

'There you go, being stupid again,' says my brain, trying to rub it in. My other brain half comes swiftly to my defence. 'Sure don't worry. It's a minor error. You're just getting used to the amount of detail on the map.'

Eventually I start to help out the nicer part of my head. After a few more hours of running in the mountains, I begin to prove it right. It takes me a while, but I get more and more used to the map as I run. I climb through Deepdale no problem, on to Grisedale Tarn, then down and over the A591 road, before climbing up through The Bog until I reach High Raise.

From here the next control, our second last of the day, is at the top of Bowfell. I approach it from Stake Pass, north-east of Bowfell's summit. Between me and the control the map shows closely packed contour lines, a mess of sheer cliffs standing right in my way. The map also shows a safe alternate path running around Angle Tarn up onto the saddle, adding a kilometre on to the most direct route, but providing a route that will keep me safe and alive.

A fellow competitor is running just ahead of me. I watch him veer to the left of Angle Tarn and head straight to climb up those contour lines and cliffs that I'm so intent on avoiding. 'Nooooooo, don't doooo it,' is all I can think. But then I reconsider. 'Or maybe he knows something that I don't know. Maybe it's like in Wicklow where there are paths that aren't marked on the map.' I watch him running towards the cliffs without the slightest hesitation. 'Oh feck it. I'm tired. And I can't be bothered to do an extra kilometre.' So I take off after him in hot pursuit.

He picks up a minute narrow path, threading its way through Hanging Knots Crags. At times, we are on all fours, scrambling up the scree. But scary though it is, it saves us ten minutes as we pop out from under the cliffs and overtake some very surprised but faster runners. Later at the camp, he reveals to me that those attempting the Bob Graham Round use this path as they summit Bowfell and the forty-one other designated Lake District Peaks. It's a secret short-cut for mad endurance mountain runners that cartographers obviously thought too crazy to map.

I finish the day in good spirits despite my initial mistakes. I feel like I've really achieved something, having navigated safely and found all the controls over the course of today. The camp too is intimate and friendly. Everyone has put up their tents and is sitting around, making their evening meals.

I don't know any of the other runners here, but I start chatting to a guy called Phillip who looks like an old hand at the sport. We swap stories about how our day went. I tell him about the scary Bowfell route through the cliffs. He's tells me about other similar routes. And what with knowing the Lake District so well, I get him to check out my proposed route for the course that we plan to run the next day.

But despite my elation at finishing Day One, it has taken its physical toll. I spent ten hours twenty-one minutes completing today's course. After so many hours of running up and down mountains, every movement of mine is slow and sore. And even though I am totally exhausted, I barely sleep. The wind rattles the sides of my tent and threatens to blow it over, keeping me wide awake all night.

I get up the next morning, barely able to move after a night spent on hard ground. Outside my tent door I can also see bad weather threatening with stormy clouds circling menacingly above. I'm half thinking of wimping out. It's going to be another marathon and a bit. It's going to involve lots of steep mountains and perilous rocky descents. And whereas at the start of Day One I had no idea what to expect, today I know exactly what lies ahead. And I know it's going to hurt.

In the end, I persevere. Everyone else in the camp is getting up and getting ready to run. I know they are also tired and in pain. So how could I possibly quit when it's obvious that they are suffering just as much as me?

Once I start to run, much to my surprise, I'm absolutely fine. My legs loosen up, my aches and pains subside and soon I'm sprinting downhill at speed, remembering why I love mountain running so much.

But the weather doesn't look good. Clouds are gathering ominously as we clamber over the boulders towards Scafel Pike's summit on the way to the control on Lingmell. It blurs my vision for a few minutes, before opening up to present stunning views the length of the Corridor Route.

As I run off the summit, I meet three other runners who are also on the course today. They too are suffering from the effects of yesterday. One looks so rough that I offer him a Panadol painkiller. He gladly takes it and swaps it with me for one of his chocolate eggs. We continue to run together towards Green Gable and on to Brandreth. It is fun to run alongside others after the hours spent running alone. It also makes a welcome breather from having to concentrate so intently on navigation with the others now showing me the way.

From Brandreth, the course leads us across the Haystacks to a control on High Crag summit. I have no choice but to climb up the scarily steep and narrow zigzag path that ploughs its way to the top of High Crag.

But it's not just the sheer drop that is frightening me. The higher I climb, the stronger I can feel the wind blow, trying to yank me off my feet. Storms are brewing over the Lake District and High Crag is the wrong place to be at a time like this. I hunch over as I continue to climb upwards, crouching down to avoid the wind. Eventually, after a few scarily airborne moments, I make it to the summit. But I can scarcely stand up in the gale. I hurl myself against the summit cairn, clinging on to its stones with my bare hands.

After a few aborted attempts, I finally manage to resurrect myself. I run away as fast as I can, heading west from High Crag towards High Stile. But I get buffeted again by the wind as it sweeps sideways across the ridge. Normally I want to be lightweight and thin for such mountain running events. But it's at times like these that I wish I was ten kilograms heavier so that I can physically weight myself to the ground.

Finally I make it off the mountain to the tranquil and sheltered setting of Buttermere Valley. As I run through the village, I pass a tea shop and bakery, all decked out for hungry hikers. I'm magnetically drawn to the cream cakes sitting in its window. But I know that if I go into the shop, I'll never come out ever again. I have to drag myself away from visions of warm tea and biscuits, vanilla ice cream and comfy chairs. 'You've got three more controls to visit,' I keep telling myself. 'Then you can sit down and rest.'

The storm clouds break as I head up Robinson. I try to put on waterproof clothing, but these are waterlogged within seconds. I quickly get cold and miserable. I stop eating. I stop drinking. 'What are you doing Moire? Why are you putting me through this?' my brain starts to bitterly complain. 'You could have left me down in Buttermere with those scones and cakes and buns. 'Don't worry.' my other brain's half starts pleading. 'There's not far to go now. Only High Spy, then past Derwentwater and the finish is just below High Seat.'

But despite the short distance left, things go from bad to worse. The rain starts to pelt down so hard that it washes a contact lens out from my eye. I am left half-blind and left looking like a ravenous drowned rat. It's not a good look for a girl.

I manage to find my way to the rest of the controls, reading the map by holding one hand cupped over my blind eye. When I eventually cross the line, I am about to fall apart at the seams. An official is there to collect my control card. But instead of talking about the course or the rain, all I can muster up is "I need a hug." Of all the requests this official has received thus far today, this is definitely one of the most bizarre.

"Well I'm sure your boyfriend will give you a big hug at the end..."

"No, you don't understand, I need one now," I say as I lunge towards her and grasp her with my two arms, smothering her in my sopping and sweaty rain jacket. She is so lovely and warm and comfortable. Fortunately, she doesn't seem to mind.

"Would you like a cup of tea?" she asks me once I loosen my grip and let her go. I'm about to burst into tears, I'm so happy about this tea offer. "I've some HobNobs in my bag," I sniffle in return. I arduously take off my rucksack and find a packet of biscuits at the bottom to share them with her and the tea. The biscuits, though, are ground to dust after having run a marathon and a bit. But it doesn't matter. I pour out the dust and lick it out of one hand as I warm my other hand with the plastic cup of tea.

I soon discover that I did well to just finish Day Two of this ultra mountain ordeal. Out of forty-seven runners in total, eighteen have retired from today's course. Some hitched lifts to the finish. Many of them got sucked into that tea shop at Buttermere. I figure that it must have been all the shite weather training I've been doing over Wicklow's boggy wet terrain that helped me do so well. I come in seventh that day overall and first lady home, in a time of ten hours thirty-nine minutes.

The third and last day is a short sprint in comparison to all that we have covered over the first two days. It is a mere thirty miles, just over a marathon. And the weather has cleared to reveal gloriously blue skies. It is a beautiful day to race back to the finish, via the long climb up Nethermost Pike, past Grisedale Tarn to Hart Crag, over to Red Screes and down its dangerously difficult but fun descent to Kirstone Pass. From there is it five kilometres over several mountains to Mardale II Bell, on to Adam Seat and Selside Pike, before finally running east of Haweswater Lake back to Bampton Village.

By now, after two days and twenty-one hours of mountain running, my body is falling to bits. Nearly every part of my body, from my battered feet to my half blinded eye, is screaming out for the finish. I'm surprised, however, that my knees have held up considering the brutally steep slopes we've been descending. The Wicklow Mountains, where I've been doing most of my training, have nothing to compare with the near vertical slants that I have been hurtling down.

I obviously think these thoughts too soon. I'm less than half the way through the final day and suddenly the side of my right knee packs in. Nothing dramatic happens. I've not twisted it or turned it or bashed it against some rock. Instead, I just lift my knee to run another step and suddenly it goes. But I'm out in the middle of nowhere, so I've no choice but to continue on. There

176

might be another twenty kilometres or a half marathon to go. But if I have to hobble on to the finish, then that's what I have to do.

The more I run on it, the more worried I get. What have I done to it? Will it get better soon? What if this is a permanent aliment and I will never run ever again? My mind extrapolates all my worries and blows them into endemic proportions.

I get to the finish after eight hours thirteen minutes of running. Over the three days, I have completed the one hundred mile run in just over twenty-nine hours in total. I finish in eleventh position overall and I am the first lady home by five and a half hours.

This is adequate proof to me that I can navigate alone.

But by running the Great Lakeland Three Day, I have joined Andrew in the injury ward. I initially arrive home hobbling, in denial that there's anything wrong. After one week of rest, I have to admit that my knee is not getting any better, so I am forced to go see a physiotherapist. She ascertains that my Iliotibial band or IT band has tendonitis, causing the lateral pain in my knee.

It's the middle of May. I'm in too much pain to run. I have to rest my leg, get sports massages and do regular stretches and exercises. Whether I'll get all this done and my knee fixed before the end of the month is looking more and more doubtful.

And whether a Wicklow Round attempt is even possible towards the end of May seems increasingly unlikely.

11. A Morning of Mist

I miss the May deadline. But I'm still determined to give the Wicklow Round a try.

The knee injury was bad timing. May is the perfect month for the Wicklow Round. At that time of year, the heather is still low, still short and shrivelled from surviving the long winter months. By May, the long winter nights are also well and truly gone, with a mere five hours of darkness as we head towards the year's longest day in June. But my knee prevents me from trying the Round.

Even if I am fit enough to attempt in June, it ends up a no-go. Downpours and gales hit Ireland at the end of the month, turning the Wicklow range into a muddy swimming pool full of flooded streams and thick mist.

July is my last ditch chance to attempt the Wicklow Round this year. The days are already getting shorter. The heather is growing higher, having gorged itself on abundant summer light and showers. August would be too late and too dark. It is definitely a case of July or bust. All I have to do is find a suitable day in that month when the weather is right.

I search and find four websites that provide weather updates for Wicklow. I have to find a day when it will be calm and dry enough to do the Round. On a near-neurotic basis I check the forecast on the hour. But what I see only makes me more worried. One website says sun, whilst another says showers. One stays committed to its forecast for the whole day, whilst another changes its prediction every four to six hours. I go through utter elation as I see sunshine predicted and then utter depression as the next site foresees deluges and storms. All this, whilst right outside my window, it rains, torrentially, incessantly, annoyingly.

I hate rain. Rain makes mist. The only thing I hate more than rain is mist.

Mist hides the mountains. To attempt the Wicklow Round I need to see for miles. I need to see the top and bottom of every mountain peak. I need blue skies.

I have been out in the Wicklow Mountains when the mist has descended without any notice, just like the freezing fog that subsumed me without notice when I ran along up Lugnaquillia. One minute, the mountain is right in front of me and I can see my route straight ahead. And then in an instant, the cloud comes down and the mountain is gone, erased by a sheet of whiteness.

In such conditions, I can get lost, so lost, especially when I am all alone. Even though I now know how to navigate, I can still end up slowing down and losing precious time when I can see less than fifty metres ahead.

But what frightens me the most is the fact that people have perished out there on those mountains. The mist comes down, the weather changes. People get lost and cold and die. Some of the most difficult mountains I am to cross on the Wicklow Round have a high probability of mist and I know that in their time, those peaks have claimed lives.

But I need more than clear conditions on the actual day of my attempt. I also want dry weather for at least a week beforehand. Wet weather can swell rivers, making them deep and wide, full of fast flowing water and slippery rocks underneath. My route brings me across three such rivers, three possible water obstacles. If rain fills them to the brim, they will be nearly impossible to cross on my own.

Not only do I need dehydrated rivers, but I also need dry terrain. The slightest bit of damp or drizzle and the Wicklow

Mountains become one big boggy mud-bath. Running up wet bog is extremely tiring, if not near impossible. And whilst going up is hard, going down through such mud can be distinctly dangerous. The mountains are dotted with boulders and cliffs that I can skid into or slide over. I therefore need a few days of weather devoid of water to deprive the bog of their slippery edge.

But this is Ireland we are talking about. There is a reason why the grass is so green and the scenery so stunning. It is because we are the blessed recipients of a near daily supply of rain, freshly delivered from our neighbouring Atlantic Ocean. Praying for one whole day of dryness is one thing. Asking for a whole week of drought is demanding a miracle.

Slowly but surely, after weeks of obsessive forecast checking, a space opens up in the weather. For the first time, the websites agree with each other, suggesting simultaneously that Sunday 20th July could indeed be the warm weather solstice that I am praying for. I am not going to get an optimal week of dry weather beforehand. But at least the day itself promises to be rain-free and clear.

On Saturday 19th, I make my final preparations. I put aside my running clothes. I pack up my bag. I check my map, compass and altimeter to make sure that they are working. I secretly hope to have no need for my navigational equipment. I know the route and mountains so well by now that I could easily run without them. But if the mist comes down, I will totally rely on them to help me find my way. So, just in case, I carry them.

Lastly, I gather together my twenty-four hours worth of food and water: sandwiches and crisps, nuts and gels, brownies and energy bars, as well as twelve litres of water and eight pints of milk. I meticulously separate them into zip-lock bags marked with stage names and stage times. "Stage 1: Start to Sally Gap. 90 minutes". "Stage 2: Sally Gap to Ballinagee Bridge. 3 hours". "Stage 3: Ballinagee Bridge to Drumgoff. 4 hours 20 minutes". From experience, I know that for every hour out there, I have to eat something small. The stage times therefore tell me the number of food items needed in each bag. For every hour, I need to drop one piece of food into the zip-lock bag and to have half a litre of water ready to keep me going.

The route will take me deep into the mountains, far from civilisation. But there will be moments when I will reconnect with people, time when the route will come off the mountain and cross roads that cars can reach. There I will pick up food and water and any extra gear. A gallant team of friends has volunteered to drive to these points and provide me with such sustenance and support. My boyfriend, Pete, will drop me to the start. Brendan, an elderly gentleman from the mountain running crowd and an avid supporter of my Wicklow Round attempt, will meet me at Sally Gap. Andrew will stay with me for ten hours, from Ballinagee Bridge until Glenmacnass. Then Pete will come back and support me from Sheepbanks Bridge until the end. Andrew plans also to join Pete towards the end, to see the final stages of the run.

That Saturday, I drive around Dublin to drop the bags and drinks to my team. Brendan is full of enthusiasm as ever and seems more ready for the Round than I. "You'll do great. It will be all good. I'll see you tomorrow morning at Sally's Gap!"

As I hand over my bags to Andrew, the mood is more sombre. "I wish I was also going out there tomorrow," he says. I wish he was coming along too. This was never meant to be me attempting to complete the Round on my own. We had planned on doing this together, as a team, just like the team we were when winning the Rogaine. But what with the knee ligament injury and the persistent colds, it was simply not meant to be.

I am very aware that Andrew is the one who has brought me to this moment: he designed my training plan, he trained alongside me, he taught me how to navigate and suggested the whole route. It is just as much his Round tomorrow as it is mine.

From the Wicklow Round list of rules, I read *"Any attempt to be recognised must first be publicised in advance on the forum section of the Irish Mountain Runners Association (IMRA) website and afterwards by supplying a list of splits"*. The rule is clear. I have to announce my attempt to all of Ireland's mountain runners for it to be valid.

Up until now, I have kept my Round attempt a semi-secret. I have mentioned my intention to the organisers, Brian Bell and Joe Lalor, when verifying the rules and checking possible dates. I have spoken with some experienced and respected mountain runners discretely, with those who know the Wicklow Mountains intimately and the many clandestine paths around them. And of course my support team knows my plan. In fact, Andrew, Brendan and Pete are the only ones who know the minute details of where I will be and at what time during the whole Round.

Apart from these few, I have not spoken to many people about attempting the Wicklow Round. I have not even told my parents of my intrepid plans. They think the business of running up and down one mountain is already dangerous enough. What would they think if they heard their daughter will try to climb twenty-six of these mountains in one go? What would they do if they knew I will try to scale some in the middle of the night? My parents already worry about me and about the next crazy thing I will try. They shook their heads when I bolted off to

Africa and stayed there for seven years. This Wicklow Round attempt may be just one stunt too many for their elderly and fragile minds. So I decide not to tell them, not to cause them any undue stress, or unexpected heart attacks. And seeing that they live on the other side of the country, I figure that they will probably never find out. I will tell them all about it later, over the phone and after the fact.

There are other reasons why I do not want to talk too much of a Wicklow Round attempt. I know that there those who doubt that the Round can ever be done. I know there are cynics who think that a solo attempt is madness, that the only way to successfully finish the Round is by doing it in a team. I also know there are doubters out there who think that only men can do it, that a woman could never complete such a mountain endurance challenge. So the idea of attempting the Round, on my own and as a female, will probably attract substantial scepticism from fellow mountain runners. I know that if I hear these opinions, I might begin to believe them. And if I start thinking they are right, then I may never have the courage to go out there and to try to prove them wrong.

However my silence about my intentions to attempt the Round is probably due to a deeper reason. During those long days of training out on the Wicklow Round route, I spent a lot of time alone with the mountains. I began to get to know them and to understand them more and more. I saw how each mountain is different in shape, form and composition, how they differ in their responses to weather, time and season. I slowly started seeing each mountain as having a distinct personality. And I soon unwittingly found out that they were all bigger, stronger and much wilder than I. They could unleash freezing fog and blow in fierce winds. They could dare me down sheer cliffs and taunt me up steep climbs.

And yet, whilst they could be brutal and frightening, they too could be calm and forgiving. It was at these quieter, gentler moments in their moods that they showed me spectacular sights that only mountains can bestow. Holding me up high above their heads, I would see golden sunsets from their sparkling summits. I would watch lakes glisten at the bottom of their secret valleys. I would breathe in fresh mountain air, distilled in the purist heavenly silence. I wanted these moments in the mountains to be mine and only mine. I wanted the mountains to show these scenes to me and no one else but me.

I had become utterly possessive of the mountains. And in turn, I have become protective of the Round. I want the Round to be just about me and the mountains. The whole challenge has become a tumultuously jealous and private love affair.

As a result of my high level of secrecy, I take the rule of publicising the attempt "*in advance*" to be a mere twelve hours before the start. On the post, I play it cool and downplay the whole thing. I write on the IMRA mountain running forum:

"*Seeing that there's such lovely weather this weekend, I think I'll give the Wicklow Round a wee go tomorrow. Thought I'd put the note on the forum so that, if I do get round, it can be seen as a recognised attempt... following the rules and all that.*"

There are no times, no locations, no phone numbers, no contacts. It is not necessary for others to know where I will be or when. Subconsciously though, it is more the mountains than the mountain runners that I am afraid of giving too much information to. If the mountains know my potential whereabouts, they could scupper all my plans.

Everything is in place. My team has my supplies. They know exactly when and where to meet me. My own gear is packed and ready. All I have to do now is wait.

The phone rings. I wonder if it is someone who has read the forum message and wants to wish me good luck. I pick up the receiver. "Hello?"

"Well hello dear, it's your mother." Normally I'd be happy to get a call from my mum. Today though, it's a different matter. If she asks about my plans for the weekend, I have no choice but to lie. My parents still don't know about the Wicklow Round. There is no way they could have read the forum though. They still don't understand the internet.

"Hello Mum, how's things?"

"Oh grand Moire, thanks for asking. Listen, we're on the road at the moment. We have a bit of business in Dublin to do tomorrow, so we are driving down right now to spend the night at your house. We'll see you soon!"

WHAT? My mind goes blank, my stomach twists in two, my legs go weak. What am I going to do?

Mum hangs up the phone. 'Oh God, I can't tell them,' I say to myself before they arrive. 'They'll worry too much. No, forget the worrying. I bet you they won't even let me out of the house to go do the Round.' But how am I going to sneak out of my own home in the middle of the night, carrying a rucksack and wearing running tights without them wondering what is going on? I can't exactly pretend I am off to the pub or going dancing in that sort of get-up.

Before they arrive, I decide to come clean. 'Damn it.' I think, 'I am thirty-two and I'm old enough to go running around the mountains on my own in the middle of the night *if I want to.'*

"On your own?" Mum asks with a noticeable element of distress. She's barely in the door and still trying to catch her breath. "Yes," I reply, before eventually pleading, "But it will be really safe, because the team will know exactly where I'm

185

meant to be and at what time. And I will be carrying an emergency GPS tracker and my mobile phone and a survival bag... and I'll be fine." She doesn't seem convinced. She looks worried. She always worries. Even though I'm always fine.

Dad, on the other hand, hasn't said a word. He is leaning back in his chair, an old man thoughtfully smoking his pipe and nursing his freshly brewed cup of tea. He has heard the whole Wicklow Round plan whilst I stammered it out, as I tried to pacify my mum.

I'm not too sure what my father's silence means. Is he so worried about me that he has lost all capacity to speak?

He continues to puff on his pipe and without mentioning me or the Round, he slowly begins to reminisce. "I remember when I sailed across the Atlantic and back. Terrible storm we had off the Bermuda Triangle. Lost the rudder and everything."

Dad has always been a passionate yachtsman. Already at the age of seventy-one, he has spent the last six years of his retirement sailing around the Canaries with Mum in tow.

"And what about the gales we had off the coast of Morocco?" Mum chimes in, now lulled by the memories of their own outdoor tales. "We nearly got the boat tangled in all those fishing nets. Oh my goodness, don't you remember?"

It is already midnight and there is no sign of either of them going to bed. They are enjoying too much the recollection of all those sailing memories. I'm just glad that they are distracted and not talking about my own crazy plans.

But more importantly tonight, I think they are trying to tell me a few things: that they too love the outdoors and the risks that lie out there; that they too need hair-raising adventures even in their seventies to keep themselves feeling alive. They are trying to show me that I may be more like them than I even realise. And, in my parents' own unique way, without directly saying it, I feel they are trying to tell me that they see themselves in me. I think they are trying to let me know that they are proud of me.

Even if I was originally searching for their tacit approval, Mum and Dad can't really argue with my scheme: I am already packed and ready to go and Pete has just arrived at my front door. It is 1.45 am on Sunday morning and Pete is about to drive me to Kippure and the official start of the Round. I kiss my parents goodnight and get into Pete's car.

It is a clear night. A full moon shines bright against the black sky. It is a beautiful, simply beautiful night.

After many thoughts and discussions with Andrew about what time to start and what mountains to run at night, I eventually decide to start at 2.30 am on the dot and to run up Kippure in the dark. From there, I will descend down the tarmac service road to Sally Gap where dawn will break around 4 am. My training times suggest that with such an early morning start I will be home by 10 pm, completing the Round just before darkness falls again.

As Pete and I sit in the car at the bottom of Kippure, I notice that the one hundred metre television mast on top of this mountain is covered in mist. It is normally visible from miles around with its flashing flare on top warding off low-flying craft. I'm not worried that I can't see it though, as I figure the mist will eventually pass. I am confident in the weather forecasters and their concurrent predictions of good weather for today.

Pete sits quietly beside me in the driver's seat. He has just landed off a plane from New York and, here he is, in the small hours of Sunday morning, helping me live my dream. We have been together now no more than eight months. And though my year's quest has been to hone me for this epic attempt, Pete's

187

challenge for the year has been simply dealing with me. It seems to him that every weekend has had me out in Wicklow, running up this hill or that. And whilst all I can think about is the mountains, all Pete wants is a Saturday night out or a weekend away, every once in a while. Those weekends I have been unable to give, so busy I have been with my preparation and so infested I have been with Selfish Runner's Syndrome. I have tried to explain to Pete why Wicklow, why the training and why the Round. It is only now, sitting in the car, that I realise I have been trying to explain something that even I don't fully understand.

But like every worthwhile guy, he has stood by his woman, backing her and her wild plans. Now tonight, he can finally let this girl loose. He is letting her find out for herself whether this crazy dream can really become reality.

As the clock strikes 2.30 am, Pete and I hug goodbye and I set off along the sandy track towards Kippure. I am so happy that I am finally fulfilling all these months of anticipation that I start running off too fast. My heart beat rises quickly from the pace and sheer excitement. 'Slow down, slow down,' I start panting to myself. 'There's still so far to go.'

Slowing myself up, I soon come to the end of the sandy track. From here, I know that there is a faint trodden trail up through the bog that leads right to Kippure's summit. I shine my head torch beam around in all directions, but in the overwhelming dark and mist the trail is nowhere to be found. Not to worry. I look at my map, take a bearing and follow the compass needle.

But I do worry. I'm still not confident in using a compass to navigate in the mist. I still want the reassurance of being on that trodden trail that leads directly to the top. Despite the direction the needle shows, I veer off to the left and right whenever I see the faintest shadow of a path. It is a dangerous strategy. Such changes in direction could soon make my compass bearing futile.

Every deviation off to the left and right proves in turn fruitless. The trail is nowhere to be found. I soon realise that the mist has created that lunar landscape that I so dread and it shows no sign of passing. Through the eye of my head torch, all I can see around me is a barren scene of bog and heather sloping ever so slightly uphill.

I left the main sandy track less than ten minutes ago. But in those intervening ten minutes, I've totally lost my nerve. That one hundred metre mast at the top of Kippure, that mast that towers over Wicklow is still nowhere to be seen. I look at the map. In addition to Kippure, there are also little hills to the left and right that I have never noticed before. Have I gone off bearing? Am I heading to one of those insignificant summits instead? Has my compass broken down without me knowing it?

Or more seriously, am I about to fail so early on? Are the mountains and the Round going to defeat me before I even reach the first summit, before I have even put up a worthy fight? With the hill still sloping up and my altimeter still showing that I am gaining height, I have no choice but to continue on up, to go wherever my compass leads me.

Slowly, from nowhere, I start to hear a distant ghostly hum droning out the night. Still half asleep and ever more scared, my mind races to figure out the sound. And before I know it, *BOOM*, a strobe-like flash lights up the fog, illuminating for a split-second my surroundings. To my left, there is a gully that I recognise. Just ahead I see a concrete post and fencing. *BOOM!* It's the perimeter around the TV mast. The mast is straight ahead! Its main structure is still hidden by the mist, but the strobe light on top is still perceptible through the haze. Now I realise where the hum is coming from. It is from the generators, pumping out power to fuel each one of the mast's epic light explosions.

I have reached the top of Kippure at last. One mountain down. Only twenty-five left to go.

Already I am behind time, five minutes lost to slowing down in the dark and the mist. Five minutes doesn't really matter though given all the hours that still lie ahead. Happy that I am finally on my way, I find the tarmac service road that leads off Kippure and run down it, back to the main road. I am beginning to look forward to running all the way down this road to Sally Gap, to meet Brendan there at sunrise.

Parked at the bottom of Kippure, whilst waiting for the hand to strike 2.30 am, Pete has grown worried at what he is about to do: leave his girl, in the middle of the mountains, in the dark and cold, all alone. We had agreed he would travel home to bed as soon as I started. Instead, he decides to change the plan and instead patrol the road around Kippure. Eventually Pete pulls up at the Kippure service road entrance, at the junction with the main road.

Jogging down the Kippure service road, I see a car pull up just where I am about to pass. I know the area around Kippure is a popular hangout for thieves and joy-riders. They frequently come up from Dublin in the middle of the night, driving around dangerously and creating general havoc. 'Maybe that car down there is full of criminals,' I think. 'Maybe they have seen my solo head torch and figured out that I am all alone. Maybe they know that the only way back to the main road is through this service entrance and are blocking my exit so they can rob and rape and pillage me. Mum was right. This was a bad idea.'

Frantically, I search and pull out my emergency GPS tracker from my bag, just like the one we carried over in Scotland for the adventure race. There is an SOS emergency services button on it. One touch will raise the alarm with the police and they will come to my aid and save me. Tentatively, I continue to run on, the tracker in my hand with my thumb hovering nervously over the pad. But with ten metres to go, I recognise the car. "Pete, what are you doing? Go home! I'm fine." It suddenly occurs to me that he is probably more nervous about this whole Round thing than I.

Pete doesn't go home, but continues to stalk me for the next half an hour. He drives up and down the road, checking that Brendan is in place at Sally Gap, before finally pulling over as I run down the road and giving me the all clear.

But in reality, all is not clear. My plan says that I am to run down the main road, the sun is to rise and the mist is to fade. The mountains have a different idea. Yes, I am to run down the road. But as I round the final bend before reaching Sally Gap, I hit a wall of solid mist, denser and thicker than what I found on Kippure. I look behind me and see Dublin City, enjoying a warm and clear sunrise. It suddenly occurs to me that the clear weather predicted by the websites is true for Dublin but not Wicklow, even though it is less than a twenty minute drive away.

I had sworn to Andrew that, if there is mist, there is no point in me trying the Round alone. I'm just not confident enough or fast enough through the mist to make it around in such conditions. But despite these firm assertions, I know this morning that it is now or never. The heather is getting higher. The days are already getting shorter. Next weekend's weather might not be any better. But more than this, more than anything else, I want to do the Round and be finished with it. I want it to give me back my life. I can't face missing Saturday nights out any more because of long Sunday training runs. I'm tired of

191

trying Pete's patience with my refusals to go on weekends away because of possible Round attempts. I am tired of scouting routes, preparing gear, watching and waiting for a break in the weather. Mist or no mist, there is no going back.

I am practically beside the car before I see the warm red glow of Brendan's brake lights through the fog. He ushers me into the backseat so I can refill my bag with food and water. We look at each other. And then we look at the mist. We are both thinking the same thing. Nobody in their right mind would go out in those conditions, let alone at this time of the night. We both know it is crazy. But we both know I have no choice.

Thankfully he does not try to dissuade me. Instead he gives me this advice. "Take it slowly," Brendan says. "Navigate carefully. Don't get lost. The mist will burn off. You will make up the time."

Saying my goodbyes to Brendan, I jog thirty metres along the road to find the start of the path leading up Carrigvore, my second summit of the day. I know the start of the path is marked at the road by a large rock and a signboard. But so poor is the visibility that I can find neither the rock nor the board. So just like on Kippure, less than an hour ago, I am forced to abandon my attempts to find the path and forge my own way up through the heather and the bog.

My altimeter clicks as I climb through the contours, reading 682 metres as Carrigvore finally levels off on top. It was a clear day when I had done my original training run. From this height, I had previously seen the four next summits of Gravale, Duff Hill, East Top and Mullaghcleevaun, all laid out in a line. But now, on my day of reckoning, there is nothing out there but grey. The secret walker tracks I had planned to use between these four summits can no longer be found. Instead, I have to depend on my map and compass and trust that they will bring me from summit to summit without leading me too far astray.

For the next four hours, all I look at are my map, compass and altimeter. At the top of each summit, I check my map and set the compass bearing. Then I hope, beg, bargain and pray that the bearing will lead me to the foot of the next mountain.

Coming off my sixth peak, Mullaghcleevaun around 6.30 am, the mist is still thick. So as usual, I set my bearing for the foot of the next mountain, Moanbane, the seventh summit on the Round. I keep an eye on the compass and run. And I run. Soon I realise that I have run too far and that where the mountain of Moanbane should be seen going up, all I can see is a slope still going down.

The problem is not the compass. The problem is the ground. The terrain between Mullaghcleevaun and Moanbane is Wicklow at its worse. These two mountains are bridged by pure Irish bog, wet and soft underfoot. Water has carved out great holes in the earth, producing peat hags that I must detour around. With so many holes in the ground, it is impossible to run in straight lines and follow the compass bearing as required. I go off to the left a little to avoid a bog hole, but forget to go to the right for a while to compensate for my minor change of course.

I must have taken quite a number of steps to the left because, before I know it, I am lost. I had been running on a bearing, expecting for the ground to flatten out at an altitude of 600 metres when I reached the bottom of Moanbane. With my altimeter reading 590 metres and with the land still sloping downwards, I know I have missed the mountain's base.

Frightened at the prospect of being well and truly lost, I quickly become disorientated in the mist. I study the map, but my head can't work out where I am. I panic and call Andrew.

193

He'd know what to do. Andrew is waiting for me at the main road down near Ballinagee Bridge, the end of my second stage, but still an hour's run away. "I've lost Moanbane Mountain," I scream. But the connection cuts and the line goes dead, just when I most need network coverage.

With time ticking away, I take a deep breath, lay the map on the ground and re-orientate it with the compass. I soon realise that I have drifted south, so I head back north to a height of six hundred metres. Andrew soon calls back. Through the poor reception, he calmly listens to what I have done. Then he tells me to head due west. From there, I'd find Moanbane. True to form, he is right. I have lost ten minutes, but have found the mountain that I had foolishly mislaid.

I am lucky to have even reached Moanbane alive. Less than half an hour before hand, I had been plodding up Mullaghcleevaun. Like many other mountains in Wicklow, this mountain is smothered in bog, thickly spread on like butter on bread. From my training runs, I had learnt that the best way to cross such a bog is to go around its sides, treading on any grassy mounds or dried up patches. The bog on top of Mullaghcleevaun has no sides, no grass and today, no patches of it dry. A brown-black slick of mud lies instead before me, separating me from my intended summit. It is wet and slippery, but with a bit of care, I find it just about crossable.

I had heard of bog-holes but never seen one before. Bog-holes are pits filled with soft mud into which you rapidly sink like quick sand. It looks like a puddle in front of me, a bit of water sitting on top of firm bog underneath. By the time my knee disappears, I know it isn't surface water. I am finding my first bog-hole ever, at 6 am on Mullaghcleevaun, in the middle of my Wicklow Round attempt.

Fortunately, I saw a survival programme on the Discovery Channel a few weeks before the Round. The host had lowered himself into quick sand and described in detail how to get out. "Don't panic. Float yourself up horizontally. Crawl your way out." 'If it worked for him,' I figure as I slowly sink into shock, 'it could just work for me.' So, trying very, very hard not to panic or hyperventilate or burst into tears, I try to float my way up and slowly swim out of the bog-hole. With no one else around to pull me out, I eventually heave myself out by grabbing on to a few tuffs of heather and pulling my body forward with all my might. Once back on terra firma, I take a deep breath, check that my shoes are still on my feet and not at the bottom of the bog and continue on up Mullaghcleevaun still shaking from what had just happened.

After my brief emergency call to Andrew, I finally find Moanbane. At the next summit, Silsean, the last peak before the road, I take a quick look at my watch. 7.45 am. After five hours and fifteen minutes of running, I am exactly one hour behind schedule. The loss in time is bad, but not irredeemable. I know that as long as I am off Tonduff North Mountain before 10.30 pm, I will still be able to complete the Round. Tonduff North is where Andrew nearly killed himself falling off a cliff. I have to get to that hidden path through Raven's Glen before dark if I want to make it safely off that mountain.

My overall plan allows me to slow by two hours. I have still one hour left to play with.

But who cares about the loss of an hour? I am just relieved to be still alive. I could have disappeared forever in Mullaghcleevaun's bog. I could have died from exhaustion wandering around in circles looking for Moanbane. I'm still so far from finishing the challenge, but I am already feeling very proud.

Andrew is waiting at the farmyard gate, watching me stumble through the field of ferns leading towards the road. I am so happy to see him, see somebody, see anybody. But I don't want to stop too long and waste too much precious time. But still, I have so much to tell him, about all that has already happened since the start. "I fell into a bog hole. And then I lost the track. And then I lost Moanbane." He hands me milk and food and water as I prattle on. Patiently he gives me some much-needed two minutes worth of attention to get me mentally settled again.

I have stopped at Ballinagee Bridge, on the tarmac road between Silsean and Oakwood. Looking up at Silsean, my eighth peak, there is nothing but mist. Oakwood, where I'm now headed, is also a complete white-out. But down at the bridge, everything is clear. "It's a lovely day in Dublin," Andrew informs me, Dublin being less than forty kilometres away. "The mist is burning off everywhere. It should also clear up here."

I hoped that the mist would clear at Sally Gap at 4 am this morning. That was four hours ago. By now I have to accept that, for the moment, the mist is here to stay. It may clear sometime, somewhere. But until that time and place, I will continue on regardless, just me and my map and my compass, up the remainder of the Wicklow Mountain peaks.

12. DARKNESS

With my bag full to the brim with gear and rations, I head for the next peak on my map, Oakwood Mountain. It will be four and a half hours before I see my support team again.

My bag is weighed down from all the food and water it is now holding. But this is what I have to carry and consume if I want to survive this run. Every hour, my body burns 600 calories from the sheer exertion of this ultra mountain endeavour. This spent energy I must constantly replace if I'm to make sure that I don't run out of steam.

I've already worked out that I need to consume in total 14,000 calories just to fuel my one day Wicklow Mountains excursion. That's how much a woman is supposed to eat in an entire week, not in twenty-four hours. 14,000 calories is like eating one hundred and thirty-three bananas or twenty-six dark chocolate bars or three kilograms of crisps. That's a lot of calories. That's a lot of eating.

But just try stuffing all these bananas, bars and crisps into you whilst simultaneously trying to run up and down mountains. It's not as easy or appealing as it may initially seem. However, after much trial and error on my training outings, I have worked out a digestible eating and drinking regime that I plan to follow for the Round. According to the plan, I will drink half a litre of water every hour and have something small to eat. I will eat sandwiches and cake, nuts and chocolate, pork pies and cold pizza, sports gels and bars, all of which I have meticulously packed so that I can easily access them on the go.

But I'm not eating.

This morning's mist has not only slowed me down. It has also inadvertently messed up my eating and drinking plan. My stomach has felt sick since the very beginning, so worried have I been about the misty conditions. And whilst concentrating so intensely on my map and compass, I have simply forgotten to eat. For the first five and half hours, up until Moanbane Mountain, I have barely consumed a thing.

As I approach Oakwood, I have been going for over six hours. But despite having burned thousands of calories already, I don't feel hungry at all. In fact, the less I eat, the less I want food. It's a vicious circle. But I know I have no choice. I have to eat.

I begin stuffing food into my mouth. But I find it impossible to swallow. I chew and chew, but instead of going down into my stomach, the food ends up stored in my throat and cheeks. My stomach and I are not on good terms. The more I make myself eat, the sicker I become. Try as I might, I cannot correct the mistake I have already made. And for the rest of the Round, I am to regret not force-feeding myself from the start.

With Oakwood straight in front of me, I wade through King's River and then head up through the forest at the mountain's foot. Through the trees I can just make out the familiar white haze of mist waiting for me on the open mountain. Oakwood is a mischief for mist. Anytime there's the slightest bit of rain or cloud in Wicklow, Oakwood is the first to snap it up. So it's no surprise to me that I'll be climbing this mountain too in a white haze, like all of the other mountains this morning.

As I emerge from Oakwood forest, I can see less than twenty metres ahead. And in those twenty metres, all I can see is a bog infested land plastered in knee-high heather perpetually sloping upwards. In fact, it looks just like every other mountain

I've already climbed this morning. Now that I come to think of it, *all* of these mountains in West Wicklow look the same when doused with a good dose of mist. For all I know, I have been going up and down the same mountain all morning. For all I know, I could still be on Moanbane or all the way back at Kippure.

But out of all the mountains on the Wicklow Round, Oakwood is definitely different, so I know I'm in the right place. Oakwood stands out from all the others because it is definitely the most boring. It has no dramatic cliffs or nearby lakes or convenient picnic places. There is nothing to see and nothing to do, except tediously trudge through its heather and bog. You can't even muster the satisfaction of getting to the peak and beating your chest in pride. The top is so flat and uninteresting that they've not even bothered to put a cairn up there to signify the summit.

No one comes to this dull place. And with no walkers plying up this mountain, it means that there are no paths for me to follow. And with no paths, I have to trip and slip my way through the marshes and mud, whilst keeping a close eye on my compass to make sure I'm still taking the right course.

Eventually I can't go up Oakwood any more. I've either died or reached the top. I check my heart rate monitor. It is still registering my pulse. I'm not dead. So this must be the top. I tick the mountain off my list and look for the next one in line. The Round says I'm to visit Table Mountain, less than three kilometres away south west from Oakwood's drudgery.

It may be only three kilometres away in distance, but it's the most difficult section to navigate on the Wicklow Round. The terrain between Oakwood and Table Mountain is covered in two metre high bog stacks, scattered across mythically flat and marshy land. Bog stacks are pillars of peat left over after all the other bog around them has been eroded away. These bog stacks annoyingly lie in the most direct route, forcing wayfarers to weave their way around these obstacles. But with such multiple enforced changes in direction, any direct compass bearing between Oakwood and Table Mountain will soon be rendered useless.

Even without mist, I can barely see over or around these columns of bog. So I decide to take a totally different course rather than a straight line. Instead of going as the crow flies, I will zigzag my way to Table Mountain by going via big features I know well.

I first aim for Art's Cross, a large memorial overlooking Glenreemore Valley. The site itself commemorates an important part of Irish history, Red Hugh O'Donnell and Art O'Neill's escape from Dublin Castle in 1592. To flee the British, they headed into the Wicklow Mountains. Art however died there, perishing from the cold. Now placed a third of the way between Oakwood and Table Mountain, this memorial cross dedicated to this event is perfectly placed to help me find my way. From the cross, I will take another bearing to Three Lakes, my second waypoint. And from Three Lakes, it's a third and final leg straight up Table Mountain, the tenth mountain out of twenty-six on the Round.

Any training runs I had previously done up Oakwood had always been in mild clear weather, with Arts Cross visible from miles around. But like everything else today, the cross is tucked well and truly away under a misty armpit. It will prove difficult to find. My map suggests that the cross should be at an altitude of 590 metres on a small spur jutting out above the valley. I take a quick look at my altimeter and try to not drop below that height.

After about twenty minutes of trekking, I am meant to see the cross. But there's no sign of this crucifix to be found in this murky mist. I panic. I pray. If I lose this monument, there is nothing else out here that can tell me where I am. I can't face being lost again, barely less than two hours after getting lost around Moanbane.

And then, from out of nowhere, I catch a glimpse of the cross out of the corner of my eye. It is directly above me. How did it get there? Either the map is wrong or my altimeter is out by thirty metres, but neither the cross nor I are where either of us is meant to be. Regardless, I quickly thank God for the apparition, then quickly scramble back up those thirty metres to the cross's base.

I now turn my compass dial to 222 degrees and make a beeline for my second waypoint, Three Lakes. I remind myself that I am only looking for two lakes at that place as opposed to three. I've always figured that the discrepancy between the name and reality is due to some cartographer's perverse sense of humour or their inability to count. Regardless, I know the two lakes I am looking for are tucked away behind six foot high mounds of bog. I'll have to be right beside them before I can see them properly.

By now I am so used to looking at nothing except my map and compass that I hardly even notice it happening. But one minute, everything is white and hidden. And the next, I can see absolutely everything! It is like someone performs that trick where they remove a white table cloth at high-speed and they leave behind all the cups and cutlery precisely on the table. But this time, the table cloth in question is covering the whole of the Wicklow Mountains. And hey presto, the cloth is whipped away and all the mountains are still in place. And then I see it, right there in front of me, less than two kilometres away. There it is, Table Mountain.

At 9.52 am on Sunday morning, the clouds around me dissipate and simply disappear. I look up and straight above me, I can see a picture-perfect crystal blue sky. I've been deprived of my sight for so many hours that I cannot help myself but cry out from sheer joy. My arms instinctively stretch up to try to touch the sky above. I want to hold it and hug it, so deliriously delighted I am to finally see it there. Never before have I been so relieved to be able to see again.

For the first time today, I put my compass away. I have concentrated on navigating in the mist for seven and a half hours. Now I can finally get back to the business of simply running and enjoying the sights and sounds of the Wicklow Mountains.

From Table Mountain, I turn south towards Camenabologue, the eleventh mountain on the Round. I am now off the blanket bog and on a safe walker's path that leads nearly all the way to Lugnaquillia, the highest peak in the Wicklow Mountains. I breathe a sigh of relief. I've had a lot of problems already this morning due to the unforeseen mist. Now that the mist is gone, I feel like everything will be okay for the first time today. It takes me fifteen minutes to go from Table Mountain to Camenabologue, exactly according to plan. I even start to eat again and regain a little energy. And I can see exactly where I am going. I am now heading towards Lugnaquillia. It might be a whole four kilometres away, but I can see it straight ahead.

I am feeling so relaxed that I even take a moment to check my emergency GPS tracker. This is the same device that I nearly used to call the police out this morning when Pete turned up unexpectedly at the bottom of Kippure's service road. Fortunately, there is also another button on the tracker beside the SOS emergency services one. It is an OK button that allows me to check-in with others and tell them that I am safe. I now press this OK button and a mobile text is automatically sent to my support team with my GPS coordinates and a message. It tells them and assures me, that everything is going well.

I continue to run up towards Lugnaquillia. After about ten minutes, I notice a helicopter coming out of nowhere. It dives and swoops over my head, then comes to an absolute standstill right over Camenabologue Mountain. It hovers right over the place where I pressed my OK button just a few minutes ago. 'Oh Jaysus,' I say to myself. 'Did I press the wrong button, the emergency services one and call out mountain rescue instead? I hear those helicopter fees are loads of money if you make a hoax call.' I start to panic. What am I going to do? I don't have time to be rescued off the mountain. I've got a Wicklow Round to finish. Then I work out the best strategy given the situation. I decide to run away.

Much later I realise that Camenabologue is on the edge of the Irish Army's artillery practise range. It was most likely an army helicopter out performing its routine military manoeuvres. It had not the slightest intention of saving me. I hadn't pressed the wrong button. It was just my over-stressed mind playing tricks on me. Looking back though, I wonder if I could have hitched a lift with the helicopter to the top of Lugnaquillia. But that would, of course, be cheating.

Once I'm out of helicopter range, I finally relax into my run. And for the first time today, I have time to take in the sights. To my right, I can see the Glen of Imail with its rivers and greenery. To my left, there lies the valley of Glenmalure with its wooded slopes topped off by the cliffs of Ballinaskea. And straight ahead, I see Lugnaquillia. It stands majestically aloof, high above the others, its broad grassy slope invitingly leading

203

to its flat towering top. It's rugged out here, yet awe-inspiringly beautiful.

The mountains have finally calmed down. After a morning of strife, of throwing mist in my face and watching me fight back, they have now declared a momentary truce. And I do not waste a single moment. I lap up this transient tranquillity now bestowed upon me and revel in the magnificent mountains set all around.

I have been on my feet now for around nine hours. But I don't feel tired. Instead, much to my surprise, I have a new lease of life. Being able to see the mountains all around reassures me. Knowing where I am and where I am going comforts me no end. And being able to see the mountain views distracts me from the journey at hand. With my mind enchanted by the scenery, my legs soon fall into a meditative rhythm. I march on and on, up and up, closer and closer to the next mountain top. My arms move back and forth in time, propelling me upwards and onwards in tandem with my feet. I am mountain running. I am happy.

It is at times like this when I'm in the mountains that I tend to reminisce. Looking back, I used to love running in Dublin's Phoenix Park, on its flat expansive lands. But after three years of mountain running, the monotony of the flat now fails to inspire. I now need the shapeliness of the hills, their mountainous summits, their deep-seated valleys. I need the grass and the heather, the mud and the rock. I need the deer, sheep and mountain goats to keep me company. I need to wonder if the sun will shine or the mist will fall. I need that sense of looking up and fearing I won't make it, that sense of looking down and feeling it's a long way to fall. I need to know I am alone in the mountains, whilst always knowing that I am at home.

I realise that after three years of mountain running, the mountains are no longer just an inanimate training ground. They have now become my mentor, teaching me what life is really all about. Each week they pull me out from the hustle and bustle of real life down below. And in the void of their surroundings, they give me the space to reflect and learn about who I really am. Because out here in the mountains, I can be me: a girl who craves challenges, who pushes the limits, who hunts for adventure. In the mountains I can feel strong, independent and free.

I touch Lugnaquillia's summit cairn, the cold, rough stone bringing me back to the task at hand. It's approaching midday on a bright sunny Sunday in mid-July. And for the first time today, I see other people on the mountain. They are walkers out enjoying the Wicklow Mountains, talking together as they approach the summit. I'm in too much of a hurry to engage in conversation, so I quickly turn around and run towards my next mountain. We acknowledge each other as we pass each other by. Most of them look at me and smile sympathetically. I begin to wonder why. 'They can't possibly know what I am doing. There is simply no way they would have heard of the Wicklow Round.'

So why are they smiling at me? Is it because they know how much fun I am having as I run like a child at full speed down the hill? Or is it out of pity on the presumption that, because I'm running, I am feeling more puffed than them? Is it because they think I am running after someone and are secretly looking forward to watching the race? Or is it just from the sheer friendliness that is created in the mountains, when like-minded mountain loving people meet and want to acknowledge each others' presence?

Whatever the reason, I return their greetings and continue on downhill. I summit Corrigasleggaun and Carrawaystick in quick succession, successfully finding the faint walking trails that lead between them and that weave their way around the bog hags. As I round one bog stack, I see Brian Bell climbing up the mountain in the opposite direction. Brian, together with Joe Lalor, is one of the founding fathers of the Wicklow Round. He is also the owner of the hand that emerged from the tent pitched beside the river when I did my first ever navigational race in Ballydonnell. And like how he encouraged me against the odds to keep going at the Ballydonnell race, he cheers me on again as I run down Carrawaystick Mountain. "You're doing well. How are you feeling?" he enquires as I run towards him. "I'm feeling fine. Lost some time in the mist this morning, but I should make it up OK." He knows there's no time to stop for long chats, so he waves me on my way.

I finally come off the open mountain that I've been on for the last four hours and drop down into the cool forest at Carrawaystick's base. From here its wide forest trails all the way to Drumgoff, the most southerly point on the Wicklow Round. Drumgoff is nothing more than a crossroads marked by a welcoming pub. It's this pub that Andrew and I were tempted to retreat into during the Rogaine when we got attacked at night by those killer ferns. But Drumgoff is the most civilisation I've seen for hours and it's the place where I will now reunite with my support team.

I eventually reach Drumgoff one hour seventeen minutes behind my predicted time. Most of this was lost due to the morning fog. Once this cleared, I did not lose any additional minutes. So I am not worried. I still have plenty of time to do a sub twenty-four hour Round.

Andrew is there waiting at Drumgoff. He looks at all the food I still have left in my bag. He can see that I have not been eating. He is not amused. "You have to eat. Between here and the next mountain, just slow right down. Walk. Eat. Take your time. Refuel properly." I nod in submission, knowing that he is right. So I set off for Mullacor Mountain from Drumgoff on a mission to feed myself. I drink a pint of milk. I eat a banana. I wolf down a packet of crisps. Then I suck on an energy gel. I still have some boiled egg sandwiches that I am meant to consume as well. But after that concoction of milk, bananas, crisps and gels, I cannot even stomach the egg smell. The thought crosses my mind to hide the sandwiches deep in the forest. Then Andrew will think that I ate them and he'll stop force feeding me food.

Four other mountain runners are waiting for me at the top of Mullacor. They heard via the forum that I was out attempting the Round and they have come all the way out here to cheer me on. It is good to see some familiar and friendly faces. But all I can manage is a wave and a faint smile. I don't have enough energy for small talk. I'm also very aware that I am still seventy-seven minutes behind schedule thanks to this morning and I don't want to lose any more time.

From Mullacor I run on to Derrybawn, the sixteenth mountain on the course, then down the steep, slate slope into Glendalough.

Glendalough today is not the peaceful place I visited during the Rogaine. Andrew and I arrived here late that evening when all the tourists had already gone home. What with it now being mid afternoon on a sunny summer Sunday, Glendalough is heaving with day trippers. For the last twelve hours, I've been steeped in isolation and tranquillity in the middle of the mountains. This Glendalough circus scene in comparison comes as a sudden shock to the system. I look and smell terrible in comparison to these freshly spruced up tourists. I feel so out of place. Though my support team are waiting for me here, I don't want to hang around. I grab what food and drink I need, then run as fast as I can out of Glendalough valley.

I start to head up the steepest climb on the Wicklow Round, the ascent up Camaderry. I plod my way methodically up the slope, my hands on my knees pushing myself higher with every stride. I can see Glendalough down below. From above, the tourists are like scampering ants in a hive of holiday activity. But up here on the mountainside, there is no one else apart but me, steadily making my way around the whole of Wicklow.

By now, I have covered sixteen of the twenty-six mountains, more than half required. However I know that the ten remaining peaks will take longer to summit as they are more difficult than the ones I've already climbed. The next few mountains after Glendalough involve steep, long and tiring ascents, up hundreds of metres at a time. On these mountains, there is no other option but to walk slowly and sure footedly until I reach each mountain top in turn.

Gavan, another fellow mountain runner and friend decides to join me on my ascent of Camaderry. He is dressed in shorts and T-shirt and is out for a proper mountain run. But after twelve hours of mountains, my legs can't muster up the speed that he is going at. I let him go on. But before he speeds off, he takes out his camera to record this poignant moment. And even though I don't feel too bad at the time, I look terrible in all the photos.

Despite my drained appearance, I still manage to catch up on the schedule. At the top of Camaderry Mountain, the Round's seventeenth peak, I am now only sixty-three minutes behind time.

I jog down the road off Camaderry to begin my ascent of Tonelagee. It is close to 4.30 pm in the afternoon. I have been going for fourteen hours. And I am beginning to tire. I notice my fatigue first when I try to take some food out of my bag. I'm looking for a brownie I remember packing, but I can't remember where I've put it. I fumble through my jacket and bag pockets, but it is nowhere to be found. Then I start getting upset about the brownie, as if my life depends on it. My tiredness is making me forgetful and increasingly irrational. Try as I might, I cannot find or get over that fateful brownie incident.

Fortunately the brownie search distracts me from the growing pains in my legs. And thanks to the distraction, I reach the top of Tonelagee before I know it.

Going up Tonelagee is easy. But descending off this mountain is notoriously difficult to navigate. Even when I'm mentally alert, I can make mistakes and still go in the wrong direction, just like when Andrew and I tried to run down this mountain in the middle of the night. With my energy levels ever depleting, I have no option but to stop for a few precious minutes at Tonelagee's top to mull over what direction to go in. Even when I do take the correct bearing, I struggle to find the boggy paths leading off the mountain, so well hidden they are in the entangled heather. Just when I need a perfect descent, I mess it up. I somehow find myself straying off the path and end up in ankle tripping heather. But I'm in such a daze that I can't work out where to look for the path again. I don't know whether to wander left or right, or just to continue down. Eventually, by pure chance, I stumble upon the track. And with its retrieval, I start becoming aware of my ever increasing demise. 'Come on now girl,' I say to myself, trying to jazz myself into action. 'You've already come so far. Let's keep it going. Just eat and drink, just concentrate and navigate and you'll be fine.'

Things are starting to slowly unravel. After being only sixty-three minutes behind on Camaderry, I am now down by one hour fifteen minutes at the bottom of Tonelagee. In the space of less than two hours, I have lost twelve precious minutes. I start to make the mental calculation. I know that above all, I have to reach the third last mountain, Tonduff North, before nightfall at 10.30 pm so that I can go via Raven's Glen. I can therefore be a maximum of two hours behind schedule and still make it on time. Any later than that and I'll end up there after nightfall. Then I will undoubtedly have to press the SOS emergency button and wait for the mountain rescue helicopter to save me whilst I dangle dangerously off the cliff Andrew nearly killed himself on.

I cannot lose any more time. But I am finding it impossible to keep up the pace. My feet ache from the pounding. My legs are shocked into submission. They scream as I force them uphill and cry as I send them back down again. My back is straining from the weight of my bag, full of what I need but which I can no longer physically carry. My shins are criss-crossed with lines of dried blood after running through miles of skin-removing heather and gorse. But I keep going regardless. I have come so far. I have to finish.

After summiting Scarr, I make my way towards Knocknacloghoge via the Inchavore River. A month ago, torrential storms hit the Wicklow Mountains causing this river to breach its banks. Fortunately, four weeks on, the waters have subsided and I am able to cross the river unharmed. But though the river levels have gone down, the rain's legacy continues to haunt.

Six weeks ago, I timed how long it would take me to travel from Scarr to Knocknacloghoge. At that time, the terrain underfoot was fine. There was soft green grass growing on the slopes of Knocknacloghoge swaying gently in the mountain breeze. There were also rocks and clumps of burnt heather dotted across this mountain side. But back then I was mentally fresh enough to avoid these.

However the past month's rains, combined with the summer sun, has caused a frenzy of ferns to spring up. In places, the ferns reach shoulder height. They force me to use my arms and legs and energy I don't have, to fight my way forward. Up higher on the mountain, the ferns have grown slower but still are booby-trapped. They wrap their stems around my legs and pull sharply to try to trip me up. I go to avoid them, but end up stumbling into the jagged edged burnt heather. The branches lacerate my legs and open up old wounds. I stagger on and head straight into the rocks and go over both of my ankles. I grimace from the pain and the unending line of torment.

I emerge from this torture having lost another fifteen minutes. Still I press on.

I push and push my way up Luggala, the twenty-first mountain on the list. I have only three more peaks, Luggala, Djouce and War Hill to summit before reaching Tonduff North, the mountain I must escape from before sunset. Then in the dark I will run the last two mountains, Prince William's Seat and Knocknagun, before finally finishing. But even though there are only six more mountains to be climbed in total, it already feels too far to go.

By now I am at my physical and mental limits. My outer leg skin is torn asunder by the thorny foliage below. My feet have endured so much pain that I can barely feel them any more. They have been stepped on constantly for the last eighteen hours. They are begging for a sit down. But even if I tried to sit, I can't. I am now super glued into a pose suitable only for going up and down mountains. Stopping would mean too much pain. So I keep going, just to keep the pain at bay.

And whilst my body gradually disintegrates, my head is slowly crumbling as well. I physically fight back the tears as I crawl up Luggala. I feel so sore and miserable and alone. All I want to do is break down and cry. All I can think about is the fact that Pete will be waiting for me at Sheepbanks Bridge, just thirty minutes away. I so badly need a hug. In fact, the only thing that keeps me going at this point is the prospect of that embrace. I just need him to tell me that everything will be all right. I need him to remind me that I can still do this.

Deep down, I still believe I can finish the Wicklow Round. But I know that time is ticking. And the pressure is on more than ever to make it off Tonduff North before dark. I have to ignore what my mind and body are telling me and switch to automatic pilot: no more thinking, no more complaining. Just keep on running until I finish the Round.

Coming off Luggala, the heather here has also grown high. Just like the ferns that shot up on Knocknacloghoge, I don't expect the heather to have reached such heights in such a short space of time. Its hard bark purges the remaining skin from my legs. I try to run around it, but am too tired to stay upright. I am so exhausted that by now my balance has all but disappeared. I lurch forward, fall sideways and skid backwards as I go downhill over the grassy mounds and uneven heather coated bog. Picking myself up each time drains me of the little energy that remains.

But I can see Sheepbanks Bridge below. Down there is Pete. Down there is the sustenance I need.

As I come closer to the Bridge, I start to see a small group of people waiting for me. I am confused. Pete is the only person who is meant to be there. So who are all the rest? I begin to hear

212

their voices as I come down the mountainside. "Come on Moire, you can do it." I don't recognise them at all. They turn out to be other mountain runners who have also heard through the IMRA forum of my Wicklow Round attempt. Because I am behind schedule, they have had to wait around two hours longer than they initially expected. I feel terrible for having kept them. I feel under pressure to keep up a brave face.

I finally reach the Bridge. They huddle all around. "How are you feeling? You're doing really well." I appreciate their support. But after so many hours of being alone, I feel disorientated by the crowd. Moreover, I don't want to distress them with the terrible details of what I've just dragged myself through. "I'm doing fine. All good, thanks," I reply. I quickly get down to the business of restocking my bag for the next mountain section.

Pete silently hands me the food and water I need. He is not sure either about what is going on. The last he saw of me was at Sally Gap at 4 am this morning. It is now 9 pm at night. I've been in the mountains for nearly nineteen hours. I'm bleeding and sweating, I'm dirty and smelly, but I'm determined to continue on. My determination momentarily distracts me and I forget to ask for the hug that I've been longing for for hours. All I can think about now is getting off Tonduff North before dark. And with time slipping away so quickly, there is no time even for a hasty embrace. I run away from the Bridge after less than two minutes' break.

With renewed intent, I run towards Djouce Mountain. But even with my new resolve, I know my plans are futile. I look over to the west and see the mountains where I was in the small hours of this morning. And directly over them, there is the sun, setting decisively on me and my Wicklow Round.

I summit Djouce and then War Hill in quick succession. It is 10.10 pm. The sun will set at 10.30 pm. Already Tonduff North has become a mere silhouette in the summer evening sky.

I know I am too late.

Tonduff North is just over two kilometres away, but it will take me at least half an hour to get there because of the rough terrain. I take the direct line off War Hill, but I hit more high heather without a path in sight. I struggle to emerge from the heathers' hold as I reach out and try to grasp Tonduff North before it disappears into the dark. And just like when I was afraid to jump into the water at the Adventure Racing World Championships, my fear of the dark now appears out of nowhere just when I least expect it. I didn't think it was an issue. I was able to cope with the dark before, but that was when I was out in the mountains with others like my adventure racing team or Andrew. But now that I am alone in the mountains, in the total pitch black, my phobia violently reappears.

As the sun sets, the wind picks up and starts to blow a haunting sound. I am surrounded by darkness and figments of my imagination that are plotting to tear me down. But I battle on. I eventually reach Tonduff North at 11 pm. By now, it is pitch-black. I am two and a half hours behind schedule but still theoretically within reach of completing the Round within twenty-four hours.

But I don't know how to get off this mountain. The way I was planning via Raven's Glen is now sealed off by the dark. I am so mentally exhausted that I cannot even read my map and figure out an alternate route. I start to panic. My throat clogs up. I choke back the tears that are welling up from sheer fright.

I call Andrew who is waiting for me close to the base of Raven's Glen.

214

"Can you see Kippure's mast from where you are standing?" he asks. Kippure was the first mountain on the Round, the one I climbed in the mist before dawn. It has a mast on top with a bright strobe that, when it's clear, can be seen from miles around. I am so close to the finish at Kippure's base that I can almost reach over and touch that beckoning light. "Head straight for the mast instead, Moire. Go west instead of east. We will wait for you at the road that leads up to the mast."

It's another short distance of two kilometres between Tonduff North and the road leading to the mast. But it's straight through marsh lands, waist-high peat cuttings and masses of knee-high heather. But I've no choice. I have to come off this mountain and cross this terrain. I tentatively start my descent off Tonduff North, my narrow beamed head torch searching out for me safe footings. But I cannot look down at the ground and look up at the same time to keep the mast in sight. Repeatedly I place my feet wrong and tumble into the bogs and streams below.

Eventually, I fall into a hole that is just about my size. Inside it is dark and warm, hidden away from the howling wind. Instead of getting straight back up again, I go to pull out my survival bag and curl up inside. I think of my emergency GPS tracker and consider pushing the button for mountain rescue to come. I am comforted by this thought. But I am also slowly losing my mind. Fortunately, my basic instincts start to override my thoughts and send out red alerts. 'You must keep going. You have to reach the road. You must get off this mountain terrain, whatever the cost.'

I am now running on empty. Only a lethal cocktail of tiredness, fear and adrenaline are fuelling me forward. But the sleep monsters are not far behind. Soon I see pairs of little lights all around me. They dart from left to right, come closer and then retreat. The lights are pairs of eyes reflecting off my head torch through the darkness. Though I know what they are, my drowsy mind starts playing tricks. I start thinking that these eyes are high enough off the ground to be those of hyenas, like the ones I saw during my time in Kenya so many years ago. And if there are hyenas, there must be elephants and lions out here as well. I start to panic. But I don't have the energy to run away. Fortunately my rational mind is still functioning, conserving itself for times such as these. "They are only deer, Moire. Don't be afraid," it says. It reminds me that I am in Ireland, not Africa. And it tells me to just keep going. It doesn't matter how long it takes me. I just have to keep going. I must get back to safety.

After what seems like eternity, I see the car lights on the road. I've made it. I'm safe. And as my feet touch the tarmac, the immensity of what I have just gone through hits me. I sit down on the roadside and start to violently shake. I've never before been so afraid or so alone. I've never before seen myself in such a pitiful state. I am physically and mentally destroyed.

But there are only two mountains left out of twenty-six. There are less than fifteen kilometres to go after completing already over eighty-five. It is only 12.15 am. I still have two hours and fifteen minutes to complete the rest. I am so close to the finish.

But I just can't go on.

I have run for nearly twenty-two hours. And there is nothing left inside me. Andrew and Pete look at me in dismay. "Are you sure you don't want to finish?" they both ask in turn. They know how much I have invested and how much I want this. They know how far I have come and how close I am to the end. But just asking me to take one more step makes me beg them for mercy.

I haven't the energy to tell them how I'm feeling. My head hangs from my shoulders from exhaustion and impending failure. I can't speak but they can read the signs. All I can do is shake my head from side to side. No, I cannot go on.

I know others would have continued, like many adventure racers who I have met. They have a drive that forbids them from ever stopping. No matter how physically beaten up they become, they are strong enough to combat any pain, to march beyond their known limits.

But there is a part of me that doesn't want to push myself beyond those boundaries. I don't want to beat my mind and body up so badly that I end up suffering a multitude of mental and physical scars. Today I wanted to do battle with the Wicklow Round. And in the end, I got what I wanted: a day long fight with the Wicklow Mountains. If I press on now, I will start hating the Round, hating the mountains and hating running. Life is too short for that amount of hate.

Andrew and Pete bundle me into a car and prepare to drive me home. But they too have had a nerve-wrecking time whilst waiting for me to appear off the mountain at midnight. They had left their car headlights on, hoping that I'd see the beams and the road from the mountain. I eventually arrive back to the cars safely. But when they try to start Pete's car, his battery has run out of power. They try to push the car to jump start it, but they end up pushing it into a deep ditch with me sitting motionlessly inside. After a series of attempts to extract the vehicle, there is nothing else for it but to abandon it for the night in an area well known for vigilantism.

And all this time, I am sitting in the front seat, mentally numb, physically shattered, just waiting for a lift home.

We eventually get home around 1 am. I am covered in so much mud and blood that I can't go straight to bed. So Pete runs

217

for me a bath. He lifts me up and cradles me into the water. But instead of washing, I curl up into a ball and fall into a comatose sleep in the bath. Pete sees what's happening. He is petrified in case I drown. But I am so happy to be finally lying down and to be feeling warm again. I'm impervious to the muck and sweat that is covering me from head to toe. In fact, I'd prefer not to wash in case I brush against the layers of bruised and battered muscles that now constitute my body.

I finally get to bed and wake up late on Monday morning. I have taken the day off work. Breakfast is a minimal affair. My mouth is still raw from eating too much sugar and my stomach upset from the force feeding regime. I decide to make myself just some strong coffee and then go to the internet to check email. Even though it is less than twelve hours since I collapsed on the road, my inbox is already full of condolences. People have somehow found out that I have not made it and want to extend their sympathies. 'But how do they know what happened?' I ask myself. The only place they could have possibly found out is from the IMRA website, so I click on the link to the forum. There are even more messages posted there, from mountain running friends as well as people I barely know. All of them are praising me for my effort, for my courage and determination and are congratulating me for getting so far.

There are also some supportive messages saying "I know how she must feel." It's a casual remark, nothing meant by it, but it makes me start thinking. How do I exactly feel? At this moment, I have no idea. I look inside and all I see is numbness. It's like someone has died and I've just heard the news and don't know how to react. In the same way, I've tried the Round and I didn't make it, but I don't yet know what to say or feel. Maybe it's because I'm still too tired this morning to have the luxury of feelings. All that is there is an unspectacular sensation of nothingness.

'So how *should* I be feeling now?' I wonder. I read more messages and realise that I should feel disappointed. I should be feeling down and distressed that I came so close but yet didn't fully make it. But it's definitely not disappointment that I am sensing. If anything, it is sheer relief. Relief that I went out and tried the Round, that I gave it everything I have, even though it simply wasn't sufficient. Just the knowledge of this starts to illicit a certain peace inside me, an acceptance that even in failure, I have done enough.

But this peace doesn't last long. As the day progresses, I start to regain again my energy and senses. And with my strength restored, I am hit by the immensity of the act that I tried to complete the day before. I start remembering the physical pressures I inflicted upon myself. I start realising the mental games I played on my mind. I start evoking the intense fear and pain I pulled myself through to keep going over all those mountains.

The memory is too much. I break down in tears. For the rest of the day I sit curled up on my sofa, sobbing my heart out. I am in mourning. I am mourning my failed attempt of the Wicklow Round. Something died yesterday. I am still to find out what perished.

When I woke this morning, I was in shock. Now I am in deep depression. But the crying does me good. Thanks to a day's worth of tears, I soon come to accept what has happened. After receiving a few more forum messages, I decide to set the story straight. Forty-eight hours later, I sit down and write non-stop for six hours about what really happened out there. I explain why I even tried the Round to begin with and how I prepared myself for it. I recount the seven hours of mist on the

Sunday morning. I tell of running happily and freely up as far as Glendalough. And I reveal my total demise and my terrifying descent off Tonduff North.

And I tell them, for now, I've had enough. I have no intention of going back out there in the near future and trying it all again. The heather and ferns are too mature, the light is now fading and the summer is drawing to a close. Another Wicklow Round attempt is definitely not on the cards.

I tell them too that I want my life back. I have spent so much time training, preparing, waiting to do the Wicklow Round that, now that I've tried it, I want some space to do other things with my life.

And with those six hours' worth of words, I draw a line under the Wicklow Round.

Struggling up Camaderry on my first Wicklow Round attempt. Photo courtesy of Gavan Doherty.

13. Unfinished Business

I draw a line under the Wicklow Round. But it is impossible to cross it out completely.

September sees the end of another mountain running season. It's a chance to take a few weeks off and to momentarily escape from my strict training regime. But it's not long before thoughts turn to next year's season and the races that I plan to run. If I want to be fit and fast for those races, I have to start back training soon. I know it will take me at least six months to prepare for them properly.

But which races do I want to do? There's no shortage of contests to choose from. But none of them seem to appeal. Instead, my heart keeps drawing me back to one that features on no official calendar... I want to do the Wicklow Round.

The physical aches and pains are long gone since that fateful day in July. Instead my head has spent weeks and weeks minutely dissecting what happened, trying to find out where exactly I went wrong.

First of all I conclude that I attempted the Wicklow Round too late in the year. I tried to do the Round in July. But by then the vegetation had already soaked up the sun and rain from the early summer months. And because of this delay, ferociously high ferns and heather had grown in several sections that severely blocked my way. If I was going to try again, it would have to be earlier. I'd have to try in May or June, when the vegetation is still low and not yet fully awake after its winter sleep.

When I tried the Wicklow Round in 2008, it was just one of many runs that I did that year. Not only had I run the Great

Lakeland Three Day in the Lake District at the start of May, but I had also run many IMRA mountain races such as Carrauntoohil and Lugnaquillia. I competed too in the Mourne British Championship, the Three Peaks World Long Distance Challenge and defended the twenty-four hour Irish Rogaine Championship, all in the space of April, May and June. I would have probably raced more if I hadn't injured my leg and endured an enforced four week racing clampdown. By being so busy running so many other races, it meant that I was missing perfect opportunities to do the Wicklow Round. If I wanted to really accomplish the Round, I would have to devote an entire year to it. There would be no vying for Championships or titles. My training, my energy, my race schedule would have to solely geared towards completing the Round.

The next thing I would have to change is my clothes. During my last attempt, I wore three quarter length tights that reached just below my knee. This running attire left exposed most of my lower leg to the whims of the Wicklow Mountains' vegetation. I can still vividly recall the pain of descending off Luggala Mountain as I approached Sheepbanks Bridge. The heather ripped right across my bare shins as I ran right through it, gouging great chunks of flesh straight out from my legs. Blood streamed down my shins, leaving only pure pain to course through my veins.

I don't want to go through that again. If I was to try one more time, I would have to opt for full length tights, the ones with zips at the ankles. These I could hoist up to my knees whilst I warmed up ascending a mountain. But I could also pull them down to my ankles for protection purposes whilst running through evil foliage.

I also need to change some administrative aspects if I am to attempt again. Three days after my Wicklow Round attempt, I found myself at the pub after an IMRA race. There I bumped into Joe Lalor, one of the Wicklow Round founders. We talked about my Wicklow Round attempt and all that happened out there. During our conversation, I told him in particular about how impressed and humbled I was by the many IMRA members who turned out to support me on my way. However, I also told him how at times I found their presence overwhelming after being out for so long in the mountains on my own. I told him how I tried to put on a brave face for all these gallant supporters, whilst inside I was suffering and crying. "Is it possible," I asked him, "to do the Round quietly, without any of such hype and curiosity?"

Joe and I agreed that the Wicklow Round will always be different for different people. Some will want everyone to know and will indeed thrive on their support and presence. Others will simply shun such publicity and will only want their nearest and dearest around them. Joe and I agreed that people attempting the Round should have the freedom to do it either way, be it publicly or in private.

As a result of our discussions that night, an IMRA Wicklow Round sub-committee is formed to debate such administrative details. They agreed that as long as there was an official notification to IMRA before hand, either on the public IMRA forum or via an email to the same sub-committee, the attempt if successful could still be recognised. I know that if I attempt again, I will choose the quieter, low-key option to keep publicity to a minimum. I would send just a simple email to the IMRA sub-committee, rather than announcing my intentions on the IMRA forum.

Whilst dissecting my performance, I also come to realise that I had started off too fast on my first Wicklow Round attempt. The secret to ultra distance running is going slow, *really* slow, especially at the start. Last time, even as I headed up the first mountain Kippure, I saw my heart rate shooting up as I tried to run along. My urge to go fast was probably the reason that I slowly died when I passed half way, from Tonelagee Mountain on. If I was to make it round in one piece, I would have to stick to the pattern of walking up all ascents and jogging down the other side. And I would have to adjust my schedule, aiming to arrive at mountains a few minutes later than the times I set before. It would mean that I would have to go back out to those twenty-six mountains and run between each one of them all over again. However, this time I would have to run at a slower speed and heart rate and use these new times as my targets. And these new splits I would have to adhere to religiously throughout any possible Wicklow Round.

And if I am to contemplate trying the Wicklow Round ever again, I would definitely have to do something about the mist. After racking my brains about how to solve this conundrum, I come up with two potential strategies. My initial strategy is to constantly train in thick misty conditions and to just get used to navigating in it.

Mist is not hard to come by in Wicklow, so I inadvertently get plenty of practise. One day I set out for a long hill run and, as if on cue, the mist comes down en masse. I'm all alone in the mountains, in the tricky area around Oakwood and Three Lakes. But I get so worried by the weather in such a navigationally difficult area that I end up freaking out. And even though I find my way home without major problems, I do a long detour and end up unintentionally registering a longer run. By coincidence, some other mountain runners I know are out on the same route that day. They navigate the area with confidence and don't seem fazed in the slightest way.

I'm so depressed by my comparative inability that I go round to see Mel, my Mourne Mountain Marathon partner. She kindly listens to my woes. "And they were able to run for twelve hours in the mist, Mel," I tell her. "And I was only able to run for seven hours and only covered forty kilometres." Mel looks at me bemused. "You know that normal people don't go out in such conditions. *Normal* people would have stayed at home. Normal people can't run for seven hours or cover a marathon distance on their training run. You know Moire, normal people... don't mountain run." Mel is adept at bringing me back to reality. And wanting to know how to navigate in zero visibility through the mountains in the middle of winter is not a normal thing to do.

After listening to Mel's advice, I work out the only other alternative to my mist dilemma. I am going to have to find a way of avoiding it entirely.

The only way of completely avoiding mist is making sure the weather is perfect. The weather forecast should state there will be no rain and that the visibility will be fine. But herein lays a problem. The weather forecast I had when I tried the Wicklow Round last July said that there would be no rain at all. But I know what I saw out there that day was definitely mist. I surmise that the Wicklow Mountains have so much water content locked in their bogs that they can defy the weather forecasts and can conjure up mist from out of nowhere. This is particularly the case in the west part of Wicklow where I am meant to spend the first half of the Round.

But there is another way. Mist normally appears in the morning. The sun rises and its heat hits the cool night moisture on the mountain terrain, thus manufacturing mist. So what if I was to start later in the day? Then the temperature difference would be less and the probability of mist would be reduced.

And didn't the mist clear around 10 am that Sunday morning when I was close to Table Mountain? Therein lays my proof.

The more I think about this option, the more I realise that there are also additional benefits to starting later as opposed to 2.30 am in the morning. By starting during the day, not only would I potentially miss the mist, but I would also be fully rested and more able to stay awake. Last time, I set off in the middle of the night. This meant I attempted the Round on the back of little or no sleep. Then when I was coming off Tonduff North towards the end, I was entering my second full night without rest. No wonder I was so weary and hallucinating towards the end. On top of everything else, I just needed to go to bed.

With the mist dilemma dispensed with, I am only left with one last problem that needs solving. But I am not sure if a solution exists. The problem I have is with my head. I've now come to accept that my physical demise during the Round was attributable to a rapid deterioration in my mental state. The same thing happened to me after the failed waterfall jump in the Adventure Racing World Championships when I collapsed after mentally giving up. As night time threatened during my Round attempt and I progressively became more tired, my mind proceeded to go on a manic rampage. Worried thoughts of failure, of negativity, of loneliness and of hopelessness completely subsumed me whilst I traipsed up Tonduff North. "You're too far behind time now," it said to me. "God, you've really fecked this up. Why did you even start this Round when you knew you'd make a mess of it like this? Now everyone will laugh at you for thinking you could even make it. But sure, you probably won't hear them laugh, because you'll never make it back. You're going to be lost out here in the mountains forever," it rattled off with a wicked, haunting laugh. It was these thoughts that wore me down, drove me to submission and ultimately made me give up.

My mind is where my greatest weakness lies. I've tried hard to stop these thoughts. I tell myself that they are irrational and untrue. But it is crazy how believable those words sound when I'm out there in the mountains and I'm tired and hungry and stressed and pushing myself to the utter limit.

I've tried time and again to stop them, but every time I've failed. If I want to try the Wicklow Round again, all I can do is learn to accept them and control them as best I can. I try to recall these ridiculous thoughts when I am back home and well rested and fed. When I remember them, I can laugh at their expense and remind myself of their folly. So if I find myself again in those irrational moments, I find it easier to remind myself of reality. 'You'll be fine,' I can tell myself. 'That's really silly. Eat a chocolate and you'll be grand. You are doing really well. You're not lost at all. What you're looking for is just over there. This isn't frightening. Nope, it's really fun!'

One by one, my head walks through each and every mistake from my maiden Round attempt. And in doing so, I find solutions to each and every one. I start to conclude that if I had only done the Round differently the first time through, I would have finished it no problem.

I make my mind up. I'm going to try the Wicklow Round again.

"But I thought you said that you never wanted to go near the Wicklow Round again," Pete retorts when he hears of my proposition. "You said you had come to peace with it. You can't be serious that you want to try again?"

"Yes, I know I said that," I plead. "But that was straight afterwards. But I've had some time to think about it. And I now know where I went wrong. You see, if I just try earlier in the year and if I change what I wear and if I go slower and avoid the mist and if I just focus on running the Round instead of other races, then I'll be able to do it."

Pete is not convinced. He saw the aftermath of the Wicklow Round last time. He saw how shaken I was straight after and how beat up my body was. For several weeks after the ordeal, he also watched me become moody and erratic, quick to tears and anger for absolutely no reason at all. He doesn't want to have to deal with all that again. He doesn't want to see me going through such unnecessary torment once more.

"But Pete, I've come this far. I've done all the homework. I know the route backwards. I know all the mountains off by heart. I know exactly what I should eat and when. I know how to pace myself around."

Pete has seen this part of me before, this utter doggedness that won't let things go until they have come to a natural end. He knows that if he is dealing with this belligerent side of my personality, then he is fighting a losing battle. But he continues to portray his scepticism. He wants to make sure that I really want to put myself through this all over again.

"I know I can do it," I continue to plead. "If the mist had not been there that morning, I would have definitely been off Tonduff North Mountain before sunset and I wouldn't have got stuck coming off it at night. I came so close the last time that it would be crazy not to go out and try it again."

Deep down, I know I can succeed the second time around. What makes me so convinced is that the last section I didn't complete on my first attempt is one of the easiest sections on the whole Round. In fact, I did all the big hard mountains and then gave up with less than two paltry little hills left.

Pete always thought that the Wicklow Round was a crazy thing to do. But he knows too that he'll get no peace if he doesn't let me go back out there once more.

"But what if you don't get around the second time? Then what?" he asks.

"I'll stop. I promise I'll stop trying," I implore. I've just inadvertently given myself an ultimatum. I have to get around this time, or else I never will.

I have only one last shot at the Wicklow Round. I'm so desperate to get around. I have to get everything right.

One of the reasons why I may have failed the first time is because, after Andrew got injured, I decided to go it alone. A solo attempt is seen as a much more difficult endeavour than trying the Round as a team. Running in a team means you can take turns in navigating. This allows you to take momentary mental rests and at times just follow your team members' lead. Being in a team also means that you have other people right there around you at moments when you're feeling low. If only I had someone with me going up the last of those mountains, I wouldn't have broken down.

I am so desperate to complete the Wicklow Round that I wonder if this time I should just go with someone else. If I had been in a team last time, I am sure my team members would have convinced me to continue on after Tonduff North and to have gone on to finish the Wicklow Round. If I had been in a team last time, I am sure the morning mist wouldn't have fazed us. There would have been two or three of us there to navigate and to keep each other going.

I am also vividly aware that I might need a partner because of my change in plans. My new plan is to start the Wicklow Round around midday instead of in the middle of the night. The last time I started in the night to minimise the amount of night navigation involved. The logic was that I would travel for a mere ninety minutes in the dark at the very start. Then if I was going fast enough, I could finish the Round before a second night began. But by starting around midday this time, there is no way I can miss an entire night. Rather I will definitely be going through a section of the mountains for at least five hours of darkness.

I still haven't gotten over my fear of being in the dark on my own. I'm extremely nervous about navigating in the night for the five hours that are required. It's so easy to get lost and disorientated when there's no light. Paths are harder to find and hills look closer than they really are. There are also the night noises that terrify me too, squealing deer and eerie owls. I still remember their darting illuminated eyes from the first Round attempt, an image that haunts me to this day. The only time I've been comfortable in darkness is when I've been with other runners. If I am in team, then I will be able to bear the night and finish the Round in one piece.

Quite unexpectedly, a chance to run with a teammate comes up over a friendly post-race pint. It is December, five months since my first Wicklow Round attempt. Paul is there at the pub, Avril's brother, Paul who is now my friend, who first introduced me to the sport of mountain running.

"So what are your race plans for next year, Moire?" he casually enquires.

"Not too sure at the moment," I coolly respond. "Maybe give the Wicklow Round another go."

"Not a bad idea, seeing that you came so close last time. Was thinking of giving it a go myself next year, if I can fit it into my own plan."

I'm intrigued to hear that he too is thinking of trying the Wicklow Round. The Round has been lying somewhat dormant for over two years. Thus far few have shown any interest in giving it a go. In fact this year I was the only one who tried. We chat some more about what I learnt from my previous attempt. And then I mention the changes to my plan.

"I'm thinking of starting at midday Paul, you know, be fresh at the start from a good night's sleep. But the only problem with this strategy is that I'll definitely have to go through a full night of navigation. I'm not looking forward to trying that on my own."

"True enough, it's not the easiest thing to do. Listen, I'm not interested in a solo attempt either. I like the company of others, the craic involved when there's a team. If you'd be interested in joining up for an attempt, I'd be more than happy to do it with you."

It is a very attractive offer. Paul is a highly experienced long distance mountain runner, as well as good company and a trusted friend. And I'm so desperate to make sure that I complete the Round this time, that at this point I don't care if I go solo or as a team.

We shake on it. We agree to do the Round together.

But as soon as I leave the pub, there is something that just doesn't feel right. It's got nothing to do with Paul. It's something to do with me. For more than a month after, I mull over our agreement to run together the Wicklow Round. And in the end, I renege on my promise.

"I'm sorry Paul, but I just can't do this," I try to explain. "You see, I tried it solo last time and I came so close to finishing. If I go together with you now, it's like I'm admitting that I can't do it on my own. And even if we do get around together, I'll always want to get back out there again and see if I can do it alone." My thoughts then turn to Pete and our agreement. "Paul, I've promised that I'll only try the Round one more time. And, if I've only one more chance, I've got to go solo. "

Paul's not convinced. He's a great team player and heartedly convinced of the merits of working together as a group. But what can he do, but accept. I feel like I've let him down, but he'll just have to find someone else to run with.

Fortunately, there are others who are also thinking of giving the Wicklow Round a go. Paul soon finds himself two other great teammates, Jason Reid and Paul Nolan. They too want to give the Wicklow Round a shot, but also want to do it in a group. All of these guys are incredibly fast and competent mountain runners, creating a much more suitable team composition than Paul and I would have ever made. I feel relieved that things have worked out in the end.

Though it is still early on in the New Year, word starts to circulate amongst mountain running circles about those considering giving the Wicklow Round a try. People soon find out that I intend to give it a second go. Rumours also abound that Paul and his team are forming for a similar attempt. Soon two other individuals reveal that they intend to try separately, Adrian Tucker and Eoin Keith. Both Adrian and Eoin are well known Irish ultra distance mountain runners, both of whom would be well capable of completing the challenge with ease.

But what makes all the talk the more interesting is the fact that nobody has yet completed the full Wicklow Round. Of all the three attempts before now, none came in under the prerequisite twenty-four hours. A ferocious ongoing debate is whether or not the Wicklow Round is even possible. Have the founders of the Round made it too difficult? Is the distance too long? Are there not too many mountains to climb? Is it fair to ask for the course to be covered in such little time?

The list of those hoping to attempt the Wicklow Round this year contains some of the best long distance mountain runners in Ireland. Surely if none of them can do it, then no one can.

It would be easy to get swept up in all the Wicklow Round gossip. But I have work to do. I have to set my new plans in motion and get ready for my second attempt.

The first thing I have to do is get back out there. It is hard revisiting all those mountains again and reliving all those memories. In January I go back up Kippure for the first time since that fateful night. But unlike that time when I couldn't find the summit, I find with ease the path that leads all the way to the top. The whole way up Kippure Mountain I can also see its mast, not hidden away at all like during the actual day of the Round. Days later, I make my way over to Mullaghcleevan and pay a visit to that bog-hole where I nearly got stuck forever. It being a clear day, I now note a route where I can pass through grass so that next time I can circumnavigate that bog of death.

I have a few more months of training before a Round attempt is possible. So I take the opportunity to investigate some alternate routes between mountains to see if I can shave off some precious seconds. After my hair-raising experience of running through razor sharp heather coming off Luggala last year, I decide I need to find a better way of descending from this mountain. I eventually opt for a quicker route around Luggala's cliffs, crossing the Cloghoge River close to The Guinness Estate and Luggala lodge. It still is not an ideal route though. The boggy path I follow clings close to the cliff edge. I notice that it is slippery in places, so tell myself not to run too fast or else risk skidding straight over the edge. But for someone not so comfortable with heights or coming close to cliffs, I am happy to finally face one of my residual fears.

But I have yet to face my biggest nightmare. The choice of going solo means I must run through the mountains alone overnight. I have to convince myself that I can do it. I have to teach myself to stay calm in such conditions.

To start off with, to wean myself in, I begin taking small opportunities to sit outside on my own in the dark. One night, I find myself in such a situation. I am alone in a forest on a night navigation course. I warily sit myself down beside a tree. Tentatively I switch off my torch and wait to see what happens. Slowly my eyes adjust to the dark. I tilt my head back and see the moon above shining through a smattering of stars. Their light is so bright that they illuminate the trees. My ears too open up in the dark. I can't see the river, but I can hear it. Its trickle is a sound I would never stop and hear if it was the full light of day. And as I sit there, I realise that the darkness isn't that bad. It is just different to the daytime, something I can not only get used to, but actually grow to love.

I start to see my fear of the dark as a case of mind over matter. I just have to convince myself that the darkness is my friend. Fortunately, I get a chance to try out this new theory one night as Jason and Paul Nolan, Paul's teammates, agree to go for a night training run over part of the Wicklow Round course. At this stage, I'm still uncertain about going into the mountains alone at night, so I'm glad to have the company.

We opt to run from Drumgoff to Glendalough, over Mullacor and Derrybawn mountains. We enter the forest beside Drumgoff to begin our night-time run. The trees cast large shadows around us, but between their tops I can just make out the moon. Even though there is but a quarter showing, it is enough to light up the track and for us to switch off our lamps. I am telling myself not to panic. And it's working. I feel calm and composed as I begin to realise that the night is in fact a safe place to be.

And what with having trained on this route now for more than a year, I know where we are going even without any artificial light. I recognise the ascent to Mullacor along the forest edge and through the grassy mounds. I am familiar with its flat marshy summit and the descent off it via the well eroded ditch. Even in the dark, I can just make out the wood above Glendalough and know that I must stay high above it. In the moonlight, as we run off Mullacor, I can see Derrybawn extending off to the left. And as we traverse Derrybawn, I recognise its mini ups and downs on top and the steep rocky route off its summit.

The run is less than two hours long, but it has reversed years of my irrational fear of the dark. I now know that I can do this. It's just a case of keeping calm, trusting my map and compass and trusting myself. Having a splinter of moonlight also helps immensely when navigating at night. I secretly pray that the night I choose to do this for real that the moon and the stars will shine benevolently.

I continue to train every weekend, notching up long runs of four, five, six, seven hours. Compared to last year, I'm pleasantly surprised to feel much fitter than before. My training times also tell a similar story. I'm going faster now despite running at the same intensity. It's not that I'm doing anything radically different this time in terms of my training. From asking around, I'm told this is quite normal since I've been at the sport for several seasons now. They say that after four years of long distance running, my body is steadily increasing its ability to endure longer and harder runs. It's not something that comes quickly or that I can force. It's just a slow build up of endurance, a maturation of my mind, body and soul.

And just as I feel fitter out on the mountains, I'm also more relaxed whilst on my weekend training runs. I feel more and more comfortable running alone around the mountains. I don't get as stressed as I used to when there's mist all around, though I still do take extreme care. Even in bad conditions, I am confident enough to cope. And I am happy enough to explore new routes through the mountains, whilst being competent enough to find my way back home again. Time, experience and consistent training are slowly forming me into the unique state required to complete the Wicklow Round.

I am also slowly coming to realise that I was chancing my luck trying to do it last year. In a way, it makes me glad that I did not get around the Wicklow Round first time. My failure makes me properly respect the challenge that is laid down. And it makes me appreciate that only those who are dedicated enough to the task will in the end succeed.

I spend hours and hours in the mountains, preparing myself for the Wicklow Round. During those long hours spent out there, I soon discover that I'm learning much more than just mountain running. The mountains seem to take each opportunity with me to teach me something new. In fact, they seem to intuitively sense what I need to know and they teach me as I run.

Most days, they teach me the importance of child-like simplicity as they show me their rugged beauty. I am amazed how such spectacular scenery can induce feelings of awe from deep within me. Sometimes they remind me of the importance of humility. On such occasions, they show me their size and superior strength, a timely reminder of my own littleness in life.

Sometimes, the mountains even sense when I'm feeling depressed or when I need help to get back on my feet. It's at such times that the mountains let me do the impossible for just a fleeting moment. They let me run faster, climb higher, or navigate better than ever before. By allowing me to excel for a brief second, the mountains in turn restore my confidence, reignite my vigour and encourage me to keep on running forward with my life.

I prepare as much as I can for another attempt at the Wicklow Round. But there are some things I know I simply cannot control.

Just like the last time, I will have to wait for the right weather. I cannot head out if there are high winds or rain or violent storms. I have to wait for it to be dry and calm. But Ireland is notorious for having bouts of bad weather that last for weeks on end. Since I plan to do the Round in either May or June, this gives me only a nine week window for a patch of clear weather to appear. Nine weeks without good weather is ludicrous in most parts of the world. In Ireland, it is the norm. So it could be very well the case that I devote my time and energy towards the Round for months, but that my weather window doesn't open and I never get the chance to run. This is the risk that I must face.

Having the right people in the right places during the Round is also a crucial part of the plan. I had no idea of how important this would be before doing the Round last year. But if it hadn't been for my support team of Brendan, Andrew and Pete I wouldn't have got as far as I did. Brendan helped me calm down at Sally Gap when the mist was all around. Pete was there providing me with food and drink, as well as being the bearer of that elusive hug that kept me going towards the end. And Andrew pulled me out of multiple navigational messes, first when I lost Moanbane at 6 am and then when I got stuck on Tonduff North in the dark.

It's a big thing to ask someone to support you on the Wicklow Round. You have to know that they'll be in the right place at the right time. They have to be responsible and trustworthy. They have to know the mountains well.

You're also asking a big time commitment from them. They have to drive all the way down to Wicklow and hang around for hours on end just so that you can spend a single solitary minute picking up food from them. Most people are doing other things with their weekends as opposed to hanging around Wicklow and waiting. So being able to get a number of people you know and trust to give up half their weekend is a difficult thing in itself.

Fortunately Andrew, reliable as ever, blocks out several weekends in anticipation of the event. Brendan is retired and free and available most days. Pete though has many time commitments and is unsure if he'll be around. I dearly want Pete to be there. I know out there he'll say the right thing to pull me through, come what may. I've already prepped him with phrases to use if he sees me faltering in the slightest. And I'll need someone to provide hugs like him in case I'm wavering at all.

There is also the mental part of me that I cannot control either. It's the part that first revealed itself during the Adventure Racing World Championships in Scotland. It's that side of me that, when it's cold and miserable and tired, simply wants to give up. And I know that if my head says no, my body will rapidly follow suit. It's a Jekyll and Hyde transformation that I've no idea how to control. I'm scared that it'll happen again on this ultimatum Wicklow Round attempt. And if I listen to it, I'll forever regret it. The only way over this is to make sure I don't reach that level of misery. I must make sure I stay warm and happy and not too tired, so my mind has no reason to deteriorate.

But anything can happen out there. Even if I make the best plans to keep my mind and body content, I know that even the best made plans can be still foiled. But I am confident that I have changed my plans as much as possible to maximise my chances. What is left over I give to sheer luck, to the good humour of the mountains and the benevolent will of the gods.

The day after my Wicklow Round attempt back in July, I curled up on my sofa and cried. For the rest of the day, it was like something had died a terrible death. Yet at the time, I had no notion what it was I was mourning.

Nearly one year on, I think I've worked out what died that day. What died was my innocent belief that anything is possible if I want it enough and try hard enough to get it. I wanted the Wicklow Round so badly. And when I tried it last time, I naively believed it was easily within my grasp. But crossing those dark mountains in the middle of the night made me profoundly realise that my fervent desire could never make up for my obvious human limitations.

Also that day in July I felt pure unadulterated pain like I've never suffered before. I am now also vividly aware of the real dangers that exist and the risks that I will bear. Stepping up to the plate a second time, I know exactly what agony and fear I'm going to go through again. Ignorance was definitely bliss all those months ago. But this time I am going into this attempt with my eyes wide open, totally aware of what those twenty-four hours have in store.

But maybe it is good to be aware of what lies ahead. It seems like a responsible maturation has happened, which will make a successful Round more meaningful to me in the end. Knowing that failure is feasible makes the whole challenge

239

more appealing. But knowing that failure is also a real possibility makes me increasingly nervous as the months of May and June fast approach.

But it is time to pull myself together. I learned the hard way in 2008. All I have to do is put all those lessons I learned last time into practice. And hope the best.

This time, I will get it right.

Paul Mahon, Jason Reid and Paul Nolan at Wicklow Gap during their 2009 Wicklow Round attempt. Photo courtesy of John Shiels, actionphotography.ie.

14. AROUND WE GO AGAIN

I will be ready from the 9th of May on.

This is the first Saturday of the year when I can possibly attempt the Wicklow Round. All the Saturdays in April have nights that last eight to nine hours. But by the second weekend in May, the days are already an hour longer, making the nights only seven hours in length. Saturday 9th May is also a date of particular appeal. That night, there will be a full moon. And when the moon is full out in the mountains, I don't even need a torch light to see everything as clear as day.

After much anticipation, the weekend finally arrives. But I am not able to try the Wicklow Round. The weather forecast says it will rain. In the end, there is no rain, only gales. But I can't go out in such high velocity winds. I would spend too much time and energy trying to battle my way forward. The winds would blow me straight off the mountain tops and sides.

So I wait. I don't know how long it will take, but all I can do is wait for the weather to come good.

This is the worst thing about the Round. It's not the training or the preparation. It's the waiting for the right weather. Mountaineers attempting to summit Everest every year have a similar ordeal. They have just a short two week weather window available to them when they can make the climb. With no control over the climatic conditions, all they can do is sit and wait and be patient and be ready to go when the weather turns right. And if it doesn't happen in that two week period, then they have no choice but to put off the attempt until next year.

But it's only when I have to really sit and watch the Irish weather that I realise how dreadful the conditions in Ireland can be. Through the whole month of May, there is not one day when the weather is dry and clear. Instead it is a never ending litany of rain and wind and fog and gales.

Weekend after weekend I psyche myself up to go out. Every Monday morning, I call up my support team to put them on stand-by. They in turn rearrange their weekend plans so that they are free to help out. But as the proposed day approaches, the weather forecast refuses to budge. It predicts rain or wind or mist. Time and again, the weather predictions force me to call off all plans. And then I have to deflate myself again for another week as I reluctantly accept that I can't go yet.

I find it hard to endure all these ups and downs. I have decided not to do many of the mountain races that I love in case they end up conflicting with a possible Wicklow Round attempt. This year's mountain running season has started and already I desperately miss the racing. Normally when I'm not competing, I would still go out and do long relaxing mountain training runs on my own. But even this I cannot do, as they would tire me out too much and render me unfit to go if a break in the weather finally comes.

And with each day I wait, the ferns and heather grow higher and the bogs get wetter. However, in a way, the wait is also a blessing. It means the days are also slowly but surely getting longer. And before I knew it, there is an extra hour's daylight on offer as I move ever closer towards the end of May. The nights are now six hours in length, a sign that we are closer now to the year's longest day.

But it isn't just a race against the foliage and impending shorter days. I have another reason to be in a hurry to get out and do the Round.

It is 2009 and the global financial crisis has hit the world with force. Ireland too has suffered from this economic catastrophe and the country's economy has ground to a steady halt. My own place of work has been hit by the downturn, with insufficient funds to continue working. Sure enough, I am soon informed that my contract will not be renewed. By the end of May I will be jobless, in a country where work is increasingly hard to come by.

Fortunately, just as doors close in Ireland, opportunities open up elsewhere. I am presented with a chance to move to Vietnam and to start a new life there. Negotiations proceed and it soon turns out that I have to move countries by mid-July at the latest. This means that if I have not done the Wicklow Round by then, then it is never going to be.

The Wicklow Round is my last bit of unfinished business before my imminent migration. I also start to see it as my final farewell to the mountains that I love. I don't know when I'll see these mountains again. But I know on the Round I'll be visiting each and every one.

It is mid-May. And I am as prepared as I could ever be, both mentally and physically.

I know my route backwards. For the past year, the Wicklow Round map has been stuck up on my kitchen wall. During the week, I'd learn by rote the route in the comfort of my own home. Over the weekends, I would then go out to the mountains and physically travel over each and every section. Over the last year and a half, I've covered every part of the route at least five times. The times it takes me between each mountain I also know off by heart. The excel spreadsheet with all my splits has been saved on my desktop so that I can test myself randomly whilst working at my computer.

My gear is well tried and tested. It is as perfect as I can make it. I know exactly what I'm going to wear. I've decided what I'm going to carry and when. I have bought the latest equipment to make sure my gear doesn't let me down. I know exactly how much food and water I'll need and I know how to pack them for easy access. My previous support team of Pete, Andrew and Brendan are prepped with the exact details of where I'll be and when.

However, even with all this meticulous preparation, I still know that the Round can throw anything at me. Second guessing these unexpected eventualities is in itself a worrisome ordeal.

Towards the end of May, after thirty days of wind and rain, the weather is starting to look like it might improve. I check with my support team about their availability for a possible Round attempt in the last weekend of May. It is at this stage that I hit a hiccup in the plan. Brendan unfortunately isn't available as the 30th and 31st May clashes with a major orienteering festival held once every two years in the south of Ireland. And even worse, Pete, my boyfriend, is not in the country that weekend. I so want him to be there on the Round. He knows what to say to me to keep me going through thick and thin. But there is nothing I can do. Neither Pete nor Brendan is available. I have to make alternate arrangements.

Fortunately Pete has some South African friends, Lara and Mark, who are willing to help out. They are relatively new to Ireland and have flexible job schedules that allow them to lend a hand at any time. When they first hear about what I am trying to do, they are simultaneously amazed and appalled. But once their shock levels die down, their intrigue soon wins them over. They offer to assist. In the end Lara and Mark, together with Andrew, now constitute my Wicklow Round support team for round two of the attempt.

I check availability with my support team for the last weekend of May. It transpires that a start day of Friday 29th

May suits everyone, with Mark and Lara free on Friday and Andrew available all day Saturday.

Whilst I am busy making my plans, others too have noticed that the weather is taking a turn for the best. I soon hear that Paul and his two fellow teammates, Paul Nolan and Jason Reid, are also preparing to head out for a Round attempt. But they have their sights on Thursday 28th May, a day before my own intended date.

To my utter surprise, I breathe a sigh of relief. They will head out before me.

Talk and pressure has been mounting over who will be the first to complete the Wicklow Round. Already one person, Adrian Tucker, made an attempt in April. He got more than half way round, as far as Wicklow Gap, before calling it a day. Now people are noticing the impending fine weather and know that, after three years in existence, the Wicklow Round might be finally slain. Someone might just go out soon and be the first person to do a sub twenty-four hour completion of the Wicklow Round. But who will be this long awaited victor?

Paul and his team of Paul Nolan and Jason Reid are, in my mind, the favourites. His first team member, Paul Nolan has a remarkable track history in mountain running, having repeatedly represented his country at international level. Jason Reid is an extremely talented young runner from New Zealand and a genuinely nice, honest guy. And Paul himself, as one of Ireland's top multi-day adventure racers, is a dead cert to pace and pull his team around the first sub twenty-four hour Round.

I ring Paul on the Monday to wish him every success on Thursday. It is then that he tells me there's been a change of plan. "Nope, we're not heading out on Thursday after all," he says. "Not all of us are free to head out that day. Looks like you'll be first one up to bat instead." My stomach falls through the floor. I had already felt comforted by the thought that Paul and his guys would get around the course the day before me. They would successfully finish and I would start mine knowing that the Round is indeed possible. I would begin the Round with one of the biggest psychological barrier finally removed. "No, no, ladies first," Paul says in his ever gentlemanly style. I beg for him to reconsider, but I know they have already made up their minds.

All I can do is keep calm and try to not think of the implications. I have to remind myself that it doesn't matter who's first or last, or fastest or slowest on the Wicklow Round. What matters is having the guts and determination to try it and to give it as good a go as I can. I can't think about what others are up to. I just have to focus on myself and on getting it right.

I take the Thursday off work to prepare all my gear, food and water. I take the day off too to simply relax and de-stress. I cannot leave anything to chance.

This time around, I also take the opportunity to forewarn Mum and Dad of my plans. "Best of luck my dear," Mum coos down the phone. "We'll be thinking and praying for you." She seems almost calm at the prospect of what I'm about to do. My parents have had almost a year to get used to the idea of me running around all of the Wicklow Mountains alone. Mum has even sent me a card wishing me all the best. She couldn't find a card with a picture of mountains on it. However, she did manage to find a card for a five-year-old's birthday. It has Spiderman on it instead. Spiderman climbs up things. And so does Moire, her logic flows. Fortunately she has crossed out the "Happy Birthday" message and in its place written "Good Luck" instead.

I arrive early at the Wicklow Round start on the last Friday in May. I'm back at the foot of Kippure Mountain, to where it all began so fatefully less than one year ago. Only this time the mountain is bathed in sunlight, not the darkness I remember from the previous 2.30 am start. To the south the sky is beautifully blue, with mountain after mountain clearly in sight. It is warm and sunny back down the slopes in Dublin City. Up here on the exposed Wicklow Mountains, a brisk breeze blows much of the warmth away. But the wind unwittingly gives me the perfect weather, a cool clear day just right for mountain running.

I hope to reach Drumgoff crossroads some fifty kilometres away as it hits dusk at 10.30 pm tonight. It should take me just under ten hours to get there from the start. So I plan to begin from Kippure at 12.40 pm. Starting in the middle of the day also allows the Wicklow Round to be broken into three distinct sections. The first section is Kippure to Drumgoff, the goal being to get off the navigationally difficult Lugnaquillia Mountain before nightfall. The second section is then from Drumgoff to Glenmacnass, a six hour section across Mullacor, Derrybawn, Camaderry and Tonelagee travelled in the dark. Then the third section is Glenmacnass to the finish, a race to get home before the stopwatch clocks up a full day.

Paranoid about missing my 12.40 pm start time, I arrive with Mark and Lara half an hour early. But it gives me a few moments to chat with them before I begin. I thank them again profusely for supporting me on my Round. I can't imagine why anyone who doesn't even mountain walk let alone mountain run would want to help me out with this endeavour. They've agreed to wait around Wicklow for me for a full twelve hours just to check that I'm okay and to give me food and drink. They will be with me all the way up until Glendalough, where I plan to arrive just after midnight.

"Oh don't worry. We understand," Lara says. "We're all mad, each in our own little ways." It is true enough. My madness is to do with mountain running. For others, their madness is perhaps more mainstream, maybe to do with work or family or a hobby. But everyone has their passion or madness for which they are willing to go that extra mile or two. And even if someone does not share the same interest, it is always a relief when someone else still understands the passion that lies beneath it.

"We are just happy to be here to support you in your madness!" Lara declares. This comes as a welcome relief. Sometimes I know my passion for mountain running has caused aggravation and stress. Whilst I'm running around the Wicklow Mountains, others are sometimes waiting for me anxiously to come back to base. It is such a relief to know that today I am so supported, to know that it's not a burden for them to be there. I vow there and then that I will do everything to make their inaugural Wicklow Round experience a happy one, one that Lara and Mark will remember forever.

And with that promise, I begin.

It feels so good to get going. The sun is shining and the sky is blue. Kippure Mountain is green and glistening right in front of me. And I'm out here doing what for months I've wanted more than anything else to do. My heart is beating from all the anticipation and excitement. I want to sprint right up to the first summit. But I know deep down that is the completely wrong thing to do. I have to take my time and enjoy the scenery. I have to climb each mountain slowly and skip gently back down the other side. I have to have fun out there if I'm to keep going for twenty-four hours. So I walk and jog, at a leisurely pace, steadily plodding on and on.

I must stay calm. But I feel so nervous. Everything rests on today. In my nervousness, I end up tying my shoes on too tight at the start. Within a few minutes, my feet begin to hurt. "You're less than ten minutes into your twenty-four hour endeavour, Moire," I whisper as I try to pacify myself. "Just stop for a few seconds and let them loose again." I bend over and slowly untie my laces. Soon I hear myself repeating like a mantra, "There's no rush, there's no rush," over and over. I have learnt my lesson. Rushing at this stage means that I won't finish in the end.

Mark and Lara drive around the other side of Kippure towards Sally Gap. I've told them that after fifty-two minutes, I should have reached the summit. They avidly watch the top of the mountain, anxious to see the slightest sign of me. If I am nervous at this stage, they are feeling even worse. "What if we don't see her? What if we are waiting in the wrong place? What do we do if something goes wrong?" I have given them a map of my exact route and a list of the exact times when I should turn up. I have given them my mobile number and other emergency phone numbers to call. But still it is difficult to calm their eager sense of responsibility towards me. The only thing I can do is make sure I don't deviate from the plan and reassure them each time I see them.

Mark and Lara see my blue jacket descending the mountain, brightly obvious against the brown bog and green grass. As I reach them, they give me a banana and a bottle, their first ever transition skilfully handled. Mark then drives them down the road to Sally Gap. I jog on after them and arrive there precisely on time. They hand me my main bag full of essentials for the next four hours. Then we bid farewell until the next time we'll see each other at 6 pm at Ballinagee Bridge.

Whilst they go off for coffee, I make my way up Carrigvore, the second mountain on the list. After months of experimenting, I have now established a fail proof protocol for journeying up and over these mountains. First I walk up the mountain. Whilst I walk, I eat. When I get to the top of the mountain, I look at my watch. Without stopping, I write down the time in my notebook. I then quickly check if I am in front or behind my planned times. Then again, without stopping, I check my altimeter to make sure it is reading the right height. A quick check of the map to make sure I'm going in the right direction and then I run down the mountain towards the next one on the list. Then I walk up the next mountain. Whilst I walk, I eat. When I get to the top of the mountain... and so the cycle continues ad infinitum.

Thankfully, in comparison to my previous Wicklow Round attempt in 2008, this attempt is marvellously uneventful. Apart from eating too much cold pizza in one go and feeling slightly sick on Mullaghcleevan, everything else goes like clockwork. There is no mist, there are no surprise bog holes and there is no getting lost around Moanbane.

I arrive at the Ballinagee Bridge transition just before 6 pm. I am already six minutes ahead of schedule. But instead of being happy at my progress, I'm feeling slightly worried. I need to be careful not to speed up and burn myself out like last time. Even six minutes early could spell disaster later.

Andrew has devised a cunning plan to make sure I refrain from going too fast. He has told me that the team will only arrive at a transition exactly at the planned time. If I arrive even a minute ahead of schedule, they just wouldn't be there. This means that, even if I arrive too soon, I'd have to wait around for them. It is a cunning trick to make me stay slow, especially at the start. It is a clever ploy that in the end pays off dividends.

Andrew, Lara and Mark are also checking my bag at the transitions to make sure I am finishing the food. When I arrive off the mountains with a morsel of food left, I get reprimanded for not eating enough. For the rest of the day I force feed myself from fear of being told off. It's another cunning plan that reaps its rewards, a psychological trick to ensure I consume enough calories for the journey.

I travel on from Ballinagee Bridge, up towards the heathery and boggy drudgery of Oakwood. I realise that if I finish the Round under twenty-four hours, I never ever have to visit this mountain ever again. Such a promise is too good to miss. I've simply got to finish, or risk having to visit Oakwood again.

This evening, there is not even a hint of mist on Oakwood, unlike the time before. Far in the distance, I can see Art's Cross and exactly where I am headed. It is wonderfully stress free being able to journey from memory, without a map and compass and to simply enjoy the landscape views around. Perhaps I begin to enjoy myself too much as I lose a faint path that I had hoped to find that, one that leads from Oakwood towards Three Lakes. But I successfully locate a different way through the bog that brings me closer towards my ultimate destination, Table Mountain. I reward myself with a big chocolate muffin for re-finding my way again. I gorge myself as I head up the slope, licking the paper and all. I don't think it is possible to be happier than I am now. I am surrounded by mountains and chocolate, a delectable combination of two of my most favourite things in the whole wide world.

I continue on from Table Mountain, right on schedule. This time round, there are no SOS emergency buttons or Irish army helicopters hovering above. Instead I have a peaceful evening stroll up Camenabologue and Lugnaquillia, the eleventh and twelfth mountains on the Round. Around 9 pm, as I am making my way up Lugnaquillia's slope, I encounter an elderly mountain walker marching back down it in the opposite direction to me. He's the first person I've seen on the mountains all day. "Beautiful evening for it," he calls over. I turn right around to see what he is talking about. Straight in front of him and just over my shoulder, we can see the most idyllic orange sunset. It casts a soothing silhouette over the lakes and hills below. It is a beautiful evening indeed.

It is only by being up at such heights so late on in the day that we can be party to such scenes. And it is all thanks to the Wicklow Round that I am here this evening. And though the Round can be viewed as one long gruelling ordeal, it is at times like this that I conclude that it also has a gentler side. Thanks to the Round I've witnessed sights and sounds that not many others have heard or seen. Thanks to the Round, I have lived more intensely than I ever before thought feasible.

I arrive in Drumgoff just before 10.30 pm, still right on schedule. I am utterly relieved. For months before, I had been worried about being delayed and having to navigate my way off Lugnaquillia at night. But this concern is now far behind me. But despite my obvious relief, I have no time to breathe easy. I now have a much more pressing fear to deal with.

Soon I will be entering the second phase of my Wicklow Round, the dark zone. I will attempt to journey from Drumgoff up the four mountains of Mullacor, Derrybawn, Camaderry and Tonelagee in the middle of the night. I chose to travel this part of the course at night because these are the mountains with the most visible paths on top. These trails are easy to find during the day. But because they are moulded in rutted bog as opposed to solid stone, it is also easy to wander off and lose them in the dark.

Mark and Lara are waiting for me exactly where we agreed in Drumgoff. They are happy to see me looking alive and well. I am so happy to see them too. All of us are also relieved that I am following the time schedule to the exact minute and that I am keeping to the nutrition plan.

From where they are parked, I can see the entrance to the forest that I must enter. It looks dark and foreboding inside. I need a hug. But Pete, my boyfriend, is out of the country. I turn to Lara. "I think I need a hug before I start this section," I say to her. "I think I need one too," she replies. "I can't believe I'm letting you go into this forest and up those mountains on your own. Promise me you'll be OK."

We embrace. I feel better already. "I'll be fine," I reassure her. And just by saying those simple words, I unwittingly reassure myself as well.

I put my bag on my back, switch on my head torch and walk straight into the woods. I take a deep breath and continue to walk as I disappear from sight. My months of mental preparation seem to have worked. I feel calm and serene. I look up and see the quarter moon and stars. It is so peaceful and still out here that I sense there is nothing to be afraid of. I even turn off my head torch for a while to soak the darkness in.

After forty-five minutes, I emerge from the forest onto Mullacor's open mountain and I make my way up its boggy, grassy slope. It is a mild and silent night, another unexpected beautiful present bestowed on me by the Wicklow Round.

I slip and slide slightly as I journey from Mullacor towards Derrybawn. As I head towards its summit, I am reminded of one time when Andrew and I were up here on a practise night run. We couldn't see much that night, but all of a sudden we heard a strange clatter and smelt a horrible stench. Before we knew it, we were in the middle of a herd of wild mountain goats who had settled down for the night. They were so stunned to see us that they set off in a stampede. Fortunately they headed back down the mountain rather than charging straight at us.

Tonight there are no such wild billy goats about. I only see the fleeting eyes and squeals of rabbits, sheep and deer. But this time around, I am sufficiently awake to know what they are, harmless creatures with whom I am sharing the mountains and the night.

I meet Mark and Lara again at Glendalough, spot on time at 12.20 am. All three of us are surprisingly awake given the time of day. "How are you doing?" I ask them, fearing that they are bored to tears by now. "Oh we're fine. But how are *you* doing?" they ask. "Oh I'm going grand," I reply. This is Mark and Lara's last stop for the night. They have already talked to Andrew who is taking over from them at Wicklow Gap. I bid them a good night's sleep and continue on my upward journey.

I have been on my feet now for twelve hours and am just over half way now. I feel much better than last time. Things are looking good.

I get to the top of Camaderry. It is 2 am on Saturday morning. I'm so used to being alone on the mountains by now that I presume that I'm the only one up here. But before I know it, I see three other head torches pointing right in my direction. "Who the hell would be up this mountain at this time of night?" I wonder. I start to panic. "They must be bad people coming to rape and pillage me. Why else would they be here?" But they don't move any closer. The three lights only look at me. And then they look at each other. I get the distinct impression that they are thinking the same things as me. Only they must be wondering what a single solitary head torch is doing up here all alone at 2 am on a Saturday morning. Somehow, I don't think they want to know the real answer.

I leave the three head torches to their confusion and summit Camaderry without due difficulty. I then make my way down the tarmac service road to Wicklow Gap. Andrew is waiting at the road for me. It's the first time I've seen him since the very start. "You're not looking too bad," he remarks. "This time last year, you looked absolutely terrible."

"Thanks for the vote of confidence," I reply. "Yeah, I'm feeling pretty good, all things considered." After a few minutes break, I make my way up and back down Tonelagee with relative ease. In the quarter moon, I can make out everything, the summit and its romantic heart shaped lake below. Even the illusive paths off Tonelagee turn out to be where I expect them.

Light eventually breaks as I wander up Scarr at 4 am. I have felt fine all through the night. Now I try to just relax and focus on my third and last leg, the run all the way home. But the concentration required to navigate in the dark has taken its toll. My body, which has cooperated up to now, tells me that it hurts. The newly gathered water in my bag feels heavy. My feet are aching. My legs can barely run downhill. I've blood blisters between my toes.

Days before my attempt, I saw on TV Sir Ranulph Fiennes summiting Mount Everest at the ripe old age of 65. This was his third attempt at this feat. His trick this time round was simple, a mantra of "Plod forever, Plod forever," kept him going up and up until he eventually reached the top. I need to adopt a similar chant and attitude right now. 'Keep going,' I tell myself. 'It doesn't matter if you finish before or after twenty-four hours. Just finish the Round. Just keep going.'

Up Knocknacloghoge, I gaze over Lough Dan as the sun rises so perfectly pretty in pink undertones. Once safely at its summit, I look back down and taunt the ferns on Knocknacloghoge's slopes that tripped me up last year. It is the end of May and they have yet to unfurl for the summer. I have escaped their grasp this time.

The taunting, however, distracts me from the job in hand. From Knocknacloghoge, I run towards Luggala, the next mountain on the list. But though I've run this route ten times before, I strangely start wondering where I am. "Is this the right mountain in front of me?" I ask myself. "Where is the path? Have I run down the wrong side of Knocknacloghoge? Where exactly am I?"

Tiredness has started playing dirty tricks on my mind. But there is nothing else for it but to stay calm. I stop and take a few moments to look at my map and align it with the compass. I then confirm to myself that I am indeed running towards the right mountain. In fact, there are no other mountains around that I could possibly run up. I take out a gel and suck on it for some extra energy. Then I tell my head to shut up and put up and just come along and enjoy the ride.

After Luggala, I cross Cloghoge River and reach the road close to Sheepbanks Bridge. It is just past 7 am in the morning. This time I'm in no rush, not fighting to reach Tonduff North before dark. No, this time I'm bang on schedule and so close to home. To the east, the sun is rising. It's going to be a beautiful day.

Andrew is there to meet me at the bridge and to give me food and water. It's such a lovely day that he fancies a morning walk up Djouce Mountain too, so I invite him along for the company. I lead the way as he follows behind. And he is bursting with all the latest gossip. I listen and laugh at his funny anecdotes. It is just like old times, just like the days when we trained together for the Wicklow Round and just like the time when we won the Rogaine.

It was always the plan that we would do the Wicklow Round together. However, in the end, it was not to be. However, despite his own plans being dashed, Andrew was always more than willing to help me prepare for my own attempt, both this and last year. I could never have contemplated doing the Round if it had not been for Andrew. Without his advice, encouragement, coaching and friendship, I could never have set foot on the Round. And though I was not always the most obedient athlete or faithful friend, I will always be grateful for having run and raced with Andrew. And I will always be glad that I climbed together with him at least one of the mountains on the Wicklow Round.

I bid farewell to Andrew on the top of Djouce. I run on from there, up War Hill and on to Tonduff North. By now it is 9 am on Saturday morning. It is a wonderful feeling to be out here on a bright summer's morning, with none of the time pressure I had last time of getting off Tonduff North Mountain before dark.

For months after my first Wicklow Round attempt, I spent long hours mulling over my route choice off Tonduff North. Should I still opt to go via Raven's Glen and its cliffs? Or should I head west from Tonduff North towards the Kippure mast and run down the tarmac road to Prince William's Seat, the second last mountain on the Round? In the end, I time both of these potential routes on my training runs. And I find the second route west off Tonduff North via the tarmac road is the slightly quicker option.

I reach the road. I am exactly at the place where I ended my Wicklow Round attempt last year. But this time, I show a clean pair of heels to the spot and run straight on. I jog on down the road. But instead of the speed that I showed on my training run, I am soon reduced to a blithering crawl. After the mountain's soft and forgiving boggy paths, these four kilometres of hard downhill tarmac are too much for my legs and feet. I grimace as each foot hits the road, agonizing pains shooting straight through my soles to my knees and hips. My feet are on fire. They grate themselves alive as they move sharply forward in my shoes as each one strikes the hard ground.

After nearly an hour of this torture, the road section finally finishes. I collapse into the forest at Oldboley's and plunge my feet into the first marsh I find. But my insides have also taken a jolting from the unending thumps on the hard tarmac. Straight out of the marsh, I rush to the nearest tree cover. My bowels expel everything it can find, an amalgam of sandwiches, cake, crisps, gels, pork pies, pizza, energy bars and milk all in a slurry form. It feels good to be vacated again. But I can't waste any more time.

I have only two more minor mountains to climb. With the finish less than an hour away, it is now just a case of not stopping, getting to Prince William's and Knocknagun and then onwards home to the finish. But I'm feeling really tired, as well as slightly bored. All I've seen for these last few hours is desolate bog and heather. All I've done for all these hours is walked up and run down hills. At this stage, the only way I can truly motivate myself to visit these last two desolate hills is to pretend that my favourite dog from Kenya, Elsa, is waiting for me at their peaks. Elsa, my magnificent, loving, faithful boxer, died over four years ago. My ploy works. I'm so excited by the prospect of seeing her there that I practically sprint up both summits.

I must be so focused on Elsa and these last two peaks that I barely see the mountain runner coming off Prince William's. She shouts hello to me as she breezes her way downhill. I raise my head slightly and return her greeting. But I am obviously too weary to speak properly. She doesn't hear me at all. "Whatever," she says as she whizzes past me, offended that I've ignored her. 'But, but... I did answer you,' I think to myself. 'It's just that I've been running for twenty-two hours. I've been on my feet since yesterday. I'm doing the Wicklow Round. And I'm really tired now.' But it's too late for explanations. She's already gone.

I visit both mountains. That makes twenty-six in total. I've done them all. I can finally go home. In just over half an hour, I should be at the finish line.

Andrew meets me on the forest road as I proudly make my way towards the finish. I am running along with all my might. Then I look to my side and I see that Andrew is casually strolling alongside me. "You're not going very fast, are you?" he remarks as he continues his leisurely walk. By now, I am looking and feeling like one of the many seventy year olds who grace the IMRA mountain races. And, according to Andrew, I'm running about the same speed as them as well.

Andrew gets to his car and drives off to the finish. "I'll meet you there," he says. It's only a few kilometres up the road. I look at my watch and realise that, with a bit of a sprint, I could get there in under twenty-three hours. And with a final kick, I get to the line with ninety seconds to spare. Twenty-two hours, fifty-eight minutes and thirty seconds it takes me in total.

I have just completed the Wicklow Round.

Mark and Lara are also there at the finish. Lara is so proud of me that she presents me with a bouquet of bluebells, freshly nicked from a farmer's field in Glendalough. They are beautiful. In fact, everything's beautiful. And I'm so happy. Because I did it.

I sit down on the edge of the tarmac road. I'm quite delirious by now with a happy drunken feeling. My speech is slightly slurred and my eyes are drooping from tiredness. My support team see all this and after a few minutes of rejoicing, they bundle me into the car and drive me to my house. This time too, everything goes to plan. The car doesn't end up in a ditch with a dead battery. It doesn't have to be abandoned for the night. No, the car starts first time and it drives me straight home.

I stay up the rest of the day, not wanting to miss a second of this happiness or this sheer relief. "I've done it. I don't have to ever do it again. Because I've done it," I happily keep reminding myself. But once I've had a good night's sleep, the happiness subsides and an overwhelming sense of pride starts to grow inside me. I feel proud for getting back out there after that difficult first attempt. I'm proud that I learnt from my mistakes. I'm proud that I'm not someone who says, "I can't do that," but who instead says, "I won't know until I try."

And moreover I'm proud that I'm a girl. I am a girl who was the first person to complete the Wicklow Round. So often us girls think that these things simply can't be done. But at the end of May 2009, I proved this belief totally wrong. In doing so, I hope that many more women get to experience the highs and learn from the lows that only the Wicklow Round can provide. And I hope that more women learn to believe in themselves, because when we dig deep, it's amazing what lies inside.

Less than twelve hours later, the first male, Eoin Keith completes the Wicklow Round. And thanks to a favourably long spell of good weather, Paul and his team also finish the Round less than a week later. After his April attempt, Adrian Tucker goes back out at the end of June and also completes the Round. So after three long years of waiting, by the close of the 2009 season, five men and one woman have successfully completed the challenge.

Looking back, the Wicklow Mountains and I have had some really good times together throughout my years of mountain running. But I will always treasure in particular the Wicklow Round, that one day, non-stop, whirlwind tour of the Wicklow Mountains. It's where I learnt the stamina and courage, the discipline and patience needed to ultra-mountain run. And it's also the place where I learnt how to be me and to be the best that I can be.

Summiting Djouce Mountain on the way to completing the Wicklow Round. Photo courtesy of Andrew McCarthy.

Thanks for buying a copy of this self-published book. If you enjoyed the read, it would be great if you could spread the word. Leave a review on Amazon, Facebook it, Twitter it, or simply just tell your friends. Thanks!

Interview with Moire O'Sullivan

What advice would you give to anyone who wants to start mountain running?

It's best to just turn up to an IMRA race. There is nothing like getting thrown into the deep end. Yes, you'll hate it and probably won't understand why anyone would want to do such a horrible sport. But once you've done your second or third race, believe me, you'll get addicted. Make sure you head to the pub after the race, as there is nothing like talking to a few mountain runners to get properly inspired. For more details on races, visit the IMRA website - http://www.imra.ie/events/

What races would you recommend to someone looking to get a feel for the sport?

The Leinster League summer races are what most people start off with. The League starts in April with races of around six kilometres. Races are held every Wednesday until July, with distances peaking at around twelve kilometres. If you can't wait until the summer, rock up to the Winter League that starts in January - just be prepared for a bit of mountain running in the sleet and snow.

All of the Leinster League and Winter League races are on marked trails. Where it's really at is when the races are across open-mountain and require navigation and that's something I'd really recommend people to eventually get into.

Is there a difference between training for long-distance running and your own training?

I'd consider myself a long distance mountain runner. However, I never put in crazy mileage or I would have ended up injured. I try to get in three seventy minute runs in during the week, then a long run over twenty-five to forty-five kilometres on the weekend followed by an orienteering race if there is one on. To stop injuries, I do core exercises three times a week and some yoga if I have time. As races get nearer, I do speed training and hill reps, but they are too painful to talk about.

Basically for mountain running, you need to do most of your training on the flat to get fit with steady heart rates. Mountain running is the technical part you add on top of that fitness.

Having done the Wicklow Round, is it something you would every consider doing again, perhaps as part of a team?

I loved doing the Wicklow Round. The reason I actually wrote the book was because I wanted other people to realise what an incredible challenge it is and to inspire others to give it a crack. So I think it's now the turn of other people to go out and do it, rather than me try to go round all over again.

What was it like to sit down and write your book about the Wicklow Round?

Writing it was the easy part. I had just been laid off from my job in Ireland in 2009 and had moved to Vietnam. I spent two whole months in Hanoi, living off my savings and writing every day. I spent hours poring over maps, remembering routes and races. I enjoyed remembering and writing about all the people I had met on my mountain running journeys. The only hard part was the home-sickness I felt when writing the book on the other side of the world.

I read online that a typical novel is 80,000 words. I wrote 85,000 just to be sure. Pete did the editing, a job that was badly needed. After staring at the paragraphs for so long, I needed someone else to do the chopping. I got friends and family to read the draft version, getting feedback on everything from style, content and typos (which are incredibly hard to spot).

I sent out book proposals to prospective publishers whilst still writing the actual text. That was another job, writing a concise punchy overview, biography, doing a market analysis and giving a list of chapters as well as three completed sample chapters.

Unfortunately the publisher route didn't work. So the book sat silently on my laptop for nearly two years. It was then, in June 2011, a friend suggested self-publishing. I found out it's free to release an e-book, so figured I had nothing to lose.

Next, people asked for paperbacks. I live in Cambodia. So I decided to print my books here. Though cheaper, the quality proved somewhat haphazard. I got 1,000 copies made up in total. I bought the barcode and ISBN number myself. John Shiels from Action Photography was generous enough to donate the cover shot for free and Nicky Cinnamond was great at agreeing to use her photo on the front cover.

The next dilemma was sending the books back to Ireland for sales. Posting them from Cambodia worked out too expensive. So I'm now sending them home in suitcases with friends and colleagues who're making the journey back. And then my dear friend Mel (from the Mourne Mountain Marathon) has been sending the books out when orders come in.

Marketing the book is a whole other issue. I've done announcements via Twitter and my blog. I've sent out email newsletters advertising the book. And I've encouraged those who've read it to give it a quick review. Eventually, I hope the book will get sold by word of mouth and that copies will also get passed around. Ultimately I didn't write the book to make my fortune. I wrote it to get the story out. The Wicklow Round will always be there. And I hope that, by documenting what it is and how I did it, that others will be inspired also to give it a go.

And if anyone feels inspired to write a book, I'd heavily recommend doing it. I have immensely enjoyed the learning curve, finding out what it takes to become a proper author.

I understand that your work means that you travel to many countries. Are you managing to keep up the running and have you any running challenges in mind for the future?

I always pack my running shoes when I go travelling. I was in New York at the end of September and had some great runs in Central Park. Recently I was in Seoul, South Korea and I got a quick river run in. In Cambodia, I still manage to run... though only if I manage to get up at 5.30 am. After that, I find it far too hot to even jog. The only place I've not managed to run was Afghanistan in March 2011 and that's because it would be practically impossible to run in a burka. Such a shame, as it's definitely got some of the best mountains in the world.

Having raced in so many different countries, what are the strangest things you've seen?

Kathmandu marathon was definitely one of the strangest races I've ever run. Despite the city's crazy traffic and large race numbers, the organizers do not close the roads. This meant I ran into one of Kathmandu's infamous stand-still traffic jams. I was slaloming around cars, motorbikes and tractors, eventually ending up on the uneven pavement on the side. Even the pavement wasn't easy running with pedestrians walking between shops, cyclists parking their bikes there and cows and dogs lying sprawled across my path. And once I had passed the grid-lock traffic, I ran straight into a protest march of over a thousand people. Eventually I managed to pass them, but only to find that, in my efforts to circumnavigate the crowd, I was over a kilometre off the course and running in totally the wrong direction.

What Kathmandu lacked in organization, Hanoi made up for hundred fold. There I entered the one mile Hanoi Peace Run around the city's Hoan Kiem Lake. All the roads were blocked off in preparation for the race. There were boxy police cars from the days of Starsky and Hutch with flashing red lights and wailing sirens patrolling the block. The local ambassadors had turned up en masse, even the one from Ireland. They were all kitted out in sporting uniform that they had been issued and instructed to wear on the day: baseball caps, 1970s polyester Adidas tracksuits and white gym plimsolls. There were speeches, Olympic style marches and children dancing salsa.

Us foreigners wanted to race with the Vietnamese, but we weren't allowed. Instead we had to race in the 'Alien' category with all the other expats. I managed to cross the line first and got interviewed for Vietnamese TV. I even got twenty-two US dollars as a prize for the win.

Running in developing countries is a different experience. How does that fit with your career as a charity worker?

I think the most profound thing I've learnt from running in developing countries is how fortunate I am to be able to run. Most don't have the strength because they don't have enough food to eat. Most don't have enough time or energy as they have to work all day in the fields, fetch water, look after numerous kids. Running is a luxury that so few of us can do.

So when you're complaining about going for your next run, remember those who don't even have the freedom to go.

About the author

Moire O'Sullivan is twice winner of Ireland's Mountain Running Championship. She has won the Irish 24 hour Rogaine Championships with Andrew McCarthy, as well as the two day Mourne Mountain Marathon mixed elite class with John McEnri. In 2008, she secured the IMRA fifty kilometre Irish Mountain Navigational Challenge Series title, the first time a female has won the event outright.

In 2009, Moire became the first person ever to complete the Wicklow Round, a hundred kilometre circuit of the Wicklow Mountains to be completed within twenty four hours.

When not running, Moire works for an international aid organisation. As part of her work, she has travelled to some of the world's poorest areas and worst conflict zones. Moire lived in Kenya for seven years, working with mentally handicapped children in Nairobi's slums. She currently lives in Cambodia.

For more information on the Wicklow Round, visit
http://www.imra.ie/wicklowround/

Follow Moire on her adventures at
http://www.moireosullivan.com/ and
http://twitter.com/#!/moireosullivan

And for more stunning photos of Irish mountain running, visit http://www.actionphotography.ie/

32734104R00155

Made in the USA
Lexington, KY
30 May 2014